SAGE was founded in 1965 by Sara Miller McCune to support the dissemination of usable knowledge by publishing innovative and high-quality research and teaching content. Today, we publish over 900 journals, including those of more than 400 learned societies, more than 800 new books per year, and a growing range of library products including archives, data, case studies, reports, and video. SAGE remains majority-owned by our founder, and after Sara's lifetime will become owned by a charitable trust that secures our continued independence.

Los Angeles | London | New Delhi | Singapore | Washington DC | Melbourne

Advance Praise

This collaborative team of Kaul and Chaudhri advance the conversation and thinking about the role of social media in society—and how organizations intervene—than any other work I have seen out there. The writing is fresh and the examples are contemporary, relevant, and compelling. This is a book for students and executives alike—providing key insights not just on social media relations, but on organizational and communication strategy, corporate reputation building, and corporate social responsibility. Get this book. More importantly, use it!

Craig Carroll
Adjunct Professor
New York University

This book is a modern, social media marketing toolkit for students of communication. It breaks down the vast, complex world of social media, taking the reader through it like a practical, outcome-oriented guide should. It is not a flick-through read. It is a detailed study of the landscape. It is rich in examples and case studies, making it relatable and useable in the real world.

Kunal Jeswani
CEO
Ogilvy & Mather India

Both private and public organizations have recently seen their reputations shattered as a result of online crises, social media mistakes, and not having a digital communication strategy in place. To stay on top of recent trends and developments, communicators and students can fortunately now turn to this book and get a fresh understanding of the social media landscape and how it might affect their organizations. Written by two of the foremost experts on the subject, and complemented with practitioner voices from the field, this is a must-read book for anyone interested in the new digital age of corporate reputation management.

Joep Cornelissen
Professor in Corporate Communication and Management
Rotterdam School of Management, Erasmus University Rotterdam

Understanding the value of Corporate Reputation, addressing reputational issues vs. all stakeholders, appreciating the necessity of business citizenship, and realizing how the digital and social turmoil is changing the whole game—these are the dynamics transforming today's business environment. Every crisis today is potentially global, social and viral, so what does it take to master the three interplays shaping crisis in this liquid age: between mainstream media and social media, between local and global dynamics, and between crisis planning and response? Well informed, based on a comprehensive analysis, this book will definitely help students and young professionals better understand what the fast-evolving "Reputation Complex" is about (Purpose + Citizenship + Employer Branding & Employee Engagement + Social Openness) and why it matters to the now and to the next of Reputation Management.

Pascal Beucler
Senior Vice President and Chief Strategy Officer, Global
MSLGROUP, part of Publicis Groupe

Corporate Communication through Social Media

Corporate Communication through Social Media

Strategies for Managing Reputation

Asha Kaul
Professor, Communication Area, Indian Institute of Management Ahmedabad

Vidhi Chaudhri
Assistant Professor, Department of Media and Communication, Erasmus University Rotterdam

SAGE | TEXTS

Los Angeles | London | New Delhi
Singapore | Washington DC | Melbourne

First published in 2017 by

SAGE | TEXTS

SAGE Publications India Pvt Ltd
B1/I-1 Mohan Cooperative Industrial Area
Mathura Road, New Delhi 110 044, India
www.sagepub.in

SAGE Publications Inc
2455 Teller Road
Thousand Oaks, California 91320, USA

SAGE Publications Ltd
1 Oliver's Yard, 55 City Road
London EC1Y 1SP, United Kingdom

SAGE Publications Asia-Pacific Pte Ltd
3 Church Street
#10-04 Samsung Hub
Singapore 049483

Published by Vivek Mehra for SAGE Publications India Pvt Ltd, typeset in 10/12 pt Times New Roman by Diligent Typesetter India Pvt Ltd, Delhi and printed at Sai Print-o-Pack, New Delhi.

Library of Congress Cataloging-in-Publication Data

Names: Kaul, Asha, author. | Chaudhri, Vidhi, author.
Title: Corporate communication through social media: strategies for managing reputation/Asha Kaul, Professor, Communication Area, Indian Institute of Management, Ahmedabad, Vidhi Chaudhri, Assistant Professor, Department of Media and Communication, Erasmus University Rotterdam.
Description: Thousand Oaks : SAGE Publications India Pvt Ltd, [2017] | Includes index.
Identifiers: LCCN 2017010920 | ISBN 9789386446190 (pbk.)
Subjects: LCSH: Corporations—Public relations. | Internet in public relations. | Social media.
Classification: LCC HD59 .K38 2017 | DDC 659.20285/4678—dc23 LC record available at https://lccn.loc.gov/2017010920

ISBN: 978-93-864-4619-0 (PB)

SAGE Team: Amit Kumar, Indrani Dutta, Vandana Gupta, Ritu Chopra

BRIEF CONTENTS

Detailed Contents

VOICES FROM THE FIELD
Contributors

CHAPTER 1

Atul Dhawan is the Chief Strategy Officer and Partner, Deloitte Touche Tohmatsu India LLP.

Deloitte refers to one or more of Deloitte Touche Tohmatsu Limited, a UK private company limited by guarantee ("DTTL"), its network of member firms, and their related entities. DTTL and each of its member firms are legally separate and independent entities. DTTL (also referred to as "Deloitte Global") does not provide services to clients.

Jeremy Brook is Creative Business Partner, The Zoo, Northern Europe, Google.

CHAPTER 2

Bhaskar Choudhuri is Marketing Director, Lenovo India & South Asia.

Arvind Sharma is ex-Chairman of Leo Burnett, India Subcontinent and now a Tech and Internet entrepreneur.

CHAPTER 3

Akanksha Singh is Recruitment Leader, Leadership & University, IBM India.

Kristian Andaker is General Manager, Office 365 Group Collaboration, Microsoft.

CHAPTER 4

Henjo Guitjens and Erik Martens (Director, Corporate Affairs) (HG/EM) are affiliated with MSLGROUP in the Netherlands.

Vikram Menon is the President and Country Head—OgilvyOne Worldwide, India. Responses include input from Karthik Srinivasan and Vanaja Pillai, OgilvyOne Worldwide, India.

CHAPTER 5

Truus Huisman is Vice President, Sustainable Business and Communications Europe, Unilever, the Netherlands

Susanne Stormer is Vice President, Corporate Sustainability, Novo Nordisk A/S, Denmark.

Martin Lloyd is Mobilization Director, Greenpeace Netherlands.

CHAPTER 6

Rohan Mirchandani is Co-founder and CEO, DRUMS Food International Pvt Ltd, Mumbai, India.

Karlijn Vogel-Meijer is Manager, Social Media, KLM Royal Dutch Airlines, the Netherlands.

PREFACE

JOINING THE CONVERSATION: THE 'INEVITABILITY' OF SOCIAL MEDIA

Counter-intuitive as it may sound, no new book can claim to 'start' a conversation around social media. Such conversations envelop nearly every aspect of our lives, for better or worse. Ask anyone whether social media have changed the way we communicate. The answer is a loud Yes! Do social media influence the way we work? Definitely! Can organizations succeed and remain relevant by ignoring social media? No way! In fact, some of these questions may be too naïve and the answers too obvious. Social media, it seems, are here to stay.

In a previous forum (*Social Media: The New Mantra for Managing Reputation*, 2015) in the early stages of planning this book, we brought together scholars and practitioners to contribute their perspectives on the topic. The affirmation of 'change' rang loud and clear, change that is pushing the boundaries of practice and research:

> This change manifests in different ways, for instance, the dynamics of communication (speed, format, directionality, and media consumption), the expectation and demand for transparency, openness, and authenticity, corporate attitude and tone of voice, and stakeholder influence. Underlying these developments is a reluctant but growing recognition that organizations can no longer control what is being said about them, where those conversations are taking place, and who is driving the agenda for brand conversations. Many would argue that organizations never really had any control, this perception of control was an illusion, and the choice is now being a part of the brand conversation or removed from it.[1]

Equally, it is comprehensible that organizations are not prepared for these changes, and not all changes have positive outcomes. We continue that conversation here.

So how and where do we begin to unpack what seems inescapable? Our entry points into this conversation are threefold. First, we focus on the reputation risks and opportunities confronting corporations in the digital age. In no way we are suggesting that reputation is the sole preserve of corporations, or for that matter, that business is isolated from larger socio-political, economic, and cultural landscape that is continually transforming with social media. The effects of digitalization are palpable across individual, organizational, and societal levels of analyses; however, we contend that corporations find themselves in a position that is simultaneously precarious and opportune. Building and maintaining positive reputations is the foundation for all corporate communication; yet those efforts can be destroyed in an instant, as famously expressed by Warren Buffett, "It takes 20 years to build a reputation and five minutes to ruin it."[2] The digitalization of communication and the 'always-on' environment make reputation management more dynamic, volatile, and susceptible, amplifying the trust deficit facing business today.

Second, and drawing upon extant work, we do not treat social media merely as tools with specific technical features; rather, we view them as enabling technologies that allow users (in our case, organizations and their stakeholders) to shape and influence new possibilities for corporate communication. We believe this approach is in line with how social networks position themselves and frame their raison d'être. Twitter, for instance, aims "to give everyone the power to create and share ideas and information instantly, without barriers."[3] YouTube, a Google company, emphasizes connectedness, community, and content sharing in its mission to "provide a forum for people to connect, inform, and inspire others across the globe and acts as a distribution platform for original content creators and advertisers large and small."[4] Doing so also allows us to not be trapped by fast-moving 'trends' and popular or new platforms and apps but critically reflects on the more fundamental implications of social-mediated developments for organization–stakeholder relationships, trust, engagement, leadership, and reputation.

Finally, we believe that the topics addressed in the book necessitate an integrated approach combining theory and practice. Despite the alleged 'inevitability,' social media and their ramifications are far from straightforward. Not all organizations are fully clear, convinced, or prepared to lead in the digital age; many are skeptical. Even though the communication landscape is quickly transforming, we have to be careful to not oversimplify the phenomenon.

To this end, we bring together perspectives from research and practice, from popular and scholarly sources, and from the lived experience of industry professionals, to unravel the multifaceted implications of social media for strategic communication. Covering a spectrum of topics (and subtopics) from branding and public relations to consumer engagement, employee relations, crisis communication, corporate responsibility, and the return on investment (ROI), the book provides a comprehensive mapping of key changes in the yet evolving business communication landscape together with an understanding of strategic benefits and challenges for corporate reputation.

APPROACH OF THE BOOK

Our goal has been to provide the reader with a broad and in-depth look at the digital landscape of organizational and corporate communication with implications for reputation. While research and practice of social media communication is growing by leaps and bounds, this growth has largely taken place in independent domains. In this book, we combine theory and practice in a grounded and relatable manner. Although we recognize that several academic disciplines are interested in reputation and social media research, we concentrate on the phenomena from the perspectives of communication and management. Drawing upon academic scholarship in these fields, state-of-the-art research, relevant cases, and practitioner perspectives, the book attempts to the best possible extent a comprehensive account of the many developments that continue to transform management communication.

Given the pace of technological changes, we make no claim to be exhaustive or conclusive in our arguments. Likewise, our effort to focus on the uses and consequences of social media means that we do not concern ourselves with specific features and characteristics of different social media, nor do we advance a prescriptive or normative perspective on using social media. No doubt, social media managers need to be conversant with the functionalities of relevant networks, their vocabulary, and usage etiquette/protocol; in this book, we are not providing a toolkit or 'how to' manual.

Each chapter addresses a specific topic in depth, highlighting major strands of thought in research and practice. To facilitate navigation, each chapter includes the following key features:

- Chapter objectives and learning objectives
- Figures, tables, and boxes (with case examples)
- Practitioner perspectives (Voices from the Field) to highlight lived experience
- Discussion questions
- Activities
- Chapter highlights
- Keywords
- Appendices to the chapters (with extended case examples)

Short and extended examples serve as illustrations and conversation starters to translate conceptual understanding to 'real' experiences, whereas activities and discussion questions provide an opportunity to explore new terrains and extend existing lines of inquiry across cultural, organizational, and societal contexts.

The central question guiding all chapters is deceptively simple: How have social media influenced the corporate communication landscape and what are the implications of these changes? What is different and why? What can we learn—from research and professional practice—about the drivers and agents of change, emerging opportunities and challenges, enduring questions, and uncharted territory? As readers dive deep into each topic area addressed here, they will appreciate the interlinkages among these topics and the complexities and nuances that preclude 'easy' answers. The wide-ranging implications of these developments—in academic parlance, the 'so what'—are unpacked through the lens of corporate reputation and its dimensions.

What we hope readers—students, academics, communication managers, and professionals—will appreciate is the effort to bridge academic and industry perspectives, which has also been a guiding feature of our teaching, research, and case writing, and that we find intellectually and personally rewarding.

ACKNOWLEDGMENTS

This book has been in the making for longer than we expected! With all of life's ups and downs, emergent developments that demanded attention and challenged us, our resolve (or at least, attempt) to be as comprehensive and up-to-date as possible, not to mention teaching commitments, the story of writing this book has been as fascinating as the communication and reputation dynamics we explore in the book.

Our research collaboration goes back several years from now, and it was a pleasure to work together on the book. Both of us are grateful for the support we received from many quarters, in many forms, and at many different points in time.

We thank our respective institutions and departments—Indian Institute of Management Ahmedabad (IIMA) and Erasmus School of History, Culture and Communication (ESHCC), Erasmus University Rotterdam (EUR)—for responding positively to our request for resources (more accurately, responding to our outburst, "We need support!"). And support we were able to solicit from Phuong Hoan Le and Wing Lam Lui (EUR), and Debarati Bhattacharya, Chitralekha Chakraborty, Ankit Dave, Tushar Meshram, Pratik G. Pillai, Nidhi N. Shendurnikar, Niharika Vankar (Academic Associates from the Communication Area at IIMA). Thanks to all of you for being there to help us collate literature and examples. We acknowledge the contributions of Prabha Shukla, Jasmine Nair, Richa Chaudhary, and Pearl Malhotra (FPM student at IIMA) who stepped in at critical junctures in the process. A big shout-out to colleagues and friends at Erasmus University Rotterdam for being sounding boards and perspective givers, and for the occasional nudging to 'get it done'!

Our sincere gratitude to all the participating professionals for their positive and enthusiastic response to our idea of 'Voices from the field,' for their candid and in-depth perspectives, and for accommodating requests for additional questions and edits. Thanks for enriching the discussion.

For indulging our plan for the book and sharing insights early on, we would like to thank Amrit Ahuja (India Managing Director of 20:20 MSLGROUP), Professor Piyush Sinha (IIMA) for his ideas on the ROI of social media, and Murli Poonath and Suniet Bezbaroowa for facilitating the practitioner interviews with their respective organizations.

Acknowledgements for any academic success are incomplete without recognizing the indulgences of the family members. Their tolerance of 'author idiosyncrasies' and encouragement have been commend able.

Asha thanks her parents, Mrs Vimla Kaul and Late Shri G. N. Kaul, and mother-in-law, Dr K. K. Kaul. Thank you Harsh, Anand, Rupa, Rohini, and Shivam for your support. Thanks for being there! I promise I will make up for lost time.

Vidhi dedicates her first book to her parents, Neelam and Late Mr Y. P. Arora, whose blessings and unconditional love push her forward every day and keep her grounded. For their belief in me, I am thankful to my in-laws, Ritu, Mrs Anjali and Mr V. K. Chaudhri, and dear friends and family, far and near, named and unnamed. Vivek, Surabhi, and Nikhil: you perfected the ritual of asking about status of the book and your firm prodding was especially decisive in the home stretch. I learn something new from you each day! For your love, thank you is just not enough!

Asha and Vidhi

NOTES

1 Chaudhri, V., & Kaul, A. (2015). Playing for the future: The 'digital roulette'! In A. Kaul & V. Chaudhri (Eds), Social media: The new mantra for managing reputation. *VIKALPA*, *40*(4), 455–491. doi:10.1177/0256090915618029
2 Quote retrieved from https://www.brainyquote.com/quotes/quotes/w/warrenbuff108887.html
3 Company information retrieved from https://about.twitter.com/company
4 Company information retrieved from https://www.youtube.com/yt/about/

About the Authors

Asha Kaul is Professor in the Communication Area, Indian Institute of Management, Ahmedabad. She obtained her doctorate in stylistics from the Indian Institute of Technology, Kanpur, in 1990. She is the author of *Effective Business Communication* (2000), *The Effective Presentation: Talk Your Way to Success* (2005), *Business Communication* (2nd edition, 2009), co-author of the book, *Corporate Reputation Decoded* (2014) and co-editor of two books: *Management Communication: Trends and Strategies* (2006) and *New Paradigms for Gender Inclusivity* (2013).

Her current areas of interest include genderlect, politeness, managerial, corporate and digital communication. Currently she is working on Indian cases to comprehend the intricacies involved in corporate decision-making for enhancing reputation.

Vidhi Chaudhri is Assistant Professor of Media and Communication at Erasmus School of History, Culture and Communication (ESHCC), Erasmus University Rotterdam, the Netherlands. Vidhi received her Ph.D. from Purdue University, USA. Her research interests include corporate social responsibility, crisis communication and corporate reputation, social media, and employee engagement. She has published in *Management Communication Quarterly*, *International Journal of Business Communication*, *Public Relations Review*, and *Journal of Corporate Citizenship*, among others. She is also (co-)author on several business cases and has contributed chapters to *The Handbook of Crisis Communication*; *Corporate Reputation Decoded: Building, Managing and Strategising for Corporate Excellence*; and *The SAGE Encyclopedia of Corporate Reputation*.

PROLOGUE

THE ASCENDANCY OF SOCIAL MEDIA

> It is a fact of the internet that every click, every view and every sign-up is recorded somewhere. Depending on your view, this is either very creepy or fantastically interesting.
>
> *Kit Smith*[1]

This is how Brandwatch introduced its compilation of 'amazing' social media facts and statistics. In July 2015, almost one-third of the world's population was active on social media. Among Internet users (~3.17 billion), approximately 2.3 billion were active on social media. About 176 million new social media users were added in 2015. In 2016, Internet users spent on average 118 minutes per day on social media, up from 109 daily minutes in the previous year.[2] This number is even higher in some countries such as Brazil and the Philippines, where users spent an average of more than 3 hours per day on social networks. As of 2016, 78 percent of the population in the United States had a social networking sites (SNS) account. With these high numbers of active users, social networks earned an estimated US$8.3 billion together from advertising in 2015.[3]

The most popular social network in the world is Facebook, with approximately 1.79 billion monthly active users in September 2016. With about 500,000 new users every day, six new Facebook profiles are created every second.[4] Seventy-two percent of all online adults in the United States visit Facebook at least once a month. The 1.79 billion active users make Facebook the second most popular platform on earth, just behind the search engine Google. Not only did Mark Zuckerberg make history by becoming the youngest self-made billionaire, Facebook also wrote history in August 2015 when it became one of the first social networks to attract 1 billion users. Mark Zuckerberg reinforced the magnitude of this milestone, "...it's just the beginning of connecting the whole world...A more open and connected world is a better world."[5]

As these data show, the pace of change is staggering. Where it took 30 years for electricity and 25 years for telephones to reach 10 percent adoption, tablet devices took five years to achieve the same rate.[6] Even these achievements pale in comparison to social media proliferation. With almost 500 million Tweets sent each day (or ~6,000 Tweets every second), Twitter went from its first tweet to its billionth in just over 3 years. Video sharing platform YouTube had about 1.1 billion unique monthly visitors in 2016[7] (see Figure P.1).

History teaches us that one should not fixate too much on the ranking or numbers as even the most established SNS can quickly crumble under the pressure of the changing social media scene. However, these statistics do show how modern-day society has become heavily intertwined with social media. Even though the popularity of an SNS might transform overnight, these numbers show that social media are here to stay. Life without social media has become unthinkable!

FIGURE P.1 *Top 10 (A) Social Networking Sites and (B) Applications*

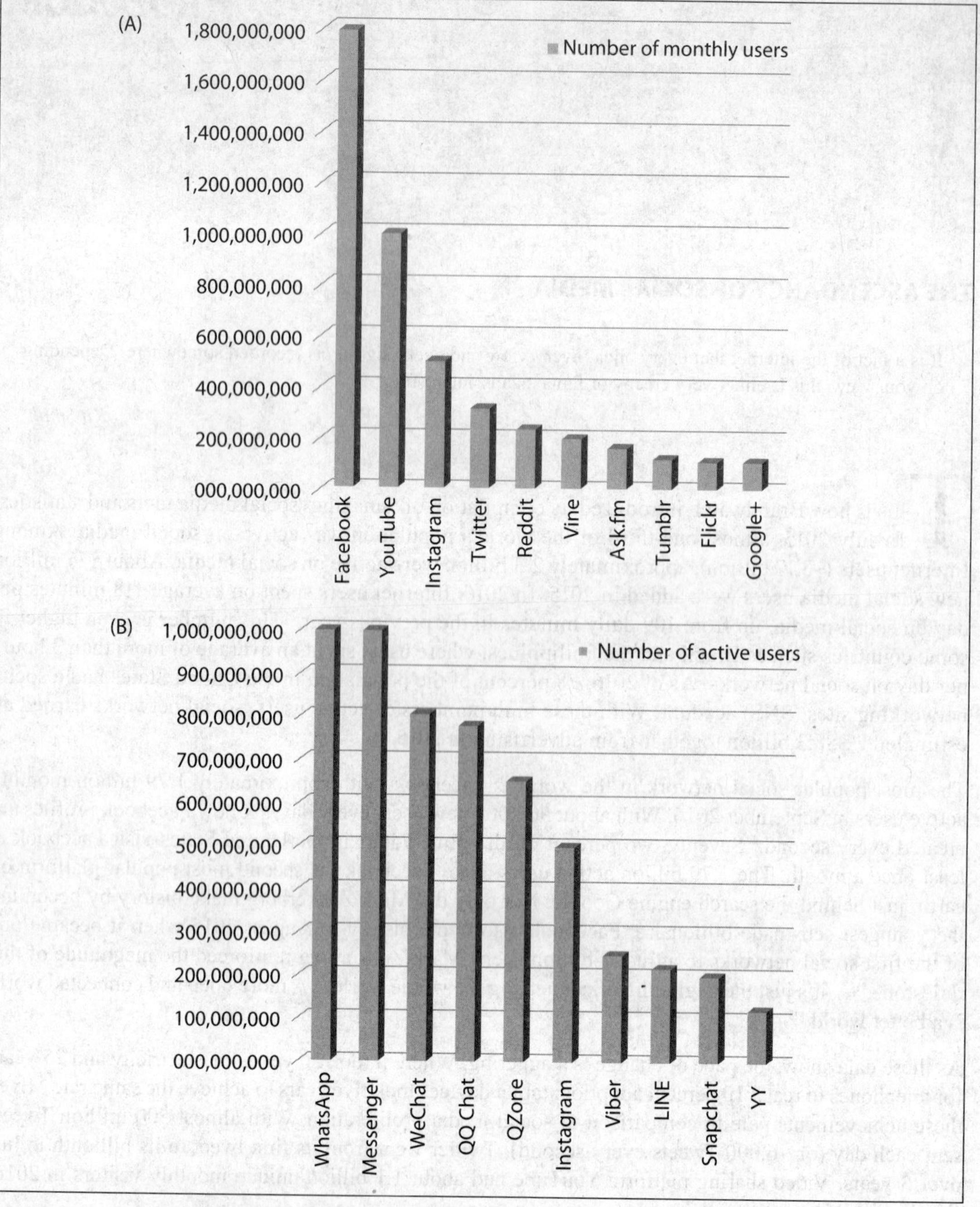

Source: Graphs created by authors based on publicly available data.[8]

It is equally important to note that even though social media are a global phenomenon, the landscape can develop very differently across countries (see Table P.1 for an illustration). In China, for example, citizens have been denied access to the world's most popular social network Facebook since 2009 due to strict government regulation.[9] In late 2016, news leaked that Facebook was developing a self-censorship/'suppression' software package that would allow it to gain entry into the 1.4 billion strong Chinese markets. The alleged software package is to be farmed out to a third party to monitor stories and make decisions about what posts would show up in Facebook feeds. While some have alleged that the company's efforts stretch its mission of connectedness too far, Zuckerberg has framed the 'yet nascent' plans as an effort "…to be a part of enabling conversation, even if it's not yet the full conversation."[10]

TABLE P.1 *Social Media across Contexts*

Top 5 Social Media: China 2016[11]	
Name	**Monthly Active Users**
1. Tencent QQ	850 million
2. WeChat	600 million
3. Sina Weibo	287 million
4. Baidu Tieba	200 million
5. Douban	200 million
Top 5 Social Media: the Netherlands 2016[12]	
Name	**Monthly Active Users**
1. WhatsApp	9.8 million
2. Facebook	9.6 million
3. YouTube	7.2 million
4. LinkedIn	4.2 million
5. Google+	3.6 million
Top 5 Social Media: Russia 2016[13]	
Name	**Monthly Active Users**
1. VK	46.6 million
2. OK.ru	31.5 million
3. Moi Mir	16.6 million
4. Facebook	21.6 million
5. Livejournal	15.1 million

As we have seen, the data are remarkable but the ramifications for corporate communication are even more intriguing. At an interpersonal level, the 'inevitability' of social media might be the norm, but the same is not necessarily true for organizations. The last few years have witnessed a 'groundswell' of interest, nudging business to view the opportunities afforded by social media and highlighting the integrated roles of leadership and culture in becoming 'social organizations.'[14] Initial—and enduring—fears surrounding the lack of control, dominance of negative information, and limited resources and knowledge to adequately prepare for the new communication landscape are allayed with the promise of big data to understand consumer needs and elevate brand experience like never before. Indeed, projections for the global social media analytics market are telling: from US$1.60 billion in 2015 to US$5.40 billion by 2020,[15] and businesses look to leverage advanced analytic techniques to be closer to their customers.

Of course, customer relationships are an integral part of a larger ecosystem within which we need to understand the ramifications of social media.

Before we delve deeper into the implications of these developments for corporate and organizational communication, we need to establish a conceptual foundation.

UNTANGLING AND ENTANGLING SOCIAL MEDIA

> We are living at a moment of profound and prolonged media transition: The old scripts by which media industries operated or consumers absorbed media content are being rewritten.
>
> *Henry Jenkins and Mark Deuze*[16]

Social media are rapidly invading all aspects of our life world. The more traditional forms of communication are seemingly becoming obsolete in a world where one can send and receive texts, videos, or photos without extra charges in just one millisecond through a multitude of social media platforms (e.g., WhatsApp, Snapchat, Facebook, and Instagram). Not only have social media brought new options for individuals to communicate with each other, they have also opened many new doors for organizations to interact with stakeholders, citizens, and other businesses.

The allure of social media derives from the ability to facilitate conversation and dialogue, foster community, enable linkages between organizations and their audiences (including employees) as well as networked communication between and among users that both produce and consume information (aka the "prosumer"). With upward of 100 million fans and 5.6 million subscribers, Coca-Cola (Facebook) and Red Bull (YouTube), respectively, illustrate the shifting paradigms of communication between organizations and their publics.

Having said that, the rise of social media also evokes feelings of uncertainty and raises questions. For example, what exactly are social media?[i] How are social media different from new media? First, the easy part: social media are part of 'new' media. Unlike traditional and analog media (e.g., newspapers, radio, and television that are not entirely redundant yet), new media signify the change to digital forms of distribution and communication. From this point on, the boundaries are blurred. We can agree that there is a thin line between new and social media where the former subsumes the latter. In other words, new media is the umbrella term where social media is a form of new media and build on the foundations of new media with some important distinctions:

> While new media allows for sharing, the development of social media and its interactive components has made the ability to comment, respond, share, critique, change and add to information possible on a broad scale. It is the increased visibility of interaction, with largely unfiltered peer-to-peer communication that cannot be easily controlled, that is central to social media. Social media is necessarily interactive, focused on social connections, and is designed with social connections in mind.[17]

This distinction points to the core challenge that make organizations wary and restless about social media—the lack of control and predictability in how, when, and where organizational messages and information are distributed, used, or interpreted.

Broadly speaking, social media can be described as online tools where users can share content, opinions, perspectives, insights, and media. A dictionary definition conceptualizes social media as "forms of electronic communication (as websites for social networking and microblogging) through which users create online communities to share information, ideas, personal messages, and other content (as videos)."[18]

[i] For purely pragmatic reasons and to avoid monotony, we use both 'new' and 'social' media in the book.

Likewise, Kaplan and Haenlein (2010) define social media as "a group of Internet-based applications that build on the ideological and technological foundations of Web 2.0, and allow the creation and exchange of user generated content."[19] The term Web 2.0 was coined in 2005 by Tim O'Reilly who envisioned the "the network as platform, spanning all connected devices [...] creating network effects through an 'architecture of participation,' and going beyond the page metaphor of Web 1.0 to deliver rich user experiences."[20]

With its unprecedented ability to "harness collective intelligence,"[21] Web 2.0 ushered in the possibility to continuously modify content in a participatory and collaborative way. No surprise then that Web 2.0 is regarded as the platform for the development of social media. Furthermore, Kaplan and Haenlein explain, "When Web 2.0 represents the ideological and technological foundation, User Generated Content (UGC) can be seen as the sum of all ways in which people make use of social media."[22]

Others refer to social networks or networking sites (e.g., Facebook, Twitter, and LinkedIn) when discussing social media. SNS, as defined by boyd and Ellison (2008), are "web-based services that allow individuals to (1) construct a public or semi-public profile within a bounded system, (2) articulate a list of other users with whom they share a connection, and (3) view and traverse their list of connections and those made by others within the system."[23] boyd and Ellison argue that the uniqueness of SNS comes from the fact that they enable users to articulate and make their social networks visible.

So, "What is **social** about social media?" asks Christian Fuchs.[24] In his conceptualization, Fuchs (2014) outlines the forms of sociality that underpin social media—information, communication, community, collaboration, and co-operative work—each related and encapsulated in the other. From this perspective, what makes Facebook 'social' is that it demonstrates multiple forms of sociality (information, communication, and community). Markedly, social media are not a unitary block, and efforts have been made to classify them according to specific functionalities, congruence with human needs, and other theoretical lenses (for a sampling, see Appendix).

The question of what constitutes 'social' is answered in different ways by others. Situating participation and participatory culture at the center of their conceptualization, Jenkins, Ford, and Green (2013) prophesize, "If it doesn't spread, it's dead."[25] For them, 'spreadability' is the defining characteristic of social media in which consumers play an active role in sharing, co-creating, reusing, and adapting content. They distinguish spreadability ("the continuous process of repurposing and recirculation") from conventional notions of stickiness ("drawing people to traditionally produced content and keeping them there") in building the case for social (spreadable) media as an expression of a participatory culture. As a "site of consumer participation," social media invite "fans and other consumers to actively participate" to create and circulate content, and to interact and collaborate.[26]

We see this optimism in the loudest voices proclaiming the participatory benefits of social media (e.g., democratization of communication, collaboration, and the creation of participatory cultures); however, they might obscure the ideological, technological, political inequities, and powers that impede these participatory ideals. Indeed, some scholars argue the need to critically review extant claims of social-mediated benefits and recognize that ultimately social media are "commercial spaces."[27] An exclusive focus on the front-end of social media (i.e., where users interact) paints a picture of involvement and participation which is "overly utopian," whereas the back-end that is hidden from view engenders new forms of "control and manipulation" in which

> Social relationships are becoming ever more distorted by hidden advertisement and other forms of manipulation; the growing ranks of the creative industry workers have to compete ever harder for work as potential clients learn to exploit free culture and drive down salaries through crowdsourcing; a gigantic surveillance machine extending the reach of powerful institutions so that they can manipulate emerging social phenomena, either intervening before they can reach critical mass, or else helping them to reach critical mass much sooner, depending on their goals and strategies.[28]

Of course, no phenomenon is without consequence or unidimensional. Social-mediated communication is no exception. For our purposes, agreeing on a definition is of lesser consequence than ensuring that we do not advance a techno-deterministic view of social media. As technology becomes deeply embedded, even mundane, prevailing definitions cannot adequately capture the nuances and dynamics of how people connect and form relationships.[29] Our approach in the book is not to treat social media merely as tools with specific technical features that are somehow 'inherently' powerful; rather, we see social media as enabling technologies that allow users (aka organizations and their stakeholders) to shape and influence new possibilities for communication. We take solace in the work of those before us who have privileged the 'use(s)' as opposed to technical peculiarities of new and/or social media. As 'old scripts' are supplanted by the new, it is helpful to remind ourselves that potential outcomes are not written 'into' social media, but contingent on their uses, as in this analogy: "The iPhone is like a pen in our hands. Good or bad, the pen itself will never write poems, but the poets will."[30]

What, then, will the story of communication in a digital age look like?

COMMUNICATION CHANGETH: THE CO-EXISTENCE OF REPUTATION PROMISE AND PERIL

In October 2016, Delta Airlines found itself in the headlines for allegedly discriminating against a black doctor on board refusing to allow her to provide medical care to a sick passenger in-flight. Dr Tamika Cross recounted the episode in a Facebook post:

> [...] the flight attendant yells "call overhead for a physician on board." I raised my hand to grab her attention. She said to me "oh no sweetie put ur hand down, we are looking for actual physicians or nurses or some type of medical personnel, we don't have time to talk to you" I tried to inform her that I was a physician but I was continually cut off by condescending remarks.
>
> Then overhead they paged "any physician on board please press your button." I stare at her as I go to press my button. She said "oh wow you're an actual physician?" I reply yes. She said "let me see your credentials. What type of Doctor are you? Where do you work? Why were you in Detroit?"[31]

The incident caused furor as people took to Twitter and Facebook to support Tamika Cross using hashtags #whatdoctorslooklike #blackwomen #discrimination and #WeDoExist, calling for a boycott of Delta and highlighting the systemic nature of bias against black female doctors. In a few days, Cross' post had more than 109K reactions, about 40,000 shares, and more than 15,000 comments forcing Delta to respond. The airline initially justified the flight attendants' request for identification but was quick to note that "the experience Dr Cross has described is not reflective of Delta's culture or of the values our employees live out every day."[32] Eventually, Delta announced a policy change eliminating the need for flight attendants to verify medical credentials as a precondition for on-board emergencies. Delta's announcement acknowledged Cross' post as the trigger for change (the feedback Dr Cross provided gave us a chance to make flying better) and was welcomed by Cross who saw the incident as opening "a very uncomfortable conversation [that] helped bring important change at a major corporation."[33]

Such cases are becoming the norm rather than the exception. As challenges come from multiple quarters and stakeholder disapproval finds new avenues for expression, organizations' ability to navigate tumultuous, always-on, environments is tested in new ways. For a firm's publics, these developments enable entry into a previously inaccessible or restricted space and make themselves heard and noticed. Direct connection with a brand or a firm in the social space presents new avenues for stakeholders to engage, collaborate, express (dis)satisfaction, spread word-of-mouth on or behalf of a brand, influence business practice—in other words, participle or actively shape firm and brand perceptions in the public sphere.

Given these paradigm changes, communication professionals find themselves "at a critical inflection point."[47] As they assume a more central role in leading reputation management, providing strategic counsel for business strategy, and building corporate character, chief communication officers (CCOs) need to be system thinkers with cross-functional capabilities. A whitepaper of the Arthur W. Page Society[48] demarcates three roles that communication professionals of the future will need to master:

The Foundational CCO	CCO is the conscience keeper of the organization, providing strategic counsel to leadership, leading the organization's reputation mandate, and ensuring that business conduct and communication is ethical, responsible, transparent, and aligned with stakeholder expectations.
The CCO as an Integrator	CCOs need to be able to work closely with other strategic functions in the C-suite (i.e., marketing, technology, human resources, etcetera) and build cross-functional capabilities. Building and maintaining reputation and stakeholder relationships necessitate holistic thinking across functional boundaries.
The CCO as a Builder of Digital Engagement Systems	CCO ability to deliver on an expanded mandate hinges on an understanding of engagement with multiple stakeholder groups. Leveraging data and digital platforms to understand motivation and create opportunities for engagement and advocacy build on authenticity and trust.

With the dramatic growth of the social web, the speed and flow of information, perhaps it is no stretch to say that leading change in a social-mediated era requires the ability to thrive in chaos! Pioneers in this space understand the need for an integrated approach that combines business strategy and communication, traditional and digital channels, organizational and stakeholder objectives, as well as intra-organizational coordination.

Motivated by the need to break out of silos and to leverage synergies across disciplinary boundaries, we have incorporated practitioner perspectives in each chapter. 'Voices from the field' help us bridge gaps between academia and industry, bring the two together to reflect on a vibrant area of study and practice. In doing so, we believe that readers can better appreciate the patterns and intersections, convergence and divergence in the way organizations approach the different functions of corporate communication—public relations and branding, crisis management, consumer and employee relations, social responsibilities, and the return on investment—in the digital age.

APPENDIX

CLASSIFYING SOCIAL MEDIA

Author(s)	Perspective on Social Media	Characteristics
Kaplan & Haenlein (2010)[49]	Social Media is a group of Internet-based applications that build on the ideological and technological foundations of Web 2.0 and allow the creation and exchange of User Generated Content.	Classify social media according to the degree of: **1. Social presence and media richness** Social presence is about the intimacy (interpersonal vs. mediated) and immediacy of the medium; media richness refers to the ability of the medium to transmit information in a given time, thereby resolving ambiguity and uncertainty, for example, blogs offer low degrees of social presence and media richness.

(Appendix Continued)

(Appendix Continued)

Author(s)	Perspective on Social Media	Characteristics
		2. Self-presentation and self-disclosure Grounded in the belief that people want to create desirable impressions via appropriate (or selective) presentation and/or disclosure of personal information. Social media permit differing degrees of self-presentation and self-disclosure, for example, social networking sites like Facebook allow for self-disclosure than content communities (e.g., YouTube) but lower than virtual game and social worlds (e.g., World of Warcraft) which nearly replicate 'all dimensions of face-to-face interactions in a virtual environment.'
Kietzmann, Hermkens, McCarthy, & Silvestre (2011)[50]	Differentiate among social media based on seven functional building blocks, the knowledge of which can allow organizations to formulate informed strategies of engagement. The relative salience of these blocks varies, for instance, the *sharing* functionality is the core to **YouTube** with conversations, groups, and reputations make a secondary role. By contrast, *identity* is core to **LinkedIn** followed by relationships and reputations.	Propose a honeycomb model with seven blocks and associated implications: **Identity:** extent to which users reveal their identities in a social media setting; privacy is a key implication. **Conversations:** extent to which users communicate with each other with implications for conversation frequency and direction (range of topics covered) **Presence:** extent to which users can know if other users are accessible which heightens the relative importance of consumer availability and location information. **Relationships:** extent to which users can be related to other users; implications for building and maintaining relationships. **Groups:** extent to which users can form communities and subcommunities; implications for group membership and protocols. **Reputations:** extent to which users can identify the standing of others, including themselves; requires appropriate metrics to assess strength, sentiment, passion, and reach of users and firms. **Sharing:** extent to which users exchange, distribute, and receive content; necessitates content management while understanding consumer motivation to share.
Yu-Qian Zhu & Houn-Gee Chen (2015)[51]	The authors propose the need to examine the congruence between social media processes and individual user needs. Understanding these linkages can help social media managers appropriately match audience needs, platform selection, and campaign goals.	Propose social media matrix based on two dimensions situating the satisfaction of human needs at the core of categorizing social media: 1. **Nature of connection** whereby profile-based connections focus on the person (as in Facebook, Twitter), while YouTube and Instagram focus on content. 2. **Level of customization** refers to the degree to which a service is customized to satisfy an individual's particular preferences. A customized message is intended for a small or specific audience (e.g., posting comments in a closed group), while a broadcast message (e.g., Presidential Tweets) is intended for larger audiences. Combining these dimensions yields a 2 × 2 matrix of social media services each of which fulfil specific personal needs: **relationship** (relatedness self-esteem), **self-media** (popularity influence, money luxury), **creative outlets** (self-actualization, competence), and **collaboration** (competence, self-actualization).

NOTES

1 Smith, K. (2016, March 7). Marketing: 96 Amazing social media statistics and facts for 2016. Retrieved April 27, 2017, from https://www.brandwatch.com/blog/96-amazing-social-media-statistics-and-facts-for-2016
2 Daily time spent on social networking by internet users worldwide from 2012 to 2016 (in minutes). Retrieved January 19, 2017 from https://www.statista.com/statistics/433871/daily-social-media-usage-worldwide/
3 Smith (2016).
4 Ibid.
5 Quote retrieved November 14, 2016, from https://www.facebook.com/zuck/posts/10102329188394581
6 McGrath, R. (2013). The pace of technology adoption is speeding up. *Harvard Business Review*. Retrieved November 1, 2016, from https://hbr.org/2013/11/the-pace-of-technology-adoption-is-speeding-up
7 Smith (2016).
8 Graphs created with information from http://www.dreamgrow.com/top-15-most-popular-social-networking-sites/.
9 Beech, H. (2016, March 21). A brief history of Facebook's courtship of China. Retrieved November 14, 2016, from http://time.com/4265665/china-facebook-mark-zuckerberg-great-firewall/
10 Isaac, M. (2016). Facebook said to create censorship tool to get back into China. Retrieved December 6, 2016, from http://www.nytimes.com/2016/11/22/technology/facebook-censorship-tool-china.html?_r=1
11 Retrieved January 19, 2017, from http://linkfluence.com/en/2016/02/08/top-10-chinese-social-media-sites/
12 Retrieved January 19, 2017, from http://www.marketingfacts.nl/berichten/social-media-in-nederland-2016-whatsapp-overstijgt-facebook
13 Retrieved January 19, 2017, from http://www.makeuseof.com/tag/top-8-russian-social-networks-makes-great/
14 For example, Bradley, A. J., & McDonald, M. P. (2011). *The social organization: How to use social media to tap the collective genius of your customers and employees*. Harvard Business Review Press. Also see Li, C. (2010). *Open leadership: How social technology can transform the way you lead*. CA: Jossey-Bass, Wiley.
15 MarketsandMarkets. (2017, January 11). Social media analytics market worth 5.40 billion USD by 2020. Retrieved January 19, 2017, from http://www.marketsandmarkets.com/PressReleases/social-media-analytics.asp
16 Jenkins, H., & Deuze, K. (2008). Editorial: Convergence culture. *Convergence: The International Journal of Research into New Media Technologies*, *14*(1), 5–12. doi:10.1177/1354856507084415
17 Pridmore, J., Falk, A., & Sprenke, I. (2013). *New media & social media: What's the difference v2.0* (Working paper on Academia.edu). Retrieved May 23, 2017, from http://www.academia.edu/1122278/New_media_and_social_media_-_whats_the_difference_v_2.0
18 Definition of social media retrieved December 7, 2016, from https://www.merriam-webster.com/dictionary/social%20media
19 Kaplan, A. M., & Haenlein, M. (2010). Users of the world, unite! The challenges and opportunities of social media. *Business Horizons*, *53*(1), 59–68. doi:10.1016/j.bushor.2009.09.003
20 O'Reilly, T. (2005). Web 2.0: Compact definition? Retrieved December 6, 2016, from http://radar.oreilly.com/2005/10/web-20-compact-definition.html
21 Ibid.
22 Kaplan & Haenlein (2010).
23 boyd, D. M., & Ellison, N. B. (2008). Social network sites: Definition, history, and scholarship. *Journal of Computer-Mediated Communication*, *13*(1), 210–230. doi:10.1111/j.1083-6101.2007.00393.x
24 Fuchs, C. (2014). *Social media: A critical introduction*. London: SAGE Publications.
25 Bury, R. (2013). Book review of Jenkins, H., Ford, S., & Green, J. *Spreadable media: Creating value and meaning in a networked culture*. New York, NY: New York University Press. *International Journal of Communication*, *7*.
26 Fuchs (2014, pp. 53–54).
27 Beer, D. (2008). Social network(ing) sites…Revisiting the story so far: A response to danah boyd & Nicole Ellison. *Journal of Computer-mediated Communication*, *13*, 516–529. doi:10.1111/j.1083-6101.2008.00408.x
28 Stalder, F. (2012). Between democracy and spectacle: The front-end and back-end of the social web. In M. Mandiberg (Ed.), *The social media reader* (pp. 242–256). Retrieved April 27, 2017, from http://felix.openflows.com/node/223
29 Beer (2008).
30 Lowry, R. (2016, July 7). These are the best iPhone photos of 2016. Retrieved November 20, 2016, from http://time.com/4393576/iphone-photo-awards-2016/

31 Facebook post (2016, October 9). Retrieved November 9, 2016, from https://www.facebook.com/tamika.cross.52/posts/658443077654049?pnref=story.

32 Kish, P. (2016, October 14). Delta releases new statement after doctor accuses company of discrimination. Retrieved December 8, 2016, from http://www.11alive.com/news/nation-now/delta-releases-new-statementafter-doctor-accuses-company-of-discrimination/336120466

33 Hixenbaugh, M. (2016, December 21). Delta apologizes, changes policy after black Houston doctor blocked from helping passenger. *Houston Chronicle*. Retrieved January 11, 2017, from http://www.houstonchronicle.com/local/prognosis/article/delta-apologizes-changes-policy-afterblack-10811268.php

34 Fombrun, C. (1996). *Reputation.* Boston, MA: Harvard Business School Press.

35 Table compiled from multiple sources: Aula, P., & Heinonen, J. (2016). *The reputable firm: How digitalization of communication is revolutionizing reputation management* (p. 3). Switzerland: Springer; Carroll, C. E. (2016). *SAGE encyclopedia of corporate reputation*. Thousand Oaks, CA: SAGE Publications; Fombrun, C. J., & van Riel, C. B. M. (2004). *Fame & fortune*. Upper Saddle River, NJ: Pearson Education.

36 Aula & Heinonen (2016).

37 Ibid.

38 See Balmer, J. M. T., Stuart, H., & Greyser, S. A. (2009). Aligning identity and strategy: Corporate branding at British Airways in the late 20th century. *California Management Review*, *51*(3), 6–23. doi:10.1225/CMR425; Carroll, C. E., Greyser, S. A., & Schreiber, E. (2011). Building and maintaining reputation through communications. In C. Caywood (Ed.), *The international handbook of strategic public relations & integrated communications* (pp. 457–476). New York, NY: McGraw-Hill.

39 Cornelissen, J. (2014). *Corporate communication: A guide to theory and practice* (4th ed.). London: SAGE Publications.

40 Aula & Heinonen (2016).

41 Argenti, P. A. (2006). How technology has influenced the field of corporate communication. *Journal of Business and Technical Communication, 20,* 357–370.

42 Gowing, N., & Langdon, C. (2016). *Thinking the unthinkable: A new imperative for leadership in the digital age.* Retrieved November 21, 2016, from http://www.cimaglobal.com/Research--Insight/Thinking-the-unthinkable-a-new-imperative-for-leadership-in-the-digital-age/

43 Ibid.

44 See report by ING *Social media has a growing impact on the news #SMING15*. (2015, October 8). Retrieved October 10, 2015, from http://www.ing.com/Newsroom/All-news/Social-media-has-a-growing-impacton-the-news-SMING15.htm

45 Corporate Communication International. (2015, October 29). *Final report: The 2015 corporate communication practices study* (Executive Summary). Retrieved November 9, 2016, from http://www.corporatecomm.org/wp-content/uploads/2016/04/Key-Findings-CCI-Study-2015-29Oct15.pdf

46 Korn Ferry Institute. (2015, July 28). *The chief communications officer: 2015 survey and findings among the Fortune 500*. Retrieved November 9, 2016, from http://www.kornferry.com/institute/the-chief-communications-officer-2015-survey-and-findings-among-the-fortune-500

47 Arthur W. Page Society. *The new CCO: Transforming enterprises in a changing world* (Digital White Paper). Retrieved December 7, 2016, from http://www.awpagesociety.com/thought-leadership/the-new-ccco-transforming-enterprises-in-a-changing-world

48 Ibid.

49 Kaplan & Haenlein (2010).

50 Kietzmann, J. H, Hermkens, K., McCarthy, I. P., & Silvestre, B. S. (2011). Social media? Get serious! Understanding the functional building blocks of social media. *Business Horizons*, *54*, 241–251. doi:10.1016/j.bushor.2011.01.00

51 Zhu, Y., & Chen, H. (2015). Social media and human need satisfaction: Implications for social media marketing. *Business Horizons, 58*, 335–345. http://dx.doi.org/10.1016/j.bushor.2015.01.006

HAPTER 1

The New Anthem for Open Source Branding

Paradox of Gaining Resonance and Ceding Control

CHAPTER OBJECTIVES

- Examine the influence of social media on branding, brand management, and brand communication.
- Assess the opportunities and challenges for branding in the digital age.
- Understand the (new and ongoing) developments in branding strategies.
- Appreciate the role of the customer in the branding process and brand activities.
- Review strategies for customer collaboration and engagement.

Keywords

Anti-branding	Consumer	Loyalty
Authenticity	Control	Medium
Brand	Culture	Paradigms
Brand entification	Criticism	Public relations
Brand communities	Dialogic processes	Social Media
Collectivism	Fans	Transparency
Co-creation	Followers	Trust
Communication	Interactivities	

INTRODUCTION

A brand is more than a trademark. It is a Trustmark. A brand is a covenant between the company and the consumer. A trusted brand is a genuine asset.

Larry Light[1]

Lady Gaga's voice breaks through the silence in the auditorium as she calls out to her fans, "Paws Up!" In response, everyone present raises their hands with the claw hand symbol. Not to project imperfections but as an acknowledgment of their love and affection for the brand, Lady Gaga. Nicknamed 'Little Monsters,' these fans wait with bated breath to be invited on stage and accorded the love Lady Gaga fervently professes for them.

What explains the enduring adulation and admiration of audiences, offline and online (~60 million, counting on both Facebook and Twitter)? At its core, the relationship in which every fan feels wanted and loved! How has she created and communicated 'THE brand' she is? Can other brands replicate her success? (Appendix A). Certainly, there are many more successes, some better known than others.

There is no denying that "branding today is a much different practice than it was even 10 years ago,"[2] and it does not take much to find all the ways branding is changing in the digital world (a Google search throws up just over 2 million results). Research suggests that social media have upended the communication patterns of consumers with brands. Many would argue that the traditional functions and strategies have become obsolete and unsustainable; others maintain that basic principles are still valid. Arguably, as things change, much still remains the same, and branding is no exception.

In this chapter, we review the influence of social media on branding and brand management, focusing on the developments and continuities, the perspectives and strategies, as well as the questions that have captured the interest of communication scholars and professionals.

First, what is a brand? The illustrious prodigy of the marketing discipline, a brand is "a name, term, sign, symbol, or design, or combination of them which is intended to identify the goods and services of one seller or group of sellers and to differentiate them from those of competitors."[3] A brand is also acknowledged as "a container for a customer's complete experience with the product or company."[4] Elaborating further, these components are referred to as brand identities, which in totality refer to knowledge or associations in the mind of the consumer under different conditions that facilitates brand recall. A brand may be a product or an organization with the ability to influence a wide spectrum of stakeholders. In this interaction between the brand and the customer, communication is the key. What and how is the brand message communicated? How are stakeholders influenced? How is engagement initiated? Together with customers, the decisions, values and activities of employees too are influenced by brands. Employees not only represent but are encouraged to 'live' these values as an organization's most prized ambassadors and advocates (also see Chapter 4). Indeed, "recognizing and reinforcing a brand's interconnections with and organization's culture and performance"[5] via strategic communication can yield positive reputation and business outcomes.

A brand is an asset and a responsibility, which allows organizations to gain the love of the customer while keeping the relationship of enchantment regulated. The challenge is to regulate these relationships with brand messages and promises. With changing times, fortunately, the core purpose of brands and branding has remained the same with major shifts in the communication process. Now there is an overwhelming emphasis on dialogue as opposed to one-way communication, many-to-many brand conversations, not to mention demanding consumers who want to be part of the brand story. How should brands respond and negotiate in this new climate? How can they manage the paradox of creating resonance with consumers while loosening, even relinquishing, control?

What makes the discussion of change so fascinating is the intellectual struggle among researchers who underscore the importance of social media for brand survival and those that refer to brands as "uninvited crashers"[6] to the social media party intended to establish connections among people and not people and brands. Arguably, there is no going back (at least at this point), so both incumbents and new entrants face the challenge of best leveraging a fragmented and heterogeneous media landscape for brand and image building. But what is the new branding paradigm? What are the new and adapted communication strategies for brand communication?

We begin the investigative process with a consideration of changes in the concept of brands and branding.

THE BRAND, THE BRANDED, AND THE BRANDING

> People do not buy goods and services. They buy relations, stories and magic.
>
> *Seth Godin*[7]

LEARNING OBJECTIVES

- Understand the contemporary changes in branding and the shift toward consumer involvement.
- Examine the implications of these developments for brand control.

Consider this: A decade or two ago, a customer goes to a store to buy a mobile phone. What are the steps she follows in the purchase decision? Based on the traditional marketing 'funnel' which was linear, she progressively moves from awareness to familiarity to consideration to purchase, and finally loyalty.[8] Starting with multiple brands in the awareness phase, and progressively reducing the number of considered brands along way, the process was straightforward. A clean and pure transaction!

Fast forward to the digital age and we find more adventure and promiscuity in the transactions. The same customer would consider a pool of available options and evaluate them (via online reviews or recommendations from trusted sources) before zeroing in on the selection. A click of the mouse and the relationship starts! Not only that, but research has also found that consumers will often go online—after purchase—to conduct further research. The post-purchase experience is a critical trigger for brand loyalty. The decision journey, characterized by informed consumers, thanks to the digital revolution, is now more circular.[9]

The point here is that purchase decisions are not purely transactional or about functional benefits. With diminishing product differentiation, growing competition, and limited attention spans, differentiating oneself from others has become ever more urgent. What makes brands (and branding) powerful is understanding how a compelling and clear vision translates to a human and emotional connect. Because brands assign personal meaning, our identities, knowingly and subliminally, are shaped and signaled though our brand preferences. When you lace up a Nike shoe or aspire to get behind the wheel of a Tesla, what are you saying about yourself? So how do brands use strategic communication to create ties that inspire trust, aspiration, and loyalty?

Think of BMW. What are the first words, associations, thoughts, or images that come to mind? What does BMW stand for? With a brand value of US$41,535 million in 2016 and its powerful core value of 'The Ultimate Driving Machine,' BMW is among the most recognizable global brands. In the 100th year of existence, the company has taken this core theme a notch higher to roll out VISION NEXT 100, "that empowers you to become the 'Ultimate Driver' – the best driver you can possibly be."[10] On social media, particularly Instagram, #BMW is reportedly the most tagged brand hashtag. Posting relevant content (e.g., photos, videos, and contests), frequent posts and updates, repurposing (or Re-gramming) user-generated content has allowed BMW to consistently drive engagement and attract new Instagram followers.[11] In the words of Harald Krüger, Chairman of the Board of Management of BMW AG, "Brands are a company's biggest USP: They combine emotion, design and heritage with the promise of high quality."[12]

The traditional approaches of brand building were centered on paid content, sponsorships, and advertisements. Arguably, the customers could easily bypass or actively choose to bypass advertisements, trusting instead recommendations from known acquaintances or other consumers.[13] Public relations (PR) professionals play a vital role in bridging the trust deficit and partner in brand building. Although PR has faced problems with its own 'brand,' often being equated to 'spin,' its goal is to build relationships between an organization and its publics.

Earlier models used by PR practitioners for communicating brands were press agentry with the help of mass media platforms to broadcast information. 'Asymmetrical' and 'symmetrical' two-way communication were other models of communication. The asymmetrical two-way communication was based on research done on targeted users to customize communication for the target segment. Symmetrical two-way communication, at least in theory,[14] was considered the holy grail for PR. It is debatable whether social media have it easier or more challenging to use symmetrical communication as a sign of being open, honest, and more ethical. What is not debatable is that a majority of consumers expect brands to be more honest and authentic, act with integrity at all-times, and stay true to its stated values.[15]

With its focus on building relationships predicated upon "reciprocity, trust, mutual legitimacy, openness, mutual satisfaction, and mutual understanding,"[16] PR has once again become the blue-eyed boy of the organization. In a changed communication landscape, PR is indispensable in the branding process to both create the brand narrative and facilitate conversations about and around the brand via third-party endorsements. For these conversations to be authentic, the onus is on the brand owners to ensure that they are:

- "Communicating honestly about products and services
- Communicating honestly about environmental impact and sustainability measures
- Acting with integrity at all-times
- Being clear about and true to beliefs
- Being open and honest about partners and suppliers
- Standing for more than just making money
- Having a relevant and engaging story"[17]

The silver lining is that social media offer a plethora of opportunities, new ways of interacting and engaging with the public at large. Dialogic loops in the communication process between the public and the organization and emphasize the manner in which these interactions can take place, the method of retention of users who engage with the organization, the process of influencing, and providing relevant information regarding the brand. Lexicon now defines the branding process as 'unstoppable,' 'furious,' and 'exciting' to the point of being engaging and compelling. Extrapolating the lexical changes to communication across social media, we evidence a shift in power from the organization to the customer and online communities.

Changes in brand communication echo the changing consumer mind-set. With more information and a greater focus on authenticity and values, consumers are more vigilant and hold brands accountable to their promises. At the extreme, brands have lost the power to act as agents of persuasion with rhetoric ability. Instead, they are being used by consumers as a platform to communicate. Earlier concepts, such as positioning, have paved the way for advocacy of a brand 'purpose' that transcends commercial imperatives. The challenge, then, is to communicate this value-driven purpose in a manner that is simultaneously creative, credible, authentic, and engaging.

A good story with a rich content can be the liberating point through which a brand relinquishes control (addressed in the section Will Social Media 'Just Do It' for Branding?). This is normally backed with a relevant message providing room and scope to customers to use the brand as a launch pad for conception, innovation, co-creation, and collaboration. There is more self-expression, greater value creation, meaningful exchange of ideas, and relationships with and among internal and external stakeholders.

Busk (2015) discusses the social media strategy of building content as a means of customer engagement with the use of all social media channels and interaction between internal and external stakeholders. One of the examples he cites is of Coca-Cola *Journey*, a storytelling engine, a digital magazine, which carries original and unique content on the company and its people. The story is narrated through a content amplification strategy that circulates the key message through Facebook, Instagram, LinkedIn, and Twitter. Leveraging the specific benefits of each platform, narratives are designed to drive engagement and delight the reader. Together with these platforms, Coca-Cola aggressively pursues search for emerging channels (e.g., Periscope). The objective of the *Journey* is reader engagement. Beginning with the premise on which the engine was launched, the company analyzes the content and its receptivity by the customers to identify what content resonates with the readers and what does not. This democratized storytelling on all platforms has helped fans and followers get an authentic perspective on the narrative of an over 100-year-old company.

> Coca-Cola supplies a fertile and rich source of stories—and stories behind the stories about the company many already thought they knew. This flexibility is the key to engaging authentically with readers, fans and followers and allows the company to be part of the world's digital conversation as it shifts.[18]

Impact of Culture on Brands and Branding

Before we proceed further, let us pause and reflect on societal culture as a governing parameter of public interactions with the organization. Though geographical boundaries have blurred with social media, the hub for initiating the branding exercise is cultural. Demonstrating cultural relevance is paramount for a successful strategy but it works in more interconnected ways. In the past and now, brands creatively draw on culture, "capitalize on cultural values, tensions, and collective ideologies to deliberately position Brands at the center of a specific cultural context."[19]

Digital technologies add another level of culture that brands need to consider. The online community creates and forms culture as they exist by propagating a system of *crowd culture*[20] that can act as an adversary claiming the audience's attention away from the brand or an ally if the brands are able to leverage their cognition and create alternative models of *cultural branding*. In the former, brands work in partnership with *crowd cultures* to promote their perception of the brand. If adopted as a deliberate strategy, it can do wonders to the brand communication. A recognized authority in branding, Douglas Holt (2016), cautions that companies need to go beyond advertisements or sponsorships because "consumers have little interest in the content that brands churn out."[21] Drawing on the power of *crowd cultures* is the future, according to Holt, because "by targeting novel ideologies flowing out of crowd cultures, brands can assert a point of view that stands out in the overstuffed media environment."[22] How important is brand culture for employees within the organization? Burberry provides empirical evidence on the point through its history of turnaround of the company that was expedited by employees internalizing the vision of the leader and the core values of sharing, involving, and engaging.[23]

Does this, however, signal a loss of brand control and act as a cause for fear?

Loss of Control

Today, there is a complete climb-down from the strategies that were guiding the branding exercise a decade ago. The golden age of branding had creative agencies employing conventional forms of advertising and other paid content. Soon came digital media with its disruptive functions. Organizations assumed knowledge of the medium and assumed that use of branded content would be a via media for them to narrate tales and establish connect with their customers. Going viral, creating buzz, developing memes were terms that still needed robust application. Billions were invested, yet by far few firms were able to connect meaningfully with customers through branded content.[24] The campaign 'HP Bend the Rules' demonstrates well the strategies of engaging customers and ceding control over branding initiatives.

In 2014, HP India initiated 'Bend the Rules' campaign as part of its global makeover plans to be recognized as a young company. It encouraged the youth to post stories and pictures of 'breaking rules' to realize their dreams and achieving success. This coincided with introduction of a new product that bends as well—the HP Pavilion × 360—a value-packed convertible PC, which easily converts from notebook, to stand, to tent, to tablet mode. A winning entry that celebrated the aspirations of the youth as enablers of purposive action was aired. Every social star collaborated with the creative process. Within four weeks, there were 45 million organic views. "HP reached their target audience with 78 percent of viewers ranging between the ages of 13–34. The HP YouTube channel visitors grew 600 percent among 13–24-year-olds and their subscribers at large increased 48 percent."[25]

From crowdsourcing brand logos and ideas for rebranding, companies are turning to their community for diverse and novel input. Mozilla's rebranding call in 2016, aligned with its open-source principles, noted: "Unlike most brand identity projects crafted by designers behind closed doors and unveiled only at the end, ours will be made entirely in the open with the advice and counsel of a global design community including you."[26] Elements of the new brand identity are being rolled out in 2017.[27]

The temptation to treat these examples as complete loss of control may be too naive. Even Mozilla was clear on its blog that inviting community counsel did not amount to crowd-sourcing or voting on ideas. However, compared to the conventional forms of communication, these changes to invite and collaborate with customers on shaping the brand signal a sea change in strategy. One might argue that brands had no choice and customers were already driving brand conversations. As the bandwidth for discussions over social platforms has increased, customers can share positive news and voice grievances. In general, emotional outpouring, another form of engagement, is gaining credence. Positive in this approach is the peep that organizations are able to manage on what appealed and what repelled in the social media space.

With the possibility to create or contribute brand content via crowdsourcing and other virtual and digital themed interactions, consumers and brands enter in a new relationship—one that empowers customers, engulfing them into the online brand community (OBC) and making them a part of the brand through a sense of ownership. This could also be christened as open-source branding.

AS THE TRUTH UNFOLDS: 'OPEN SOURCE BRANDING'

> You have to stay true to your heritage; that's what your brand is about.
>
> *Alice Temperley* [28]

LEARNING OBJECTIVES

- Recognize how brands can be managed collectively by the organization and the consumer.
- Comprehend the considerations (collectivism, transparency, and criticism) for open-source branding.

'Open source branding' is a process in which consumers have equal, if not greater, say in what the brand should look like and how it should perform. This entails a participatory and collaborative behavior with empowered consumers co-creating, sharing, and disseminating content.

What drives successful brand management in the digital landscape? The brand value proposition that cuts across competition and provides a gilt edge. Do I as an organization know more about the customers, their psyche than my competitors? What is meaningful and relevant for the customers? Answers to these questions begin with design of an engagement-centric value proposition through which organizations pursue meaningful dialogues with customers, share and embrace ideas that drive heightened levels of affinity with the brand and the branding process. In this process, trust is a great leveler levied to perceive 'openness' and 'transparency' in the organizational intent as perceived by the customers.

This new face of branding may be frightening to many. It is characterized by three distinct features of "collectivism," "transparency," and "criticism"[29] (Figure 1.1).

FIGURE 1.1 *Open Source Branding*

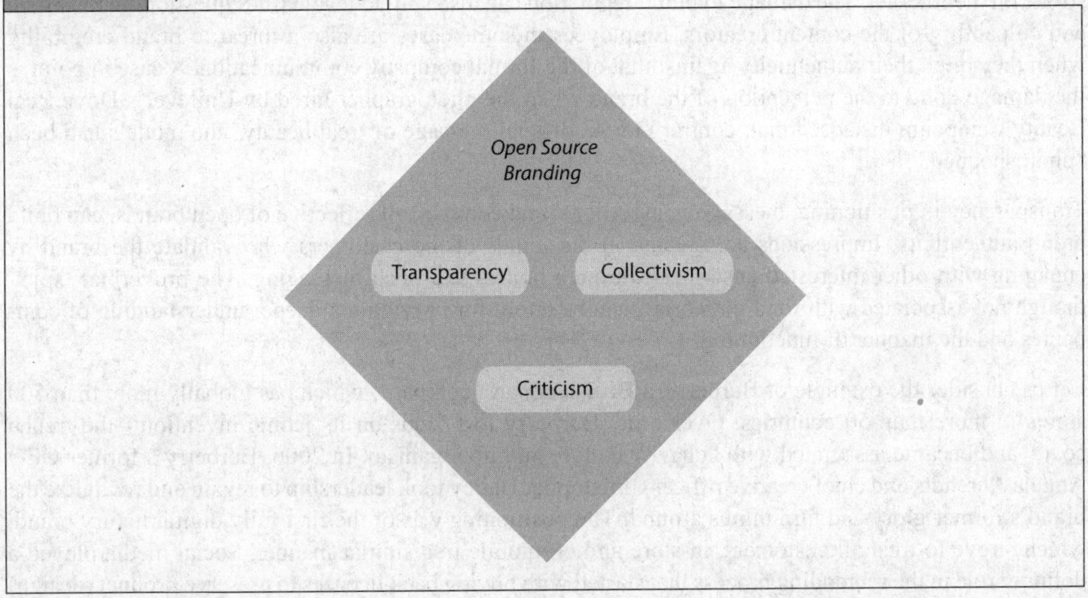

Source: Adapted by the authors from Fournier and Avery (2011).[30]

Collectivism

Virtual connections generated among disparate yet concurring people and/or micro-targeted niche segments provide opportunities to individuals and communities for sharing content and strengthening group bonds on the brand. In the social media, brand following and sharing information ensures a collaborative approach that can be spun in favor of the company and brand by acknowledging consumer rights and relinquishing control. A case in point is the Coca-Cola Facebook page, which is co-managed by fans and the company. The organization has given up control on the content of this Facebook page, which is replete with messages from people and lacks corporate messaging.

There are some brands that initiate the process from scratch and formulate the business model based on the principle of collective power of consumers to generate content and create the brand image. Political leaders such as Barack Obama (former US President), Narendra Modi (Indian Prime Minister), and Hollywood and Bollywood actors are adopting this principle to solicit comments and to share information through Twitter.

Companies scout for this consumer-generated content, which can then be co-opted for brand promotion. These organically created messages become viral sensations on the social media and create a halo effect of credibility. However, not all is positive as collectivism can often prove to be contradictory to the company vision and mission and force a company to take a path, which though favorable to the consumer, may not be company friendly. Collectivism in social media, with all its intent and purpose, is in favor of the consumer and not the brand.

Transparency

In the age of Web 2.0, where all knowledge is public, companies apparently are sitting on a time bomb of bad publicity without the luxury of concealing information that they may want to keep under wraps. This proposition is more applicable to iconic brands with the potential of being weakened by a single stroke on the Internet. The damage to brand reputation can also spill to legal issues questioning the intent and culpability of the content creators. Employees in some cases are also a threat to brand credibility when they pitch their authenticity against that of the formal company communication. A case in point is the damage done to the perception of the brand when the photographer hired by Unilever's Dove Real Beauty Campaign disclosed that, contrary to the official message of 'real beauty,' the models had been "photoshopped."[31]

Transparency in positioning, messaging, assertions, and conduct, all reflective of open brands, can build brand authenticity. Impressions are created in the minds of the customers who validate the brand by engaging with other interested customers, through honest and open messaging. The proverbial 'spin,' though not associated with fond memories, can be a tool for providing a deeper understanding of companies and the manner of functioning.

Let us consider the example of Burberry, a British apparel company, which has globally more than 500 stores in more than 50 countries. Over time, Burberry lost focus on its iconic invention—the trench coat—and became associated with "chav"[32] culture and hooliganism. In 2006, Burberry's former CEO Angela Ahrendts and chief creative officer Christopher Bailey took leadership to regain and revitalize the brand's former glory and turn things around. The positioning was of the first fully digital luxury brand, which strove to treat all customers, in-store and on mobile in a similar manner. Social media played a defining role in the rebranding process that started with buying back licenses to preserve product (design) integrity. In 2009, with the launch of 'The Art of the Trench,' Burberry became the first company to go fully digital and build a social enterprise. On a microsite, the company invited customers to post photos of themselves wearing trench coats, and to comment, like, and share content on Facebook, Twitter, and email. This strategy of establishing a connect with customers enhanced the aspirational value of the brand and inculcated brand loyalty.

Additionally, in the spring/summer of 2010, a fashion show was streamed live, giving the world free access to exclusive ramp action for the first time. Within a year, Burberry's Facebook page had more than a million followers, the largest at the time for a luxury brand, and the company recorded a 50 percent growth in e-commerce sales.[33] During Ahrendts' time as CEO, company valuations rose from £2 billion to more than £7 billion.[34] As a pioneer in incorporating technology in the fashion industry,[35] the company is recognized as one of the most popular brands on social media.[36] As on date, there are more than 17 million likes on Facebook, 6.7 million followers on Twitter, and 7 million followers on Instagram.[37]

Other companies have also stepped up their branding strategies in the desire to be transparent and truthful about the brands. Transparency provides an impetus to companies to provide truthful information. At the end of the day, a purposeful positioning of the brand is important in creating an image of trust in the mind of the customer. The brand authenticity is an indication of the level of trust the organization begets.

But what do transparency and authenticity look like, and who is to decide? Is there anything as 'complete transparency,' and can authenticity and strategic considerations co-exist? In an effort to balance these vexing predicaments, organizations have used fake blogs (Flogs), ghost blogging, ghost tweeting, and astroturfing (providing money to online influencers to create fake sentiment). Whether these are 'worth' the potential damage to brand reputation, if disclosed, is a question that all organizations and brand executives need to ask and answer for themselves. When Walmart got caught for its fake blog (*Wal-Marting Across America*) and the efforts to pass it off as an independent commentary of two people who turned out to be employees of the retailer's then PR firm, Edelman, there was widespread disbelief and indignation. In fact, the more shocking than Walmart's responsibility was the outcry that Edelman had failed to practice what it preached to clients, a lesson quickly taken to heart by the PR firm.[38]

The ascendance of open-source branding and associated considerations discussed are bound to evoke some uncertainty about how 'much' trust can be passed on to online communities and users. What works for one will not work for all, and the answers are contingent on organizational philosophy, preparedness, and risk appetite, among others. An organization with a low appetite for uncertainty will minimize engagement, and its interactions with customers will be restricted to predefined areas as customer service. As "predictive practitioners,"[39] these organizations lack sense of adventure and excitement and the outcome of their endeavors is predictable, expected and measurable.

Others deliberately embrace uncertainty. They do not rely on social media for procuring information about their brand. These "creative experimenters"[40] court engagement from their customers for singular functions and practices employing small and isolated experiments that make the organization open for scrutiny. Twitter and Facebook are popular platforms for such initiatives; companies may leverage their in-house proprietary tools as well. Such a strategy usually stems from budget constraints. Both creative practitioner and predictive experimenter strategies are quick and easy to implement for demonstration of transparency in conduct and behavior.

On the other hand, there are organizations that go all hog and embrace high uncertainty and are in the explorative mode while tinkering with social media to engage audience across functions. They are termed as "social media champions."[41] As organizations seek more significant results, they can adopt these large-scale schemes.

Lastly, we have organizations that open their frontiers across platforms seeking interaction across business areas and ask for overall feedback. These are large-scale efforts aimed at receiving constructive critique on their business. The level of uncertainty for such organizations is very high. The strategy of these "social media transformers"[42] is impactful and can reverberate vicissitudes from the conceptualization of a product, the research and design, to its manufacture, operationalization, and even the supply chain. Progression in role from champions to transformers usually lies in the leadership vision and organization-wide company philosophy toward the online community.

What is interesting is that these categories are not fixed or permanent. Organizations may shift from one strategy to another depending on the need of the hour and the ability to take risks at a given point in time. Investment in the environment and the current market structure influence practitioners to adopt one of these philosophies. Considering that social media are only a decade old, organizations are still trying to lodge themselves in this space, build strategies that will impact their present branding exercise and reputation and place the foundation of learning for future strategies.

A study[43] was conducted on 3,500 customers and non-customers of Netherlands-based KLM Royal Dutch Airlines to research the impact of social media on corporate reputation. The findings reported that the impact of news with a positive tone of voice ups a positive image of the company. Exposure to electronic word-of-mouth (eWOM) of a company revealed again a positive impression. Next, when companies 'humanize' the brand, they create a perception that is cordial and inviting.[44] Finally, interactivity encouraged positivity and developed a favorable inkling toward the company and brand, which directly impacted the corporate reputation. When the interactivity was high, it predicted a more positive reputational impact[45] and enhanced attitudinal outcomes than otherwise.

The question now is how can brands manage this new paradigm of co-existing with their consumers?

WILL SOCIAL MEDIA 'JUST DO IT' FOR BRANDING?

> If you don't give the market the story to talk about, they'll define your brand's story for you.
>
> *David Brier*[46]

LEARNING OBJECTIVES

- Identify the strategies for customer involvement in branding.
- Review the importance of communication for creating brand loyalty and trust.

"HOW? NOW. WOW!" are the three pillars of strategy at Monster.[47] These three innocent words explain how page views on content rose by 18 million, and conversions to job search jumped up 28 percent in 2016 over the previous year.[48]

'How?' addresses the question of creation of value-oriented content for the brand. If the brand message considers the audience needs and fulfills them, brand loyalty is a given. In the particular case of Monster, the 'how' relates to job, job search, and content management. The company adopts a two-pronged approach for content. The first involves search of bottom-of-funnel keywords, which provides a clue about the customer search points. The second focuses on 'how to' of the clicks, that is, the topics on which the customers will anyway click even if they think the topics are not of direct relevance. The next pillar is 'Now.' What do people want to know 'now'? The brand should be made to appear current and relevant. The brand experience through this communication is what the third pillar stands for: 'WOW!' Content of this kind is more in nature of building brands rather than just aiming at conversions through social media. For Monster then, How is for utility, Now for news, and Wow for emotions.

What makes a brand 'tick' in the social media realm? Is it the How, Now, WOW strategy? Of course, there are the 'knowns' (awareness, differentiation, compelling value proposition, deep consumer insight, creating personal connect and meaning), some of which have gained more prominence (e.g., meaningful experiences). Then, there are the 'unknowns' (understanding and communicating with Millennials, and accepting consumers as co-pilot or pilot-in-command in the branding journey). Although the 'unknowns' arouse anxiety by virtue of their novelty, even the 'knowns' are made more challenging in the digital age. How can brands tell an appealing story in a cluttered and hyper-competitive communication space? Is managing the new branding paradigm the answer?

MANAGING THE NEW BRANDING PARADIGM

Social media have created a virtual ecosystem and considerably narrowed the gap between the consumers and the organization, strengthened ties, and increased customer involvement. The platforms on which the consumers are most active are vital to establish connections but that is only the start. Can consumers be motivated to be creative? What are the processes, tools, and strategies to facilitate collective creativity? Which social media are best suited for such innovative activities?

Consumer involvement and support can provide a sense of ownership to the enthusiasts and generate brand loyalty. Though the strategies delineated below are not written in stone, they are evolving and marketers still need to test the robustness to be able to come up with a theoretically sound framework for application.

- Co-creation
- Storytelling
- Brand Entification
- Managing and Building Brand Communities
- Advergaming: Second Life
- Creating Avatars

Co-creation

Co-creation is the process of content creation through 'open innovation'[49] with the support of external players. The process of co-creation is undertaken to solicit support of customers in design of new products and has gained prominence in the last decade or so. Generation of novel ideas and selection and implementation of the most appropriate one are the two central activities included in the process of co-creation. On some occasions, consumer support is solicited for evaluation of potential ideas entreating for a higher degree of involvement.

The process of generation of ideas through co-creation is comparatively simpler as it allows greater flexibility and higher degree of freedom and creativity than otherwise. The challenge is to look for ways to incentivize the creators of innovative ideas that can range from cash or licensing contracts to non-monetary acknowledgements. Some or all of these inducements have been reportedly used by organizations to garner customer support.

While indulging in value-creating activities such as brainstorming for low-budget advertising or creating tag lines, organizations run the risk of being the subject of ridicule by consumers who may decide to hijack the process. These problems are faced majorly by organizations with a strong brand reputation or even when there is brand ambiguity and multiple initiatives. Market uncertainty may force an organization to seek inputs from consumers, which may not always secure the relevant responses. Further, the frequency of engagement has been found to be inversely proportional to the quantity, quality, and variety of input. An interesting example is of Dell IdeaStorm in which customers were found to be repeating ideas already presented or implemented by the company. In such cases, constant interaction and monitoring of ideas would be the closest that organizations can attempt.

Storytelling

Does Candy Crush Saga ring a bell? How do you move on the serpentine roads as you progress from one level to the other? By reimagining and reinventing the tools of navigation. To bring the analogy closer home, brand communication through storytelling is another form of deconstructing and reconstructing conversations and communicating with customers, adding value, and overcoming obstacles. The information architecture is shaped by designing and scripting a content saga that appeals to the customers.

The overall strategy is creation of well-analyzed and researched content and some unraveling pieces which cannot be easily addressed. What works wonders in this process is a collation of facts and figures, and structuring of content with purpose before planning the strategy. This will inevitably draw attention to what is being said and create room for personalization.

The story framework has been used by companies to create their narratives in a form that appeals and engages. STORY can also been used as an acronym to understand the process of narration.

S: Situation relevant to the reader
T: Told in a way to engage the reader
O: Opens the reader's mind
R: Relationship
Y: Yields information beyond the story

Many examples of storytelling successes and fails spring forth. As a case in point, Red Bull's digital magazine (rebulletin.com) is a storehouse of stories about sports, lifestyle, and culture that are relevant to the brand's demographic without necessarily calling out the company's products. High-quality videos and exclusive photographs have made this storytelling platform a magnet for enthusiasts who associate with the values of adventure, extreme sport, entertainment, travel, and leisure, among others. The Stratos jump by Felix Baumgartner to break the world record of the longest freefall jump of 128,000 feet above the Earth strongly etched the brand in consumer lives; the video has over 41 million views since it was published in October 2012.[50] Documenting epic moments that give "wings to people and ideas," the beverage itself is not the headline in the case of Red Bull.

TOMS shoes is another example of a brand with a social mission collaborating closely with customers to inspire collective action, and P&G's campaign #LikeAGirl allows their audience a lead role in the story. Under Armor's campaign 'I Will What I Want' is one more case of storytelling that strikes an emotional chord and draws on lived experience, seeking to empower women to rise above rejection, take back control, and push ahead. Interactive films with real-time commentary streaming in from social media featured 'athletic females' such as ballet dancer Misty Copeland and supermodel Gisele Bündchen and told the stories of women breaking through social scrutiny and pressure to pursue their goals. The multimedia campaign has fueled a positive association for brand among women ('brand for me'; as opposed to its masculine origins), a 120 percent increase in brand awareness, five billion media impressions, US$35 million in earned media, and a 28 percent[51] increase in sales.

A story helps in building connects and loyalty between the brand and the customer through brand communication. It provides flexibility in engaging authentically with readers, fans, and followers and allows the company to be part of the world's digital conversation as it shifts. The focus though is on quality storytelling, without which there is no context or connect with the reader. (For more on visual storytelling, refer to the story of Whole Foods: Box 1.1.)

Based on a study of social media pioneers and experts, research consultancy Latitude[52] published an interesting report that identified audience expectations around storytelling and best practices of storytelling. For one, they reported that with growing possibilities for interaction and real-time communication, audiences 'crave more control' on their content experiences, and many would like opportunities for contributing, changing, experiencing stories themselves. Second, they found that audiences are willing to extend collaboration by creatively donating their skills, or submitting ideas, and even participate in getting the word out. But what will the most resonant stories in the future have in common? The report proposed 4Is:

- **Immersion:** can I go deeper into the story-world, by learning more about it or by heightening my sensory experience of it?
- **Interactivity:** can I change or influence elements of the story? Can I interact with other people around the story?

- **Integration:** is a cohesive story being told across platforms? Can I interface with the real world in any way?
- **Impact:** does the story inspire me to take action in my own life, such as making a purchase or supporting a good cause?[53]

How important is the storytelling process in brand communication and building brand loyalty? It may be difficult to assign a quantitative value to the same, but it can be categorically asserted that an authentic story helps build trust and generate brand loyalty.

Brand Entification

Brand entification signifies the emotional and cognitive relationship between serious social media users (specifically Twitter) and the brands. This is inclusive of what they ascribe to the brand.

Though Twitter is only a decade old, it has over 317 monthly active users (2016) that send approximately over 500 million tweets daily.[54] Interestingly, though some of the tweets do mention product or brand names, none of the highly valued products are part of the Twitter conversation. A careful consideration to this problem is required for the solution to the problem is not novel but based on the activities in the social media space and the response patterns.

The intrusive power of Twitter in the active army of the current generation (Millennials) requires an alignment with their mind-set. An understanding of this generation, fully immersed in social media and inseparable from smartphones, with calibrated use of Twitter handles and smart engagement of users can help organizations entify their brands by elevating it to a celebrity status. Whole Foods (Box 1.1) is a good example of how the organization facilitated brand entification. Here, we discuss the specific tactics of the company in promoting their brand and building brand loyalty.

Box 1.1: Whole Food and Social Media

Founded in Texas, Whole Foods Market came into existence in 1980. After 34 years of existence, it could well boast of sales to the tune of US$14.63 billion (2014), which was an increase from US$400,000 since the year of inception. Its target customers lead a very busy lifestyle and are between 25 and 40 years of age. It has repeatedly been subject to consumer backlash for procuring material from farms with low concern for ethical food production. Being constantly pressured by environmentalists, the company has moved ahead treading cautiously while addressing concerns through its social media accounts.

In 2012, it had almost 600 social media accounts talking about the brand and 2,000 employees regularly contributing to the content. Its strategy has been primarily directed toward Twitter, where it has 4.38 million followers, roughly 60.2 percent of its total media followers. A majority (~60%) of its tweets are in the form of recipes which link the consumer to the company blog or its YouTube channel. Approximately 85 percent of its tweets contain visual messages. The Whole Foods social media engagement team is very responsive. Apart from weekends, they respond to almost 100 tweets per day. To gel with the consumers they try and adapt their voice to the customer styles.

Whole Foods is also active on other platforms such as Facebook (24%) and Instagram (6%). With a following of 1.7 million on Facebook, Whole Foods proceeds with an amalgamated social media strategy. It promotes intersecting content across platforms. There is consistency and similarity in the messages posted on Facebook and Twitter, though the bit.ly links are different, primarily to track the

(Box 1.1 Continued)

(Box 1.1 Continued)

traffic generated from each platform. Links from these platforms are provided that lead the reader to the blog/web page. Apart from Instagram, Whole Foods is also using Pinterest.

By June end of 2015, supportive audience on the social web had increased to 260,500. Awards for the 'Best Brand on Pinterest' have consistently validated the company's social media marketing on multiple platforms.

> At Whole Foods Market we are always looking for new ways to reflect the **immersive visual experiences** of our retail spaces in an authentic and compelling way in our visual spaces. Pinterest provides us a unique opportunity to create a strong connection with our customers through visual storytelling in a way that they want to collect and experience time and again—a unique value proposition of the digital world. We're thrilled to receive the Shorty Award because it validates our main digital marketing approach of establishing **online communities** with our customers focused on shared values and passions.[55] (emphasis added)

Source: Anderson (2015).[55]

The three associated characteristics of brand entification are:

1. The brand is much more than a human voice that speaks and responds. It has the status of a celebrity with high social prestige.
2. The brand allows for bragging rights in the Twitter community by helping consumers elevate their status and adopt narcissistic principles of self-love.
3. The user values are respected and the brand helps authenticate and live with these values.

Entification allows brands to get the benefit of users who censor and control negative comments, concentrate on generating and sharing positive tweets and in fact even defend the brand when attacked. The values espoused by the users are reverberated through the content that the brand projects in the social media.[56]

A common practice on Twitter is to express love for the brand in a vocabulary normally associated with celebrities. However, this is not a common phenomenon as several Twitter users are also indifferent to entificatory attributions of the brand. There are two factors that can be associated with relentless conversations on Twitter—the fear of missing out (FOMO) or the thought that life is interfering with Twitter usage and not vice versa. FOMO often drives Twitter users to share information, knowledge, and intelligence. Users are careful not to send out negative comments, which are censored, for they do not want to cause embarrassment to entified brands.

Managing and Building Brand Communities

Brand communities can be built by initiating informal social media dialogue through customer-to-customer (C2C) interactions or formal sponsored dialogue on discussion forums. These communities can be both a blessing in disguise and a curse for the organizations. The advantage of these communities is that they can build relationships that foster brand loyalties. The example of Vital Platforms provided below clearly enunciates the point.

The 'Vital Signs' platform was created by the Avery Dennison Foundation team with the Rainforest Alliance in 2013.[57] They joined hands with *The Guardian* in 2014 to influence viewership and help people see a connect between people and the planet. The positioning of the brand was envisioned to create meaning, generate purpose in the perception of the people in which they could sense a possibility of making a difference in their own personal lives. Stories were crafted with themes around sustainability, FSG certified product communities and processes while maintaining the educational intent of the content. In the process of telling all these stories, the company ensured a very high degree of transparency. While measuring brand sentiment, Avery Dennison found an increase in viewership, implying a positive correlation between building brand awareness and communication in brand communities.[58]

Successful brand communities can be build by a re-imagining and rethinking of communication patterns structured on the native organizational wisdom of identifying brand ambassadors or advocates. Research on American online consumers reports that 70 percent consumers listen to this voice on blogs, reviews, and discussion forums.[59] These brand champions facilitate development of brand communities through sharing relevant and engaging content. They are the human voice for the company, gently and positively cajoling customers to develop a positive frame of mind by redesigning content provided by the organizations. They are also entrusted with the task of managing information by understanding the communities, identifying and implementing drivers of success in OBCs, and dealing with negative messages.

While managing online C2C interaction, managers should understand the disposition of online communities they are engaging with, as well as the tenets of promoting successful interaction and of managing negative online colloquies. An example that readily comes to mind is that of Patanjali and Baba Ramdev (see Appendix B). What made the brand successful? The founder, the positioning, and the brand communication! With a curious mix of modernity and conventionalism, Baba Ramdev has an appeal for consumers across age and income brackets. His wellness sermons and easy-to-perform *asana*s (Yoga poses), revival of Ayurveda and naturopathy, and a nationalist appeal has global multinationals scratching their head in disbelief. Arguably, a combination of factors has propelled Patanjali to its current position: communication reiterating the benefits of Ayurveda and naturopathy coupled with engagement and the timing of the launch. In an age fettered by physical and mental anguish at perceived environmental ills, the transparent brand communication reiterating a return to proven wisdom and tradition has been reassuring and perceived to be authentic. Not to mention the fillip from heightened national sentiments of promoting what is Indian and shunning what is not.

Patanjali's brand communication is based on the 4 Ps of marketing: differentiated product with appeal to the Indian masses in traditional Ayurvedic medicines and remedies. Twenty–thirty percent discounted price as compared to similar products of competitors. Distribution through Ayurvedic pharmacies with a strong claim on Ayurveda and health benefits being reiterated by the brand ambassador, Baba Ramdev, himself. In spite of following the basic tenets of marketing and communication, Patanjali has recently been in the news for allegations of fake products. Big players like Hindustan Unilever, Nestle, and Colgate-Palmolive are volleying against Baba Ramdev with lab test reports on manufacture of fake and adulterated Patanjali products.[60] All fans and communities wait with bated breath to watch the unfolding of the story of the brand war. Will this incident impact brand loyalty and brand authenticity? You may want to compare and contrast this case and the anticipated results with the Maggi case (see Appendix, Chapter 2).

So far we have discussed strategies for building connects, drawing people together in the form of brand communities. We also need to consider situations when followers decide to opt out of the crowd and shift loyalty to other brands. What is it that excites this move is a question addressed by Lehr (2015) in the article titled, "The Unfollow Algorithm."[61] Addressing questions as to why are brands followed or "unfollowed," the study reports that only four percent of respondents follow brands on social media to give brand feedback, 16 percent of the respondents follow a brand because they like it, 15 percent follow brands to be notified of special offers/promotions, and 12 percent follow brands to learn about new products and services. The answers to the 'unfollow' question present the following responses: 45 percent unfollow because of too much self-promotion (e.g., when a company ignores its audience and constantly promotes its brand). Another 34 percent unfollow if it uses automated messaging (e.g., when you follow a brand and automatically receive a message saying "Thanks for following me!"). Revealing data with sufficiently interesting points for reflection!

Primary and extended brand communities

Brand communities can be categorized as primary and extended. Primary community comprises users whose attachment to and interest in specific brands is deep, commitment stronger, and involvement higher than the general category of the extended brand community. For instance, they may be troubled by negative reviews and may shoot out messages or share their anguish with other members in the community. Their bonding with the community members has put in place unspoken and unwritten governance practices because of which users may decide to step in to correct alleged misinformation or misrepresentation of sorts. With strong influencers and champions for the brand, this community is willing to address concerns of the dissatisfied customers who approach them for problem resolution. There are few problems to be addressed as long as the interactions remain within this community. When disgruntled customers are unable to secure desired responses and begin posting on YouTube or Facebook, messages reach extended communities, creating irreparable damage to the organization and the brand.

Tailoring the right message for online brand communication follows the four steps of "Intervention, conversion, value creation and harvesting."[62] Generally adopted to counter negativity, intervention is executed by employees hired for the purpose of reviewing and monitoring inappropriate comments. Arguably, in such instances, stakes are high, for there is perceived threat to company reputation in the public domain. The challenge for conversion is to handle the disgruntled community and convert them to friends and allies championing the cause of the brand. For this purpose, evangelists and moderators may be requisitioned to proactively intercept and provide speedy and convincing responses. The final technique, of creating value for the brand community, can be implemented by understanding customer needs and requirements and focusing on the positive and proactive forms of communication (Figure 1.2).

Social media have invoked companies to sign an unspoken contract with customers on 'control' of brand communication. In this space, it is not prudent to relinquish complete control. As online communication

FIGURE 1.2 *Social Media Brand Communication*

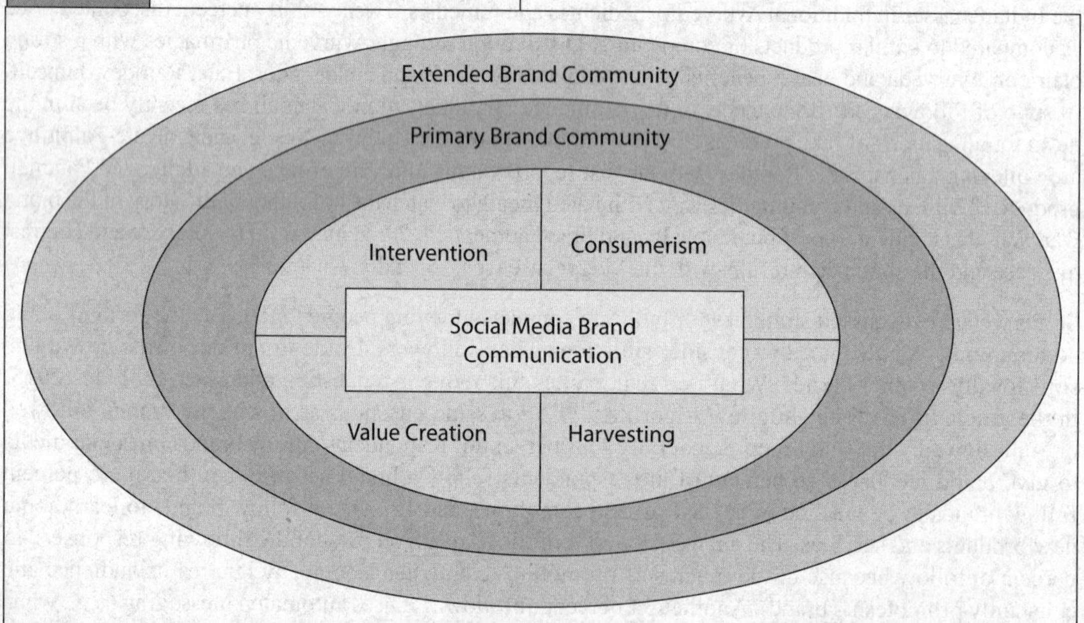

Source: Adapted by the authors from Noble et al. (2012).[63]

is about getting to know the customer better, a listening exercise on what are the customers talking about identifying their affinities and their affiliations with various brands can be a driver in building relationships. Providing solutions to pain points is a good way to commence engagement and build loyalty. Consider the example of BeingGirl.com, a website created by Proctor & Gamble (P&G) to provide teenage girls advice on female hygiene and answer questions on similar related topics. The dialogue with teenage girls addressed concerns clinically and objectively. The why, what, and how of the menstrual cycle, body changes, friendships and so on were topics that girls were hesitant in talking about. They found the dialogue and information engaging, educational and informative—which answered their innermost fears and concerns. Soon, P&G was able to create a 'teen destination' that not only drove visits and engagement but also sales.[64] By the end of the year (2007), there were over 32,000 registered users. In the same year, the site was nominated for the Asia Mobile Awards. Neither the story nor the brand purpose ended at this point. P&G has continued the zealous mission and on its 'Always' website gives advice from first periods to leaky bladders.[65] The trending campaign of P&G Always #LikeAGirl enunciates the brand purpose—to espouse the cause of girls and women through empowerment. The campaign celebrates the proud moments of living and behaving like a girl.[66]

While rethinking brand communication, organizations can align words with actions. The maxim for success is performing acts of "doing good, and get caught doing it."[67] Publics have taken message composition in their own hands with a democratization of information sharing. This is both a top-down corporate-driven process and a bottom-up customer-driven approach. The third is the ability to manage relationships with stakeholders. The only process of managing these relationships is by giving an ear to the conversations and engaging with them. The knowledge transfer is not only from the organization but also from all available sources. Good news for organizations is that social media have provided room and space for convergence of all forms of information that consumers can access from different sources.

Advergaming: Second Life

Social media are now the most proliferated media being used by marketers to promote and communicate brands. Social media have created opportunities for marketers to generate a new paradigm of communication with online computer games or virtual reality. This phenomenon, advergaming, has caught the attention of customers and is a growing field of interest for the last one decade. It allows brands to target specific users and communities espousing same values, needs, and aspirational identities.[68]

Adding a human element to the computer-generated environment has its merits of fascinating customers to the point of influencing purchase decisions and building brand affiliation. One of the major factors that allow Second Life to be used as a platform for engaging with customers is the format of user groups. These groups allow its members to connect with their fellow associates, trade information, and fulfill personal goals. It is important to understand the user in Second Life before using the strategy for branding activities. Users evaluate a brand on how well does the product category fit into the virtual world and how fitting is the product in adapting the emotions, characteristics, and attributes of the game.

Though there is conceivable potential in this space, the target audience is mostly limited to the profile of users attracted to online gaming. Unlike social media that has perpetuated across ethnicities, profiles, ages, socio-economic classes and genders, the online gaming space has a limited audience.

Consequently, one of the most popular ways of promoting a brand in the virtual world is through avatars.

Creating Avatars

An avatar is a computer-generated graphic that is technologically enabled for the user to engage with the virtual world.[69] It is a visual representation of the user, created and personalized with attributes as desired by the user.

Avatars are being used by organizations to interact with other avatars in virtual reality and are generally termed as spokes-avatars. They play various roles from being brand promoters, representatives of their organizations, act as personal shopping assistants and can even engage in conversations with the online users in the best commercial interests of their organization. Considering the freedom with which these avatars can be customized and utilized, it is a great marketing and branding ploy for organizations. Most brands anthromorphize these avatars to best suit their needs and to also imbibe the characteristics of the brand they are endorsing. What better game plan can there be than creation of an electronic personal assistant that can talk, respond to queries, form a reciprocal relationship, discuss the brand, and overall make the experience of interaction with the organization more enjoyable?[70]

Considering that brands have moved a long way away from selling on the basis of functional attributes and have accepted that the need to embody certain traits for a brand personality, spoke-avatars too need to have a personality to be able to endorse those brands. It is highly plausible that when users interact with avatars as representatives of brands, they might perceive these avatars as the personified versions of these brands. Just as in a retail environment, sales assistants are a part of the brand and shopping experience, these avatars are also guided by similar social relationship archetypes. Following from this premise then, the perception of brand interaction or the virtual shopping experience will be dependent on the nature of interface with the spokes avatar.

There has been a vivid rise in the number of organizations choosing avatars for brand communication and interaction. Undoubtedly, once the trend has been set, several organizations will eagerly adopt this route of building PR with their audience. However, not all brands/avatars would be successful in cultivating this online relationship. Credibility of the avatar is a major differentiating factor in the minds of the online community.

Considering the raw potency of this concept and the extent of opportunities that organizations can invest in this area of brand communication, it has been surprising that the addition of newer brands has slowed down, and after an initial high, there has been little progress.

Building Brand Loyalty

The afore-discussed sections point to techniques and strategies for building brand loyalty. Brand communities facilitate in building relationships between customers, customers and products, brands and the company and fostering brand loyalty. Research advocates the importance of trust—"the willingness of the average consumer to rely on the ability of the brand to perform its stated function"[71] in building brand loyalty.[72] The question, then, is how do online communities impact loyalty.

Interestingly, contradictory views have been posited by researchers on how trust can be built by social media. Some posit that social media are the best possible vehicle for reaching out to customers, while others argue that social media possess the potential of crashing the environment of people and friends.[73] Without getting into the specifics of the debate, we surmise that social media are 'people's media' which carry user-generated content with the aim of facilitating conversations and interactions among people/customers. Repeated interactions and long-term relationships[74] among customers and brand community can increase brand trust. Additionally, information sharing that reduces uncertainty and increases brand predictability results in developing trust. This is operationalized by improving customer relationship with the brand, other consumers, the company, and the products[75] and participation in social virtual communities.[76]

Undoubtedly, there has been an increase in investment in social media as a tool for brand communication and branding. However, deciphering the value of social media is still a puzzle.

Stemming from research, we can summarize starting considerations for organizations to develop brand loyalty (Table 1.1).

loyalty."[82] Social media have provided an irrefutable benefit to communicate brands because of the intrinsic nature of it being "no cost," "sticky," "effective" with an element of "humanizing."[83] This has provided an opportunity to organizations to mold their branding content in the new medium with a changed content while interacting in real time with their audience. The incessant chatter in the media space though has robbed companies of absolute control over the content. But how important is this loss of control in the process of branding? Does it really matter in the social media space?

Chapter Highlights

1. A brand embodies the dual character of an asset and a responsibility. It apportions organizations to gain the love of the customer yet obliges them to regulate this relationship of enchantment.
2. Social media have changed the communication patterns of consumers with brands.
3. Unidirectional communication is giving way to dialogic processes in which roles and responsibilities of the customers and marketers have reversed.
4. In social media, the touch points of influence and interactions provide an opportunity to organizations to shape the medium as well as the content and build interactivities.
5. Interactivities can be of three kinds: (1) Human-to-computer (2) human-to-human and (3) human-to-content.
6. Brands need to break through cultural barriers to be successful by challenging norms and still blending in by being culturally relevant.
7. The online community creates and forms culture, propagating a system of *crowd culture.* Brands work in partnership with *crowd cultures* to promote their perception of the brand.
8. Organizations can plan, strategize, and initiate 'no control' by conferring the right to the audiences to create content through ideas of crowdsourcing, virtual- and digital-themed interactions.
9. Open-source branding entails a participatory and collaborative behavior with empowered consumers co-creating, sharing, and disseminating content.
10. The new face of branding is challenging and is characterized by three distinct features of "collectivism," "transparency," and "criticism."
11. High-profile brands or dominant exemplars, also leaders in the industry, are subject to greater risk of consumer activism.
12. There are multiple threats, risks, and openings for brands in the social media space.
13. The threats may vary across product categories and may rely on ability of the organization to maintain its brand promise.
14. Some strategies to gain consumer support are co-creation, cultivating brand loyalty, brand entification, managing online brand communities, advergaming—Second Life and creating avatars.
15. Developing primary and extended brand communities are critical to the process of online brand communication.
16. Organizational PRs are the patterns for connect between the organization and the publics.
17. Websites are the easiest way to connect with the customers. PR firms also use blogs and leverage Facebook to encourage dialogue and build engagement with the larger community.
18. The core of any brand communication strategy hinges on the relationship theory, which advocates that initiatives taken under the aegis of PR should allow organizations to form relationships.

Activities

1. Based on your understanding of the chapter, do a self-positioning exercise. Imagine your brand. How would you define yourself? Think about your brand promise, purpose, and value proposition. How would you communicate brand YOU to prospective and current stakeholders (you may narrow the range of stakeholders by adding a specific context, e.g., a job interview).

2. Think of your favorite brand or one that you most admire. What makes this brand 'great'? What does the brand mean to you? What does it stand for, what are its core values and brand positioning? How does this brand communicate with you? How has this brand gained your trust and loyalty. Another version of previous exercise could be to compare a brand you like with one that you do not. What explains your responses?

3. Conduct research on a brand with which you engage (or one that you follow) on social media. How would you characterize the brand's relationship with its followers? What is your assessment of the approach of this brand to negotiate the paradox of gaining resonance and ceding control?

4. The chapter introduces many different concepts. In pairs of threes, choose a focal concept and find additional sources and an artefact (a short case, video, etcetera) that is relevant to the concept. Then prepare to 'teach' the class in a 7–10-min presentation (including Q&A). Instruct the class as if you are the expert on the concept. Your presentation should deepen understanding of the concept and show the ability to apply knowledge to a case.

5. Highlighted in the chapter and previous research is the threat from losing control. Many have argued that brands never had control. Watch this TEDTalk by Tim Leberecht: *3 ways to (usefully) lose control of your brand* (link: http://www.ted.com/talks/tim_leberecht_3_ways_to_usefully_lose_control_of_your_reputation/transcript?language=en). In pairs or in small groups, work together to create your own 'talk' (3–5 min) highlighting your arguments and perspectives on this topic.

6. Work in collaboration with local businesses or non-profit organizations (could be new or early start-ups, established brands, or those looking to rebrand) that are looking to enhance their digital presence. Employing concepts discussed, conduct a communication audit to assess current practices, understand how social media can contribute to their strategic objectives, and work with the organization to devise a brand campaign across relevant media. Conduct a post-campaign evaluation to assess results and make modifications, going forward.

7. Storytelling is becoming more critical for authentic communication that inspires loyalty and identification with a brand. Telling a unique story and breaking out of the clutter is no mean task. Compare and contrast brand stories. What kinds of stories are brands telling; how are these linked to their corporate or business values; who are the main actors in these stories; how do these stories position the brand in relation to these actors; what are the key themes and plots in these stories, and so on? How does storytelling create 'uniqueness' in these cases?

8. With a specific brand in mind, carry out an empirical research to understand consumer knowledge of the brand, awareness, positioning, favorability, and uniqueness of associations, and the brand promise. Why do customers use and purchase this brand; what do they think, feel, and do about the brand? Assess the alignment between consumer perspectives and brand image (are there potential or existing problems and what are the implications of these misalignments), and make recommendations, as necessary.

9. The digital age is forcing many organizations, big and small, to review and demonstrate relevance. Many legacy organizations have or are rebranding in the face of new challenges. Examine a rebranding initiative in-depth (5Ws and 1H—who, what, when, why, where, and how) with special focus on the role of social media.

10. The chapter discusses several strategies for consumer involvement in the new branding paradigm. Search, prepare, and present short case studies of wins and failures in each strategy. Via the exercise, reflect on your learnings about the role of customers via brand (control).

Discussion Questions

1. Have social media dramatically altered the way you relate with brands? Explain.
2. The focus on dialogue and dialogic communication is a prominent theme in literature. Social media are seen to be facilitators of dialogue. What are the assumptions in this argument (e.g., assumptions about the 'value' of dialogue; about the stakeholder–organization relationship; about social networks and their functionalities and so on)? How does your experience support or challenge these assumptions?
3. How do social media influence the image of a brand? By leveraging social media can organizations make brands more favorable to their stakeholders? Is there anything as 'too much' customer involvement in a brand to the point where the brand starts to look weak?
4. One perspective holds that social media were never intended for connecting people and brands, while another views social media as crucial for business success. How do you make sense of social media for branding? Can we speak about branding that excludes social media? Are there specific examples? Under what conditions might such an approach work?
5. What is your perspective on the tension between authenticity and transparency, namely, strategic outcomes (competitive advantage)? Does one trump the other? Are these mutually exclusive? Looking at examples you have encountered, what arguments can you make about the relevance and importance of these considerations for brand behavior?
6. How do you see the projected role of avatars as brand ambassadors? What is the value proposition of avatars, and what are the possible implications for brand–consumer connect?
7. In the quest to seem authentic and be transparent, organizations might resort to questionable practices as in the case of Walmart's fake blog(gers). What is the likely reputational impact of such activities, if exposed? Could some brands escape serious consequences? Explain.
8. Who is really in 'control' of the brand in the digital age? When former CEO of Abercrombie & Fitch (A&F) claimed that their clothes were for the "cool kids," his comments incited controversy and a stakeholder-driven rebranding campaign (#FitchTheHomeless) that went viral. Greg Karber decided to give the brand a 'readjustment' from its current identity to "apparel for the homeless" and encouraged others to participate (watch the video here https://www.youtube.com/watch?v=O95DBxnXiSo). Using such examples (and others of your own choosing), how do you explain the control dynamic between brands and their audiences? What advice would you give to brand managers to tackle such challenges?

APPENDIX A
CASE

EXCERPTED FROM MONSTER LOYALTY: HOW LADY GAGA TURNS FOLLOWERS INTO FANATICS

> We identify with each other. I see myself in my fans and my fans see themselves in me. I call them little monsters because they are my inspiration.
>
> *Lady Gaga*[84]

Lady Gaga, with more than 60 million followers on Twitter and Facebook each, has been on the *Times Magazine*'s 100 most Influential People in the world. She has, over time, methodically built a base of 'little monsters' who not only love her for her music but are also inspired by her and her ability to build a sense of community.

Lessons from Lady Gaga's experience:

1. *Focus on your one percenters*: Most of the time, businesses are consumed by trying to attract new customers rather than focusing on retaining existing ones. Gaga's philosophy of focusing on the one percent of her core advocates, her super fans has won her appreciation and a loyal following.
2. *Lead with values*: Gaga's following is supported by her ability to stand for something 'bigger' than herself and her values. As a supporter of the LGBT community, she has been a champion for the cause of those who have been marginalized and bullied by society for being different.
3. *Build community*: Building community starts with finding a common thread that brings people together. Common experiences help define a community and allow members to rely on each other for support. When companies connect like-minded people and create a feeling of intimacy between them, the companies become relevant to their customers.
4. *Give fans a name, embrace shared symbols, and treat them like rockstars*: Little Monsters is the moniker for Gaga's fans, which helps them identify with each other as part of like-minded community. Celebrating fans or customers and making them feel like a rock star is another tactic that Lady Gaga uses to perfection. She has instituted a few traditions during her performances that make her fans feel like superstars in their own right, such as inviting a fan on to the stage during her performances, giving away a symbolic key to the first in line for her performances, putting spotlight on special gifts, and recognizing standouts on social media.
5. *Generate something to talk about*: Lady Gaga understands that standing out is important and needs a good story. Whether it is the Meat Dress Lady Gaga wore to the 2010 MTV awards, her product endorsements, or contraptions for her 'Born This Way' song performances (which is about encouraging people of all races and sexual orientation to be brave and believe in themselves) everything she does, generates discussion.

APPENDIX B
CASE

REWRITING THE RULES OF BRANDING IN INDIA: PATANJALI

In 2006, the famous Yoga guru Baba Ramdev and Mr Balkrishna launched Patanjali, an Indian pharmaceutical company with focus on manufacturing Ayurvedic medicines. The brand Patanjali soon gained momentum and became a contender for the number one position in the FMCG market rubbing shoulders with FMCG giants like Hindustan Unilever, Nestle, Dabur and Colgate-Palmolive.

The meteoric rise of the brand has been credited to the founder, his vision, and the consumer association with the brand. Baba Ramdev, a veteran at Yoga, began his journey with Patanjali in a simple manner, advocating the benefits of Ayurveda, an old science that had lost visibility but was still recognized as the panacea of all physical ailments. His strategy of branding the products with a natural, organic and wellness tag captured the fancy of the consumers. The birth of the brand was, reportedly, for a good cause.

Patanjali soon came to be associated with all that was good, pure, and unadulterated. The concept of 'Ayurvedic heritage' was found appealing to the Indian masses who gradually began to shift loyalty from their hitherto coveted brands to Patanjali. Based on consumer appeal for its products, Patanjali diversified into food, toothpaste, shampoo, and other personal care products.[85]

Given the current fad of moving away from artificial foods to natural and herbal products, it was not all that difficult for Baba Ramdev to garner a following of millions of consumers. Coupled with Yoga and its benefits, consumers did not need much persuasion. As a health freak, he was frequently seen on TV promoting Yoga and its benefits. One of the customers at a Mumbai store stated, "Baba Ramdev has such a big name, so I think the products must be pure and not adulterated. I have full trust in them."[86] As a proponent of the natural, Baba Ramdev used online social media platform to engage the consumers and talk with them about Yoga and Ayurveda. More than monologue, he used dialogue and interacted with followers by organizing live chats through which he invited discussions and provided information on Yoga camps, events, and latest Patanjali products.

Baba Ramdev's involvement in various nationalistic issues (Indian), such as anti-corruption *Andolan* (movement) and Lokpal Bill in 2011, provided visibility to the leader, the cause, and the brand. Further, as a proponent of Yoga and its benefits on sponsored TV reality shows, Baba Ramdev was seen implicitly and explicitly promoting the brand.

Further, tie ups with Future Group, Reliance Retail, and BigBasket.com added to the market presence of Patanjali. The final masterstroke of the strategy was the launch of Patanjali *atta* (whole wheat) noodles during the crisis faced by Nestle when it was forced to withdraw its product, Maggi noodles, the heart-throb of the younger generation and working women in India.[87]

Appealing to the nationalist sentiment of the consumers, Baba Ramdev urged and appealed in favor of *Swadeshi* (Indian) as against MNC products. He launched the Aarthik Swarajya Campaign (Economic Independence Campaign), where MNCs are compared to East India Company, suggesting how Indian wealth is being depleted by MNCs. Tapping on the potential of the Indian FMCG market, this campaign is fettered to appeal to the nationalistic sentiments of the masses, for it is hoped that its similarity to Gandhi's 'Swadeshi Movement' will help the brand position itself as suitable to the Indian psyche.

At a time when Patanjali was facing competition from brands like Hindustan Unilever and Proctor & Gamble, which had entered into the domain of promoting the brand in regional languages, Baba Ramdev unobtrusively slipped into a similar mode. Sensing the relevance of organic engagement with the consumers, Baba Ramdev adopted the strategy of sharing content in Hindi on Facebook and Twitter. "Brands are seeing engagement ratios of 24% through regional content which is considerably healthy."[88]

In May 2016, Baba Ramdev had over 6.6 million likes on Facebook and 564 thousand followers on Twitter.[89] The brand Patanjali revolutionized the FMCG industry with its innovative and path-breaking recipes for success. Within a decade of its commercial launch, the brand grew to ₹5,000 crore business.[90] In six months, 15,000 conversations around this brand were recorded on Twitter alone.[91]

In the last five years since its launch, Patanjali's CAGR was recorded to be over 50 percent as compared to the industry which was still reeling at seven percent.[92] This growth was a result of the introduction of around 400 products across multiple categories.[93]

"If they do not take him seriously, he could be a serious threat in many categories," says Arvind Singhal, founder of retail consultancy Technopak. "It's the only product I know where someone from the lower income strata, middle income strata and top income strata are all customers."[94]

As a brand, Patanjali has not been able to keep pace with the increasing demand and enhanced customer base. In the next two years, Patanjali is expected to invest US$150 million in machinery and other fixed assets and expand capacity across India.[95]

31 Bahadur, N. (n.d.). Dove "Real Beauty" Campaign Turns 10: How a brand tried to change the conversation about female beauty. Retrieved January 10, 2017, from http://www.huffingtonpost.in/entry/dove-real-beautycampaign-turns-10_n_4575940

32 Bothwell, C. (2005). Burberry versus the Chavs. Retrieved January 19, 2017, from http://news.bbc.co.uk/2/hi/business/4381140.stm

33 Na, A. (2016, June 8). Case study on how Burberry became a digital luxury brand. Retrieved October 15, 2016, from http://www.digitalvidya.com/blog/case-study-on-how-burberry-became-a-digital-luxury-brand/

34 Dann, K., & Jenkin, M. (2015). Back from the brink: Five successful brands and why they worked. Retrieved January 2, 2017, from https://www.theguardian.com/small-business-network/2015/jul/23/five-successfulrebrands-why-worked

35 Team L. H. (n.d.). How burberry uses social media (case study). Retrieved October 15, 2016, from http://linkhumans.com/case-study/burberry

36 Na (2016).

37 Ibid.

38 Gogoi, P. (2006). Wal-Mart's Jim and Laura: The real story. Retrieved January 10, 2017, from https://www.bloomberg.com/news/articles/2006-10-09/wal-marts-jim-and-laura-the-real-storybusinessweek-business-news-stockmarket-and-financial-advice

39 Wilson, H. J., Parise, P. G., & Weinberg, B. D. (2011). What's your social media strategy? *Harvard Business Review*, July–August, 23–25.

40 Ibid.

41 Ibid.

42 Ibid.

43 Bor, S. E. (2014). The link between social media activity and corporate reputation. Retrieved January 5, 2017, from http://www.forbes.com/sites/onmarketing/2014/07/14/the-link-between-social-media-activity-and-corporatereputation/#6cc5d3536d45

44 Malone, C., & Fiske, S. T. (2013). *The human brand: How we relate to people, products, and companies*. New York, NY: John Wiley & Sons.

45 Sundar, S. S., Kalyanaraman, S., & Brown, J. (2003). Explicating web site interactivity impression formation effects in political campaign sites. *Communication Research*, *30*(1), 30–59. http://doi.org/10.1177/0093650202239025

46 Moazzez, N. (2014, January 28). 50 Amazing personal branding quotes you need to know. Retrieved November 2, 2016, from http://www.navidmoazzez.com/best-personal-branding-quotes/

47 Magnarelli, M. (2016). The "How? Now. Wow!" Framework that's helped monster supercharge its content KPIs. Retrieved January 6, 2017, from http://review.content-science.com/2016/10/the-how-now-wowframework-thats-helped-monster-supercharge-its-content-kpis/

48 Ibid.

49 Chesbrough, H. W. (2003). *Open innovation: The new imperative for creating and profiting from technology*. Cambridge, MA: Harvard Business School Publishing.

50 Felix. (n.d.). Felix Baumgartner's supersonic free fall from 128k'—Mission Highlights. Retrieved January 6, 2017, from https://www.youtube.com/watch?v=FHtvDA0W34I

51 Warc. (n.d.). Under armour: I will what I want. Retrieved January 7, 2017, from https://www.warc.com/Content/ContentViewer.aspx?MasterContentRef=6e7dfdfe-7083-415a-ac9e-35f8cf18ef69&CID=A105605&PUB=JAYCHIAT

52 Gaskins, K. (n.d.). What audiences want: Study uncovers possible futures for storytelling. Retrieved January 7, 2017, from http://latd.com/blog/audiences-want-study-uncovers-possible-futures-storytelling

53 Ibid.

54 Portal, S.-T. S. (2016). Number of monthly active Twitter users worldwide from 1st quarter 2010 to 3rd quarter 2016 (in millions). Retrieved January 7, 2017, from https://www.statista.com/statistics/282087/number-of-monthlyactive-twitter-users/

55 Anderson, N. (2015). How whole foods uses social media (case study). Retrieved January 7, 2017, from http://linkhumans.com/case-study/whole-foods

56 Sashittal, H. C., Hodis, M., & Sriramachandramurthy, R. (2015). Entifying your brand among Twitter-using millenials. *Business Horizons*, *58*(3), 325–333.

57 Moats, J. (2015). Behind the success of Avery Dennison's branded content campaign for sustainability. Retrieved January 12, 2017, from http://review.content-science.com/2015/09/behind-the-success-of-averydennisons-branded-content-campaign-for-sustainability/#
58 Ibid.
59 Olenski, S. (2013). Why integrated marketing communications is more important than ever. Retrieved January 5, 2017, from http://www.forbes.com/sites/steveolenski/2013/09/16/why-integrated-marketingcommunications-is-more-important-than-ever/#472fce232544
60 Anand, S., & Bhushan, R. (2016). HUL, Colgate, Nestle are getting fake Patanjali products tested in labs: Baba Ramdev. Retrieved January 12, 2017, from http://brandequity.economictimes.indiatimes.com/news/business-of-brands/hul-eolgate-nestle-are-getting-fake-patanjali-products-tested-in-labs-baba-ramdev/50815271
61 Lehr, A. (2015). The unfollow algorithm. Retrieved January 5, 2017, from http://www.buzzstream.com/blog/unfollow-algorithm.html
62 Noble, C. H., Noble, S. M., & Adjei, M. T. (2012). Let them talk! Managing primary and extended online brand communities for success. *Business Horizons*, *55*(5), 475–483.
63 Ibid.
64 Noorbakhsh, S. (2008). Marketing 101. Retrieved January 7, 2017, from http://www.japaninc.com/mgz_july_2008_marketing101
65 Always. (n.d.) Retrieved January 9, 2017, from http://always.com/en-us/tips-and-advice/your-first-period
66 Always. (2014). Retrieved January 2, 2017, from https://www.youtube.com/watch?v=XjJQBjWYDTs
67 Jordan, R. Cited in Capozzi, L., & Zipfel, L. B. (2012). The conversation age: The opportunity for public relations. *Corporate Communications*, *17*(3), 336–349.
68 Laskowska-Witek, J., & Mitręga, M. (2014). Brand promotion through computer games on the example of second life. *The Central European Journal of Social Sciences and Humanities*, *205*, 34–48.
69 Holzwarth, M., Janiszewski, C., & Neumann, M. M. (2006). The influence of avatars on online consumer shopping behavior. *Journal of Marketing*, *70*, 19–36.
70 Ibid.
71 Chaudhuri, A., & Holbrook, M. B. (2001). The chain of effects from brand trust and brand affect to brand performance: The role of brand loyalty. *Journal of Marketing*, *65*(April), 81–93.
72 Kim, M., Chung, N., & Lee, C. (2011). The effect of perceived trust on electronic commerce: Shopping online for tourism products and services in South Korea. *Tourism Management*, *32*, 256–265.
73 Fournier, S., & Avery, J. (2011). The uninvited brand. *Business Horizon*, *54*, 193–207.
74 Holmes, J. G. (1991). Trust and the appraisal process in close relationships. In W. H. Jones & D. Perlman (Eds.), *Advances in personal relationships* (Vol. 2, pp. 57–104). London: Jessica Kingsley.
75 Laroche, M., Habibi, M. R., & Richard, M.-O. (2013). To be or not to be in social media: How brand loyalty is affected by social media? *International Journal of Information Management*, *33*, 76–82.
76 Casaló, L. V., Flavián, C., & Guinalíu, M. (2010). Relationship quality, community promotion and brand loyalty in virtual communities: Evidence from free software communities. *International Journal of Information Management*, *30*(4), 357–367.
77 Fifield, A. (n.d.). 9 Killer branding quotes from The World's Top Billionaires. Retrieved November 2, 2016, from http://addicted2success.com/quotes/9-killer-branding-quotes-from-the-worlds-top-billionaires/
78 Leberecht, T. (2012). 3 Ways to (usefully) lose control of your brand (Online). Retrieved January 4, 2017, from http://www.ted.com/talks/tim_leberecht_3_ways_to_usefully_lose_control_of_your_reputation?language=en
79 Kucuk, S. U. (2008). Negative double jeopardy: The role of anti-brand sites on the internet. *Journal of Brand Management*, *15*, 209–222.
80 Ibid.
81 Ibid.
82 Aaker, D. A. (1992). Managing the most important assets: Brand equity. *Planning Review*, *20*(5), 56–58.
83 Wright, D. K., & Hinson, M. D. (2008b). How blogs and social media are changing public relations and the way it is practiced. *Public Relations Journal*, *2*(2), 1–21.
84 Huba, J. (2013). *Monster loyalty: How Lady Gaga turns followers into fanatics*. New York, NY: Penguin Group.
85 Kazmin, A. (2016, March 27). Yoga guru rewrites consumer marketing rules in India. Retrieved October 4, 2016, from https://www.ft.com/content/6e3ff8ea-f0d2-11e5-aff5-19b4e253664a#axzz4HOOp5Vl7

86 Limaye, Y. (2015, December 21). The yoga guru turned company boss. Retrieved October 4, 2016, from http://www.bbc.com/news/business-35097567

87 Chaturvedi, A. (2016). Brands like Coca Cola, Patanjali, and others embrace regional languages on social media. Retrieved November 4, 2016, from http://economictimes.indiatimes.com/tech/internet/brands-like-coca-colapatanjali-and-others-embrace-regional-languages-on-social-media/articleshow/52335944.cms

88 Ibid.

89 Singh, K. (2016, June 18). The unusual success story of Patanjali, Baba Ramdev, and Yoga: Part 2. Retrieved October 7, 2016, from https://www.xorlabs.in/blog/success-story-of-patanjali-baba-ramdev-yoga-part2/

90 Mahajan, C. (2016, September 9). Patanjali: A brand aligned by purpose, yet derailed by ambition. Retrieved October 4, 2016, from http://2020msl.com/blog/patanjali-a-brand-aligned-by-purpose-yet-derailed-by-ambition/

91 Chaturvedi (2016).

92 Mahajan (2016).

93 Ibid.

94 Kazmin (2016).

95 Ibid.

CHAPTER 2

ON-DEMAND MARKETING

Social Selling, Customer Engagement, and Advocacy

CHAPTER OBJECTIVES

- Understand the changes in customer engagement in the digital age.
- Examine the developments in the marketing landscape (e.g., social selling).
- Review the processes of social-mediated customer-connect.
- Explore options for consumer engagement and synergistic value creation.
- Assess collaborative techniques for social selling, customer engagement, and advocacy.

Keywords

Baby boomers	Generation Z	Prosumers
Brand advocates	Influencers	Return on investment
Brand loyalty	Investments	Shareworthy
Customer engagement	Involvement	Social selling
Preferences	Millennials	Uses and gratification theory (UGT)
Digital generation	Narcissism	Value fusion
Digital native	Newsworthy	Word-of-mouth (WOM)
Engagement	Organizational reputation	
Evangelism	Participation	

INTRODUCTION

> These days social media waits for no one. If you're LATE for the party, you'll probably be covered by all the noise and you might not be able to get your voice across. It could only mean that if you want to be heard by the crowd, you have to be fast; and on social media, that means you have to be REALLY fast.
>
> *Aaron Lee*[1]

In 2003, after the re-launch of the brand, Old Spice first introduced its body wash. As the product gained popularity, competitors too thronged the aisles. In 2006, Old Spice experienced a drop in ranks and was faced with the challenge of restoring its position by drawing on its history and expertise to make it relevant to the current generation of both men and women. With the objective of initiating conversation on bodywash among the young purchasers, Old Spice launched its "The Man Your Man Could Smell Like" campaign, with Isaiah Mustafa, the former NFL wide receiver, as the "Old Spice

15. Though engaging with Millennials is tough, it is not impossible. Listening to their conversations, being present and engaged on all social media platforms, initiating two-way dialogue, constantly and consistently messaging and being creative are some techniques for securing eyeballs and winning confidence.

Activities

1. Form groups of four and devise a social media communication strategy for engaging with the Millennials. The strategy can be based on any one that you have heard of or read about in your course. Be prepared to discuss the parameters on which you devised your strategy/plan.
2. Prepare an open-ended questionnaire for the three generations—Baby Boomers, Millennials, and Generation Z—on their use of social media to make purchases. Go and visit a mall or any other crowded place where you will be able to talk to them and discuss. Collate your findings and present in class the differences, if any, in their purchase decision.
3. Create a fictitious website for any product that you wish to sell. Use social media to generate interest. You may choose to use any medium to establish contact.

   After 15 days, assess the impact of your strategies. Were you able to generate conversation? What was the nature of comments? Who were the consumers talking about your product? How many 'likes' and 'dislikes,' 'tweets,' and 'retweets' were you able to generate? Present your analysis to class and state your learning from the process.
4. Individually or in collaboration, prepare a social media campaign for societal benefits (think about ongoing issues such as abortion, sexual assault, women, and health). Were you able to crowdsource ideas? How and why?
5. Study some lead campaigns that have been in the news. What were the drivers for these campaigns? What were the reputational benefits of these campaigns? Prepare a presentation on what you think are the reasons for the success of these campaigns. Present details for the same.
6. In your groups, study two companies each in the following sectors: telecom, FMCG, health and pharmaceutical. Study their social media strategy for consumer engagement. Aside from information on their website and social media platforms, you may contact the relevant person in the organization. Share the differences in approach and explain reasons for the same.
7. You are a Millennial consumer. Reflect on your expectations from the companies. When would you buy a product? What is your mind map? What do you expect to be the engagement techniques? Talk to the Baby Boomers (your parents) and the Generation Z (your younger brother/s and sister/s). Ask them to reflect on similar questions. Prepare a note with expectations of the three generations.
8. Study in your groups some of the campaigns that have failed in the social media. What can be the reasons for the same? Consumer apathy, incorrect environmental assessment, lack of appeal, or something else?
9. Because of the nature of business, B2B and B2C have different set of target customers. Search through the social media channels and collate strategies of different companies to build brand awareness and loyalty. Share your findings in class.
10. Divide your group into three subgroups. Each group will select a company that has demonstrated one of the three managerial approaches to social media: path of least resistance, playing their game, and leveraging Web 2.0 connectedness. You may study the techniques either on the net or interview people in the organizations. Analyze the findings. Which of the three approaches is the best and why?

Discussion Questions

1. Social media have been a blessing to organizations for promoting their products, but they are not without baneful effects. Discuss the statement, citing examples for the same.
2. Elaborate on techniques followed by companies to secure eyeballs and garner consumer support. Discuss the same in relation to choice of medium.
3. Can one message be created for all generations of consumers? Discuss citing examples of companies which have used one message for addressing all concerns.
4. Which according to you is more important: content or platform through which content is shared? You may want to reflect on the example of Maggi where a PDF file was posted on Twitter and excited flak from consumers.
5. Discuss Millennial traits and how they are different from those of either the Baby Boomers or Generation Z.
6. Explain how Millennials can be engaged citing examples from companies.
7. B2B and B2C businesses would adhere to differing social media principles to engage with consumers. Review the examples of GE and IBM cited in the chapter and compare the same to other B2C companies. Explain the differences citing reasons for the same.
8. "Willingness to Participate accords a competitive edge to a company which is not the case with Willingness to Pay." Do you agree with the statement? If yes, present your arguments in favor of the statement citing examples from social media. If not, discuss why Willingness to Pay is still more significant than Willingness to Participate.

APPENDIX
CASE

NESTLE ENTANGLED! BRAVING THE MAGGI NOODLE CRISIS IN INDIA[69]

On May 21, 2015, the Food and Drug Administration (FDA) ordered Nestle India to recall Maggi after confirming presence of high levels of lead and monosodium glutamate (MSG) in the product. The test was conducted on 29 samples, of which 15 tested positive.[70] The media reports shared the findings and detailed the harmful effects of Maggi consumption. As a mark of protest against "unhealthy" food products in the market,[71] hostile consumers began burning packets of Maggi. Recall they must, thought Paul Bulcke, CEO, Nestle, but what would be the aftermath of the recall? With a 63 percent market share, Maggi was an undisputed leader in the ₹4,200 crores (US$636.12 million) Indian instant-noodle market.[72] His concerns were manifold: Will they be able to get Maggi back on the shelf? Will they ever be able to capture consumer faith and trust? What strategies should be adopted to rebuild reputation, redefine perceptions, and regain market share in India?

On June 5, 2015, Bulcke stated in a press conference that tests conducted by Nestle and third parties on almost 1,000 batches and 600 batches, respectively, had reported Maggi as "safe for consumption"[73] with "below permissible limits of lead and MSG." The entire episode, according to Bulcke, rested on "unfounded confusion."[74]

Storm in a Cup of Maggi Noodles

On March 10, 2014, Sanjay Singh, local food inspector in Barabanki, picked Maggi noodles from supermarket shelves and sent it to nearby state laboratory in Gorakhpur city for tests. He claimed that his action was prompted by media reports on high levels of lead and presence of MSG in Maggi.[75] On April 24, 2014, the lab announced that the label "No added MSG" was false and violated regulatory norms of India.[76] The local magistrate pronounced that a similar finding had been reported in 2013. The local retailer paid a fine of ₹25,000 (US$400) for the repeated offence. Nestle India contested the April 24 ruling stating that the presence of MSG was a "natural process" and appealed for further tests. The sample was transferred from Barabanki supermarket to government referral lab, Central Food Laboratory, Kolkata.

Almost a year later, on April 7, 2015, the Central Food Laboratory, Kolkata, presented its findings and declared excessive levels of lead—17.2 parts per million—that was nearly eight times more than the stipulated norm of 2.5 parts per million. A case was registered in a Barabanki court against Nestle India. Similar tests were conducted and 14 other states also called for either full or partial ban. The central government directed the Food Safety and Standards Association of India (FSSAI) to investigate.

The Delhi government on June 3 banned Maggi noodles for 15 days. The move was followed by other states in India, such as Gujarat, Uttarakhand, Jammu and Kashmir, and Tamil Nadu.

On 5 June, FSSAI ordered product recall, directed Nestle's compliance in three days and ordered daily update on the progress.[77]

On June 11, Nestle India contested the FSSAI ban in the Bombay High Court claiming that it was solely based on a test report and "not on any risk assessment, communication or risk management."[78] Hence, the question of health risk of violation of the law did not arise. The samples that had been collected had passed their expiry date and hence could not have "drastic effects."[79]

Nestle Takes the Stage

Following the recall order, the news spread like wildfire through social media. News on social media gained traction as it reached 125 million Facebook users and more than 800 WhatsApp users.[80] On May 21, 2015, when the FDA issued orders for recall, Nestle social media sites went on a hiatus with the Twitter handle of Nestle India carrying a single post. All social media sites became active on June 1, 2015[81] and two days later began engagement.[82] In the meanwhile, consumers had shifted gears and the conversation and sentiment progressively shifted from positive to negative with such keywords as "lead," "MSG," "ban," and "withdrawal."[83] The maximum amount of activity on social media (72,562 mentions)[84] happened on June 4, 2015.

On June 5, 2015, Nestle organized its first media briefing since the controversy. The company's delayed response to the controversy was explained by the Nestle CEO, "We were engaging with the authorities"[85] who asserted that Nestle was not challenging the authorities but working with them to validate the testing methodology. Nestle "will do everything it takes…to clarify the situation to have MAGGI Noodles back on the shelves at the earliest."[86]

On June 8, 2015, there were a total of 4.43 lakh (443,000) mentions of the ban and recall on social media, including 4.37 lakh (437,000) tweets. Consumers engaged with one another in almost all social media platforms, such as blogs, forums, Twitter, and Facebook fan actions. In this phase, Twitter gained maximum traction, and statistics revealed 14 percent positive tweets, 33 percent neutral tweets, and 43 percent negative tweets.[87] Almost 60 percent of the sentiment on social media was negative (Saikia, 2015).[88]

Nestle's first line of defense was a technical explanation on Twitter in a four-page PDF with no company logo. The move was severely criticized by the various brand management firms who felt that Nestle should have attempted a more human connect rather than a robotic response. "They seem to have lost the plot by posting PDF files on Twitter. Most Twitter users access it through the phone. Who is going to see a PDF file on their phones?"[89]

Nestle began targeting consumer sentiment through graphic banners on Twitter and through video ads that were promoted on social media with the hashtag #WeMissYouToo. The video was in response to other videos published by fans with hashtags like #Maggiinasoup, #MaggiKeSideEffects, and #WeMissYouMaggi. Out of the three videos, two were also shared on the official Meri Maggi (My Maggi) Facebook page. One video showed young men talking about how life had never been the same since their 'friend' went away.[90] The video 'Mom' was the most favorite amongst the young and showed a teen talking to friends how he had never troubled his mother when his friends came over for late night parties as all snacked on the 'two-minute' noodles. The third shows a man talking about how he is now forced to rely on home delivery menus.

An official post on Meri Maggi (My Maggi) YouTube channel stated, "This one is for all our fans! Can't thank you enough for your support. Share it and keep spreading the MAGGI love."[91] Nestle received appreciation for its endeavors and the video garnered over 102,670 views on YouTube in less than 24 hours.[92]

Rebuilding Stakeholder Trust

To appease the consumers, Nestle simultaneously worked on a plan to involve all stakeholders. It took journalists to its oldest factory, which also housed its research and development center at Moga, Punjab, to showcase its production quality standards.[93] Nestle instructed internal stakeholders not to talk to anyone or share information that had not been cleared by the legal team.

The management engaged with employees and tried to involve them in overcoming the unfortunate incident.[94] The company created a dedicated web page for employees to share feedback on how the image of Maggi can be rebuilt. Through this survey, employees were encouraged to raise queries and doubts.

A strategic change in leadership took place in July 2015 whereby current MD Etienne Benet was replaced by Suresh Narayanan, an Indian by origin.

What Next?

On November 9, 2015, five months after the recall, Maggi was back in-store shelves across 100 cities in India. As part of its relaunch strategy, Maggi partnered e-commerce retailer Snapdeal to boost the sale of its *masala* (spice) variant. On day one of the announcement (November 12), Snapdeal reportedly sold a total of 60,000 Maggi Welcome Kits[95] within the first few minutes. Each Welcome Kit contained 12 packs of Maggi and other company paraphernalia (a 2016 calendar, magnet, post cards, and a Welcome Back letter).

On a dedicated website,[96] Nestle India welcomed consumers back to Maggi. The website also included FAQ section that responded to the core issues in the recall (e.g., false labels of "No added MSG" and excessive levels of lead) and a subsection with detailed test results to demonstrate that Maggi had been exonerated by the Bombay High Court following retest of Maggi samples by three accredited laboratories. In the states where the ban continues, Nestle India is reportedly working with relevant authorities.

Celebrating the relaunch of Maggi, Nestle India MD Suresh Narayanan[97] reiterated the importance of food safety and product quality, while acknowledging that "a seed of doubt had been planted" so regaining consumer trust was the priority. The organization has reportedly intensified consumer engagement mechanisms to offer 24×7 service across traditional and social media channels.

Further, the Indian MD has announced a change in company strategy whereby Nestle India would work on a three-to-five-year plan to reduce dependence on Maggi, a product category that accounted for 30 percent of sales before the crisis.

11. Are there any questions that you/we should be asking regarding the future of digital engagement? Please elaborate.

BC: Reach is certainly one. While the media are able to engage audiences, their ability to deliver brand and business impact on scale is an ongoing debate. The second is advertising fraud. It is estimated that nearly 60–70 percent of all ad inventory is not viewable or high quality. Currently, there is a lack of robust software/systems to make it happen. Thirdly, talent is a challenge. The formal/informal education system is still not geared up to deliver to needs of the industry. Fourthly, organizations have to stop viewing social media as a marketing 'thing' and view it as a company-wide response across functions. For example, it has implications for HR. LinkedIn/Glassdoor are go-to places for new recruits, influential customers want service on social media, and finance teams need to see how quarterly results are doing on groups of finance professionals, etc.

AS: The whole space is about infinite questions and slowly evolving answers.

All marketers including many who 'seem to be doing a good job' of their social media marketing/digital consumer engagement programs are still grappling with three really basic questions:

- Do these contribute to my business? If yes, exactly how?
- Do these contribute to the strength of my brands? If yes, exactly how?
- And given that these two basic questions are still unanswered, what are the right goals and metrics to track the results of my investments?

It is generally agreed that consumer engagement is better than simple consumer actions like likes. However, jury is out on whether even engagement metrics, for instance shares, contribute profitably to businesses.

The following summarizes the current operating premises of even the smartest marketers:

- Even though we do not understand exactly how social media can help our brands and businesses, with the amount of time consumers are spending on these, we cannot afford to ignore them. We simply have to continue to experiment with them and learn to use them for the benefit of our brands.
- Till we can establish their ROI in terms of additional revenues and margins and brand metrics, let us follow a pragmatic approach: Let us continue to invest 80/90 percent of our marketing dollars on marketing channels/vehicles that we know work. Let us treat the balance 10–20 percent of the budget as R&D budget and invest it in social media/digital consumer engagement. On this portion of the budget, returns today may be unclear but for our continued success tomorrow, it is very important for us to continue to invest and learn.

12. Any other comments?

BC: Social media have opened up a world of opportunities for ideas that truly stand out. It is also a great equalizer in the industry as smaller companies and emerging brands, if smart, can really ratchet up. If there's one thing that I'd end with, it is to urge companies to treat the concept of social media as much, much wider and all-encompassing than just restricting it to a singular dimension to be handled by just marketing.

AS: We live in an interconnected and integrated world. Social media efforts, therefore, always have to be seen in the context of the brand's overall communication strategy and plans and not in isolation. Coming back to the Coke Studio example, we produced music programming content that was aired on TV and could be downloaded through social media. It is this kind of integrated thinking that is key to today's communication planning.

NOTES

1 Lee, A. (n.d.). 50 Inspiring quotes from 50 top social media power influencers. Retrieved March 21, 2016, from https://blog.kissmetrics.com/50-social-media-influencers/

2 Baboushkin, T. (2013, August 29). YouTube case study: Old Spice. Social media delivered. Retrieved April 4, 2016, from http://www.socialmediadelivered.com/2013/08/29/youtube-case-study-old-spice/

3 D&AD. (n.d.). Case Study: Old Spice Response Campaign. Retrieved May 5, 2016, from http://www.dandad.org/en/d-ad-old-spice-case-study-digital-marketing/

4 Ibid.

5 Ibid.

6 Grinner, D. (2010, July 27). Hey Old Spice haters, sales are up 107%. Adweek. Retrieved May 24, 2016, from http://www.adweek.com/adfreak/hey-old-spice-haters-sales-are-107-12422

7 Ibid.

8 Killian, G., & McManus, K. (2015). A marketing communications approach for the digital era: Managerial guidelines for social media integration. *Business Horizons*, *58*(5), 539–549.

9 SalesForce. (2015). 2015 state of B2C marketing. Retrieved July 21, 2016, from https://www.salesforce.com/form/marketingcloud/conf/b2c-state-of-marketing.jsp

10 Donnelly, C., & Scaff, R. (2016). Who are the Millennial shoppers? And what do they really want? Retrieved March 16, 2016, from https://www.accenture.com/in-en/insight-outlook-who-are-millennial-shoppers-what-do-theyreally-want-retail

11 Chester, E. (n.d.) Employing generation why? Retrieved June 30, 2016, from http://www.mcosa.net/SPF-SIG%20TRAINING%20Folder/us_consulting_millennialfactsheet_080606.pdf

12 Berthon, P. R., Pitt, L. F., Plangger, K., & Shapiro, D. (2012). Marketing meets Web 2.0, social media, and creative consumers: Implications for International marketing strategy. *Business Horizons*, *55*(3), 261–271. Retrieved July 10, 2016, from http://www.academia.edu/3624287/Marketing_meets_Web_2.0_social_media_and_creative_consumers_Implications_for_international_marketing_strategy

13 Genelins, S. (2010, July 3). The shift from consumers to prosumers. *Forbes*. Retrieved June 15, 2016, from http://www.forbes.com/sites/work-in-progress/2010/07/03/the-shift-from-consumers-to-prosumers/#600c8bcb543f

14 Ibid.

15 Brown, J. J., & Reingen, P. H. (1987). Social ties and word of mouth referral behavior. *Journal of Consumer Research*, *14*(3), 350–362.

16 Starbucks. (n.d.). MyStarbucksIdea.com. Retrieved June 30, 2016, from http://www.starbucks.com/coffeehouse/learn-more/my-starbucks-idea

17 *Harvard Business Review*. (2015, October 31). My Starbucks idea: Crowdsourcing for customer satisfaction and innovation. *Harvard Business Review*. Retrieved June 18, 2016, from https://digit.hbs.org/submission/my-starbucks-idea-crowdsourcing-for-customer-satisfaction-and-innovation/

18 Muntinga, D. G., Moorman, M., & Smit, E. G. (2011). Introducing COBRAs: Exploring motivations for brand-related social media use. *International Journal of Advertising*, *30*(1), 13–46.

19 Rossi, E. (2002). Uses and gratification/dependency theory. Retrieved July 16, 2016, from http://zimmer.csufresno.edu/~johnca/spch100/7-4-uses.htm

20 McQuail, D. (1983). *Mass communication theory* (1st ed.). London: SAGE Publications.

21 Boff, L. (2016). The big brand theory: GE demonstrates value through platform-specific content. Retrieved June 26, 2016, from http://www.socialmediatoday.com/content/big-brand-theory-ge-demonstrates-value-through-platformspecific-content

22 Dahlström, P., & Edelman, D. (2013, April). The coming era of 'on-demand' marketing. *Mckinsey Quarterly*. Retrieved July 16, 2016, from http://www.mckinsey.com/business-functions/marketing-and-sales/our-insights/the-coming-era-of-on-demand-marketing

23 Knox, S. (1997). The death of brand deference: Can brand management stop the rot? *Journal of Product & Brand Management*, *6*(1), 49–55.

24 Gopaldas, A. (2015). Creating firm, customer, and societal value: Toward a theory of positive marketing. *Journal of Business Research*, *68*(12), 2446–2451. Retrieved July 20, 2016, from http://dx.doi.org/10.1016/j.jbusres.2015.06.031

25 Ibid.

26 Roderick, L. (2015, November 4). Starbucks on why its Red Cup Christmas campaign will hit home on social media. *Marketing Week*. Retrieved July 20, 2016, from https://www.marketingweek.com/2015/11/04/starbucks-on-why-its-red-cup-christmas-campaign-will-hit-home-on-social-media/

27 Brown, E. (2015, November 13). #CreativeBranding—Starbucks Red Cups stir social media furore. *DesignMantic*. Retrieved June 30, 2016, from http://www.designmantic.com/blog/starbucks-red-cups-stir-social-media-furore/

28 Whitten, S. (2015, November 13). Starbucks holiday Red Cup brews controversy on social media. Retrieved June 24, 2016, from http://www.cnbc.com/2015/11/09/starbucks-holiday-red-cup-brews-controversy-on-social-media.html

29 Ibid.

30 King, C. (2015, November 13). Starbucks' response to Red Cup controversy? Let social sort it out. Retrieved June 24, 2016, from http://www.socialmediatoday.com/social-business/starbucks-response-red-cup-controversy-letsocial-sort-it-out

31 Alyssa. (2015, November 11). Starbucks' Red Cup design was a bad idea…or was it? Retrieved July 20, 2016, from http://www.pragermicrosystems.com/blog/general/starbucks-red-cup-design-was-a-bad-idea-or-was-it/

32 Red cup controversy didn't dampen Starbucks' holiday sales. (2016, January 22). Retrieved June 24, 2016, from http://www.nola.com/business/index.ssf/2016/01/starbucks_earnings_holidays.html

33 Larivière, B., Joosten, H., Malthouse, E. C., van Birgelen, M., Aksoy, P., Kunz, W. H., & Huang, M. H. (2013). Value fusion: The blending of consumer and firm value in the distinct context of mobile technologies and social media. *Journal of Service Management*, *24*(3), 268–293. Retrieved June 20, 2016, from http://dx.doi.org/10.1108/09564231311326996

34 Narasaki, R. (2016). General electric: BtoB social selling. Retrieved June 24, 2016, from https://vimeo.com/104333919

35 Genelins, S. (2010, July 3). The shift from consumers to prosumers. *Forbes*. Retrieved June 15, 2016, from http://www.forbes.com/sites/work-in-progress/2010/07/03/the-shift-from-consumers-to-prosumers/#600c8bcb543f

36 Kaul, A., & Thappa, V. (2013). *IBM's digital influence programme*, 1–17. Ontario: Richard Ivey School of Business.

37 Fournier, S., & Avery, J. (2011). The uninvited brand. *Business Horizons*, *54*(3), 193–207. doi:10.1016/j.bushor.2011.01.001

38 Devlioti, V. (2015, January 19). Do it like the best: How GoPro rules Instagram? Wersm. Retrieved June 18, 2016, from http://wersm.com/do-it-like-the-best-how-gopro-rules-instagram/

39 Burnay, K. (2014, January 14). Why you should Envy the GoPro Instagram strategy. *Trackmaven*. Retrieved June 11, 2016, from http://trackmaven.com/blog/2015/01/why-you-should-envy-and-emulate-gopros-instagram-strategy/

40 Influencer Connect. (2015, May 19). Successful Instagram campaigns: Learning from 3 of the top brands. Retrieved June 17, 2016, from http://influencerconnect.com/successful-instagram-campaigns-learning-from-3-of-the-top-brands/

41 Chapman, M. (2014, May 20). McDonald's asks public to create products with 'burger builder' crowd-sourcing tool. *Campaign*. Retrieved June 20, 2016, from http://www.campaignlive.co.uk/article/1294903/mcdonalds-asks-public-create-products-burger-builder-crowd-sourcing-tool#xVf2biwDIh4rzRZe.99

42 Mahoney, S. (2010, April 30). BP's woes illustrate risk of green branding. Retrieved July 3, 2016, from http://www.mediapost.com/publications/article/127265/bps-woes-illustrate-risk-of-green-branding.html

43 Fournier and Avery (2011).

44 Our socialtimes. (2014, February 28). 6 Examples of social media crisis: What can we learn? Retrieved June 1, 2016, from http://oursocialtimes.com/6-examples-of-social-media-crises-what-can-we-learn/

45 Bansal, M. (2015, May 13). Here's how not to make top social media blunders on your Brand's Page. Office chai. Retrieved June 1, 2016, from https://officechai.com/learn/social-media-blunders-indian-companies/#

46 Ibid.

47 Haines, B. (2015, December 29). 14 Amazing social media customer service examples. Buffer social. Retrieved June 25, 2016, from https://blog.bufferapp.com/social-media-customer-service

48 Howe, J. (n.d.). Crowd sourcing quotes. Innosabi. Retrieved June 28, 2016, from http://innosabi.com/wp-content/uploads/2013/09/innosabi-Resources-Crowdsourcing-Quotes.pdf

49 Howe, J. (2006). The rise of crowdsourcing. Retrieved May 20, 2016, from http://archive.wired.com/wired/archive/14.06/crowds.html

50 Kearns, K. (2015, July 10). 9 Great examples of crowdsourcing in the age of empowered consumers. Tweakyourbiz. Retrieved June 20, 2016, from http://tweakyourbiz.com/marketing/2015/07/10/9-great-examples-crowdsourcingage-empowered-consumers/

51 Saxton, G. D., Oh, O., & Kishore, R. (2013). Rules of crowdsourcing: Models, issues, and systems of control. *Information Systems Management*, *30*(1), 2–20. http://dx.doi.org/10.1080/10580530.2013.739883
52 Digital Strategy Consulting. (2014, January 16). Lays expands 'Do Us A Flavour' into year-long social media campaign. Retrieved June 18, 2016, from http://www.digitalstrategyconsulting.com/intelligence/2014/01/lays_expands_do_us_a_flavour_into_yearlong_social_media_campaign.php
53 Goodrich, R. (2013, February 26). What is crowdsourcing. *Business News Daily*. Retrieved June 18, 2016, from http://www.businessnewsdaily.com/4025-what-is-crowdsourcing.html
54 PWC. (2011). Harnessing the power of crowdsourcing. Does your company stand out in a crowd? Retrieved June 18, 2016, from https://www.pwc.com/us/en/people-management/assets/crowdsourcing-paper.pdf
55 Lancaster, L.C., Stillman, D. (2016). When Generations Collide. HarperCollins: New York.
56 Miller, R. K., and Associates. (2008). Consumer use of the Internet and Mobile Web. New York. Retrieved July 20, 2016, from http://www.rkma.com/2016CUIMtoc.pdf
57 Kelley, R. (2009, April 27). Generation me. *Newsweek*. Retrieved July 20, 2016, from http://www.newsweek.com/2009/04/17/generation-me.html
58 Goldman Sachs report cited in Susan, K. (2015, June). Millennials in the marketplace: A new breed of consumers and employees. Retrieved March 26, 2016, from http://www.2020mag.com/ce/TTViewTest.aspx?LessonId=111468
59 Kaul, A. (2012). "Doing" the act: Lenovo and corporate reputation. *Emerging Markets Case Studies Collection Emerald Case Study*, *2*(8), 1–16, doi.10.1108/20450621211299547
60 Euromonitor Research. (2015, March 2). Millennials—A new breed of travelers. Retrieved June 2, 2016, from http://blog.euromonitor.com/2015/03/millennials-a-new-breed-of-travelers.html
61 Ibid.
62 Carroll, D. (2015). Marketing to millennials. Retrieved July 20, 2016, from http://www.visionmonday.com/business/millennial-project/article/marketing-to-millennials/
63 Sago, B. (2010). The influence of social media message sources on Millennial Generation International. *Journal of Integrated Marketing Communications, 2*(2), 7–18.
64 Helsper, E. J., & Eynon, R. (2010). Digital natives: Where is the evidence? *British Educational Research Journal*, *36*(3), 503–520.
65 Owyang, J. K. (2009, March). Social media playtime is over. Forrester Research. Retrieved July 20, 2016, from http://courses.washington.edu/mcdmugc/page2/page3/files/social-media-playtime-over-forrester.pdf
66 Lantos, G. P. (2014). Marketing to millennials: Reach the largest and most influential generation of consumers ever. *Journal of Consumer Marketing*, *31*(5), 401–403. doi:10.1108/JCM-03-2014-0909
67 Ibid.
68 Ibid.
69 Case prepared on the basis of publicly available material and media reports.
70 Kazmin, A. (2015, June 7). Nestlé hit by storm in a cup of Maggi noodles. *The Economic Times*. Retrieved October 29, 2015, from http://www.ft.com/intl/cms/s/0/3f46f9d4-0cd1-11e5-b850-00144feabdc0.html#axzz3qamgKa9E
71 Bose, A. (n.d.). Noodles up in flames-consumers alert but food controller clueless about tests. *The Telegraph*. Retrieved October 29, 2015, from http://www.telegraphindia.com/1150603/jsp/jharkhand/story_23536.jsp#.VjswLeN961s
72 Noodles in India. (2015, March). Retrieved October 29, 2015, from http://www.euromonitor.com/noodles-in-india/report
73 Pradhan, S., & Kalra, A. (2015, June 9). Maggi noodle crisis: How it all began. *Business Today*. Retrieved October 29, 2015, from http://www.businesstoday.in/current/corporate/maggi-noodle-crisis-how-it-all-began/story/220287.html
74 *The Economic Times*. (2015, June 6). Nestle chief Paul Bulcke says Maggi safe for consumption, says unfounded confusion over product. *The Economic Times*. Retrieved October 20, 2015, from http://economictimes.indiatimes.com/industry/cons-products/food/nestle-chief-paul-bulcke-says-maggi-safe-for-consumption-saysunfounded-confusion-over-product/articleshow/47559781.cms
75 Bommakanti, U. (2015, June 6). Who Brought Maggi Down? Two Different Names Come Up. *The New Indian Express*. Retrieved October 26, 2015, from http://www.newindianexpress.com/nation/Who-Brought-Maggi-Down-Two-Different-Names-Come-Up/2015/06/06/article2852494.ece
76 Pradhan and Kalra (2015).

77 *The Hindu*. (2015, June 5). Food Safety regulator orders Nestle to recall nine variants of Maggi noodles. *The Hindu*. Retrieved October 29, 2015, from http://www.thehindu.com/news/national/maggi-row-food-safety-regulatororders-nestle-to-recall-nine-variants-of-maggi-noodles/article7285855.ece
78 Khan, A., & Narayan, K. (2015, June 12). Maggi row: Nestle moves Bombay High Court against 'ban' on Maggi noodles. *The Indian Express*. Retrieved November 4, 2015, from http://indianexpress.com/article/cities/mumbai/maggi-row-nestle-approaches-bombay-high-court-against-fssai-ban/
79 Ibid.
80 Chhabara, R. (2015). Asia column: Lessons from Nestlé's crisis in India. *Ethical Corporation*. Retrieved November 3, 2015, from http://www.ethicalcorp.com/stakeholder-engagement/asia-column-lessons-nestles-crisis-india
81 Balakrishnan, R., & Bapna, A. (2015, June 10). #MaggiInASoup: A case study of how not to handle a crisis. *The Economic Times*. Retrieved November 4, 2015, from http://economictimes.indiatimes.com/magazines/brand-equity/maggiinasoup-a-case-study-of-how-not-to-handle-a crisis/articleshow/47599502.cms?utm_source=contentofinterest&utm_medium=text&utm_campaign=cppst
82 *The Times of India*. (2015, June 6). As Maggi stewed, Nestle PR was slow to tackle fire. *The Times of India*. Retrieved November 4, 2015, from http://timesofindia.indiatimes.com/india/As-Maggi-stewed-Nestle-PRwas-slow-to-tackle-fire/articleshow/47561579.cms
83 GenYmedium. (2015, June 14). Maggi's loyal fan base might help it make a comeback. Retrieved November 4, 2015, from http://www.genymedium.com/maggis-loyal-fan-base-might-help-make-comeback/
84 Singh, V. (n.d.). Social Listening Report. Retrieved November 7, 2015, from http://www.slideshare.net/vikashnsingh/maggi-crisis-and-social-listening-report
85 *F. Business*. (2015, June 6). After epic PR fail over Maggi, Nestle India ropes in APCO, Shivani Hegde to control damage. *F. Business*. Retrieved November 1, 2015, from http://www.firstpost.com/business/after-epic-pr-failover-maggi-nestle-india-ropes-in-apco-shivani-hegde-to-control-damage-2282788.html
86 Nestlé India comes out of hiding, decides to hold Maggi sale. (2015, June 5). Retrieved November 4, 2015, from http://www.exchange4media.com/marketing/nestlé-india-comes-out-of-hiding-decides-to-hold-maggis-ale_60295.html
87 Saikia, R. (2015, June 9). Maggi crisis—Social media glorifies the ban. Retrieved November 7, 2015, from http://simplify360.com/blog/maggi-crisis-social-media-glorifies-the-ban
88 Ibid.
89 Murthy, Mahesh. (n.d.). Mahesh Murthy, founder of Pinstorm, a digital brand management firm. Retrieved November 1, 2015, from http://www.firstpost.com/business/tone-deaf-pr-on-maggi-this-isnt-the-first-time-nestlesducked-corporate-responsibility-2280792.html
90 Maggi was referred to as 'Friend' in the video.
91 Bhasin, S. (2015, August 26). Love in the time of ban: Maggi thanks fans with #wemissyoutoo ads. *Hindustan Times*. Retrieved April 21, 2017, from http://www.hindustantimes.com/india/love-in-the-time-of-ban-maggithanks-fans-with-wemissyoutoo-ads/story-0PEvWIfEVfjg5zUwEWrFEK.html
92 Post ban, Maggi unveils 'aggressive' campaign with viral video. (2015, August 25). Retrieved November 5, 2015, from http://www.exchange4media.com/digital/post-ban-maggi-unveils-aggressive-campaign-with-viralvideo_61394.html
93 Dutta, A. (2015, August 14). Maggi mess led Nestle to rope in crisis managers. *Business Standard*. Retrieved October 30, 2015, from http://www.business-standard.com/article/companies/maggi-mess-led-nestle-to-rope-in-crisismanagers-115081301982_1.html
94 Dutta, A., & Pinto, V. (2015, July 2). This is how Nestle plans to relaunch Maggi. Retrieved October 29, 2015, from http://www.rediff.com/business/report/this-is-how-nestle-plans-to-relaunch-maggi/20150702.htm
95 Unboxing the Maggi Welcome Kit. Retrieved May 24, 2017, from https://www.youtube.com/watch?v=BZ0fCFeKmog
96 Nestle India has a dedicated space on its website to answer questions related to the Maggi recall. See https://www.nestle.in/aboutus/ask-nestle/answers/maggi-noodles-india-msg-lead-ban-recall
97 In case of a longer session, the instructor may choose to play excerpts from the interview with Maggi India MD Suresh Narayanan. Retrieved May 24, 2017, from https://www.youtube.com/watch?v=pSf_387Z5E8. Or see http://timesofindia.indiatimes.com/business/india-business/Nestle-backwith-Maggi-in-100-cities/articleshow/49731212.cms

HAPTER 3

Social Media@Work

Employees as Reputation Agents

CHAPTER OBJECTIVES

- Understand how social media are changing organizational practices.
- Examine the opportunities and challenges of these developments.
- Analyze the role of employees as reputation agents.
- Reflect on the implications for organizational communication and reputation management.

Keywords
Affordances
Blurring boundaries
Collaboration
Control
Culture
Cybervetting
Digital engagement
Employees
Employee advocacy
Enterprise social media
Ethics
Governance
Leadership
Monitoring
Reputation agents
Social media@work
Social media policy
Surveillance

INTRODUCTION

> It's 4:30 a.m. and I am at work. I work for an awesome company that produces news videos. For almost two years, I have sacrificed my relationships, time and energy for this job. And my boss only cares… about quantity and how many views each video gets. So I figured… I'd make ONE video of my own. To focus on the content instead of worry about the views. Oh, and to let my boss know… I quit. I QUIT! I'm gone.[1]

This is how Marina Shifrin announced in September 2013 that she was quitting her job, via an "interpretive dance" YouTube video set to an appropriately titled Kanye West track, 'Gone.'

The episode above is a rather dramatic but neither far-fetched nor isolated occurrence in the digital age! As social media become pervasive, organizations and their members have to contend with changes in organizational practices—from new ways of working to social-mediated employee communication and engagement—that profoundly affect corporate reputation management. Drama aside, incidents such as Shifrin's spark conversations about social media in the organizational context and their ramifications for employers and employees alike. Shifrin herself acknowledged that she took a calculated risk but that others should resist the urge to quit in quite such an "epic" manner unless they have a plan![2]

In this chapter, we look at some of the considerations around social media@work, their implications, and what is required to meaningfully integrate new ways of working into everyday organizational practice(s). How are social media changing organizational practices, interaction, and communication? How are employers using social media and for what purposes? What are the controversies and challenges surrounding the use of social media in the workplace? What are the reputation consequences and how do organizations manage these? Can employers completely control employee use of social media?

These questions are pertinent in an increasingly digital workplace. Gartner predicts that by 2020, more than seven billion people and businesses and at least 30 billion devices will be connected to the Internet fortifying "the world of digital business."[3] Twenty-five percent of the world's economy will be digital by the year 2020.[4] Given these developments and the exponential growth of social media, their integration in business strategy will contribute to rapid digitization, as well as offer new forms of engagement, interactivity, and relationships.

However, if we agree that creating a digital ecosystem ultimately rests on people,[5] we can better appreciate the complexities associated with social media in the organizational context. Perhaps this is not a surprise but a helpful reminder in the rush to leverage new media for business benefit. With this guiding thought, our point of departure in this chapter is not the social technologies or software tools that (will come to) dominate in a digital workplace but what these developments mean for everyday organizational practices, for the experiences of organization members, and for organizational reputation.

FIRST THINGS FIRST: SETTING THE CONTEXT

To say that the nature of work has changed in the past few decades nearly borders on cliché. Globalization processes, flexible work arrangements, new tools and media technologies, and changing expectations are both the antecedents and products of a dynamic work environment. With regard to digitalization, social networking platforms significantly affect employee ability to work anywhere, anytime, share ideas and information, leverage knowledge and expertise across teams, geographies, and time zones, and so much more.

Within our focus on the organizational context, we distinguish between two related developments—the first is enterprise social media (ESM), which outlines how organizations are using networking tools to work better and for 'internal' communication. Second is the 'boundary-spanning' role of employees as brand representatives and advocates and/or speaking as or on behalf of the organization. As our opening example illustrates, social media provide a space for employees to share their experiences and frustrations, allowing visibility into previously invisible or 'private' contexts. This, of course, is not a direct consequence of social media, but it gathers momentum in the digital age and presents new possibilities and risks. In this chapter, we concentrate on the latter development, which many organizations see as a red flag in managing reputation. Importantly, this emphasis is justified given our interest in the reputational challenges and opportunities.

ENTERPRISE SOCIAL MEDIA: WHAT'S IN IT FOR EVERYONE?

LEARNING OBJECTIVES

- Understand the basics of enterprise social media (ESM).
- Understand the potential of social media for employee engagement.
- Introduce strategies to build momentum for ESM.

A comprehensive definition of ESM refers to

> [w]eb-based platforms that allow workers to (1) communicate messages with specific coworkers or broadcast messages to everyone in the organization; (2) explicitly indicate or implicitly reveal particular coworkers as communication partners; (3) post, edit, and sort text and files linked to themselves or others; and (4) view the messages, connections, text, and files communicated, posted, edited and sorted by anyone else in the organization at any time of their choosing.[6]

Note that the definition above focuses not on the specific *channels* or tools of communication but treats social media as a "*platform* upon which social interaction occurs" with a focus on the communicative implications of social media use within organizations. Core to understanding the role of ESM, then, is to appreciate its perceived contribution to (improving) internal organizational communication, among and with employees. Although employees are an important, if not the most crucial, stakeholder group for any organization, social media research has primarily concentrated on customer engagement, largely because of the dominance of marketing and related implications of social media.

Nonetheless, there is a renewed understanding that as internal stakeholders, employees are the backbone of any successful business, and employee relationships are vital to positive customer experience. Internal communication is associated with higher levels of employee engagement, a culture of open communication, and employee alignment with corporate brand objectives.[7] Although traditional media tools such as email and the corporate intranet are important (perhaps more than new media in most cases), social media accelerate these possibilities with interactive, peer-to-peer, communication. Company blogs, in particular, are frequently used to crowdsource ideas, for sharing knowledge and thought leadership, project collaboration, and others. Overall, the communication possibilities afforded by ESM are many including the following:[8]

- Employee engagement.
- Breaking down internal silos by facilitating knowledge sharing and collaboration leading to innovation and new idea generation.
- Ability to build new networks within the physical organization and across virtual environments.
- As a testing ground for external/client-facing communication.
- Internal branding and developing employees as brand ambassadors and evangelists.

The potential influence of new media on employee relations and 'internal' communication explains the emerging interest in ESM. There are shining examples of organizations that have understood the potential of ESM and are using it to their advantage. For example, IBM uses social collaboration tools such as the proprietary IBM Connections for knowledge sharing and innovation. IBM's approach to collaboration and decision-making using networking technologies is well known in the form of its Jam sessions. The famous Values Jam in 2003, the first examination of the company's core values in 100 years, was the springboard for IBM's current core values as defined by IBMers. To mark its centenary and commemorate IBM's celebration of service, Jam sessions were used to crowdsource ideas and encourage participation for employee-led service projects to further strengthen its culture of service and corporate citizenship.[9]

For internal collaboration, several choices of networks exist, for instance, executives can participate in existing commercial networks (e.g., Facebook and Twitter), create their own internal networks for the exclusive use of employees, or build new functionalities (e.g., blogs and wikis) into existing systems, and so on. Another legacy firm making impressive strides on social media is General Electric (GE). GE is active on several social networks, but its internal collaboration tool Colab connects the more than 300,000 employees worldwide. Colab—a combination of Facebook, Twitter, LinkedIn, and Pinterest—was introduced in 2012 with the goal "to help employees become more efficient and to be able to reach across divisional, functional and geographic boundaries for help in solving problems."[10] In an interview, GE executive Ron Utterbeck explained the need to break silos and connect people across functions, "with Facebook, you hang with your crowd, your generation and your peeps but in the enterprise you want to cross those generational boundaries."[11] In less than a year of its launch, Colab had amassed over 100,000 users.

Admittedly, the experiences of IBM and GE will not automatically translate to all organizations. Even organizations that rely on the functionality of commercial social networks (Facebook and Twitter) instead of developing their own will have different outcomes given that these networks impose their own rules and guidelines. Under the tip of the iceberg, mixed feelings prevail among the two camps of social media enthusiasts and social media realists. A survey of business professionals hints at the possibility that ESM platforms emerge as the primary form of communication in the future. However, in the present scenario, traditional channels of communication, especially face-to-face meetings and email, continue to dominate in terms of usage frequency and perceived effectiveness for internal communication. Driving support for ESM is expected to come from generations X and Y as also enhanced usage. Business professionals who currently use ESM are more positive about their potential than those who do not.[12]

As an example, a few years ago, there was a lot of talk about Bring Your Own Device (BYOD) programs that allowed employees to use their personal mobile devices or tablets to access enterprise data.[13] The ubiquity of mobile computing and the alleged benefits of higher productivity and employee satisfaction fueled the BYOD movement, although reactions are now mixed with some calling it a passing fad, and others, a business reality. A report by Gartner predicts that by 2020, 85 percent of businesses will have some kind of BYOD program in place. For others, the risk of security breaches is high enough to discourage many organizations from exclusively relying on BYOD.[14] Nonetheless, our interest is in the implications of these unfolding developments, and it is abundantly clear that organizations are seeking ways to balance being adaptive and innovative in ways that enhance (and sometimes complicate) employee relationships and communication.

Social-mediated Employee Engagement

> In today's environment where there is an alarming lack of trust in all institutions, employees are increasingly the key prism for brand credibility and trust. Engaging them can provide companies the best way to humanize and unify their enterprise voice—a strategic imperative in today's environment.
>
> *Micho Spring*[15]

One of the loudest messages in any report on the potential of ESM is the promise of employee engagement. The potential of engagement via new social technologies resonates with organizations that understand that employee engagement yields positive business outcomes; yet digital engagement efforts are yet nascent or ad hoc. The benefits of (digital) engagement are many, for instance, employee engagement is linked to stronger business results in the form of higher customer satisfaction (+40%), profitability (+30%), and overall firm performance (+36%).[16] Besides, employee engagement is positively related to alignment with strategic objectives, satisfaction and productivity, and employee-driven innovation, among others.

Social media offer organizations a new avenue to drive employee engagement. Employee willingness to engage in supportive behavior (e.g., recommendation to buy company products and services; actively defend employer) is also much higher in organizations that are socially encouraging versus that are not.[17] Socially engaged companies benefit from high levels of engagement as employees feel more connected, informed, and optimistic about their employers.[18] Indeed, at such companies, leaders are at the helm of building engagement and positive relationships using ESM. Often, however, organizations struggle with the practical know how. Most organizations do not have a coherent strategy for digital employee engagement and the returns (ROI) on social media investment remain anecdotal.

Thinking about digital engagement, current efforts concentrate on (*a*) internal collaboration and (*b*) digital/social empowerment (Figure 3.1), and a very few organizations use (*c*) employee advocacy as an engagement mechanism, putting employees in the driver seat and empowering them to represent the organization on their personal social media accounts.[19] This form of advocacy is arguably the most difficult for organizations; "only corporate cultures rooted in trust can do employee advocacy well."[20]

FIGURE 3.1 *Forms of Digital Employee Engagement*

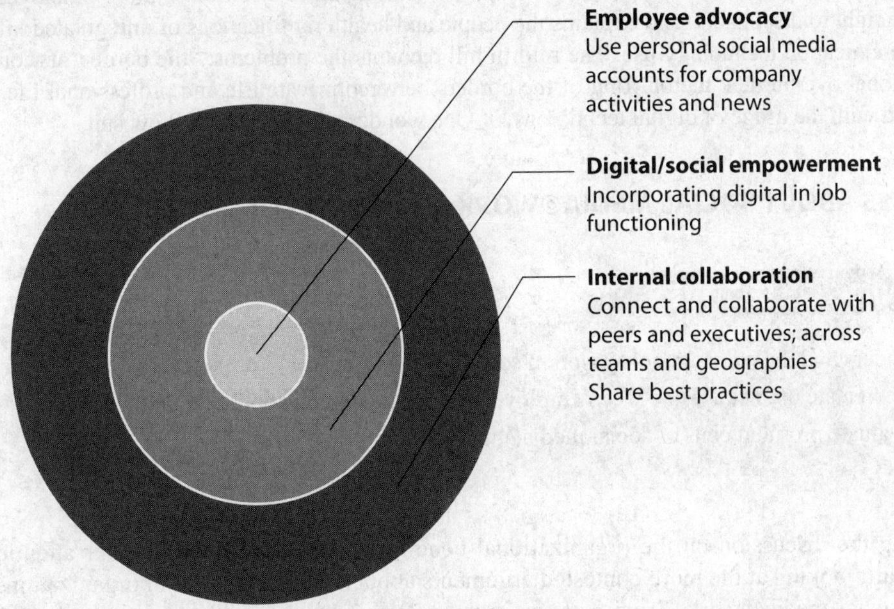

Source: Li et al. (2014).[21]

There are exceptions. Online retailer Zappos encourages employees to use social media as part of the company commitment to 'delivering WOW' customer service and engage consumer communities. Employees are encouraged to tweet (and trained to use Twitter) about company culture (using such hashtags as #ZapposCulture and #Zapponians) and share useful resources both on and off the Zappos networks. The belief in empowering employees for their boundary-spanning/advocacy role stems from CEO Tony Hsieh's commitment to putting people first and a strong culture as the bedrock of corporate success.[22]

Indeed, empowered employees (what some have called HEROes or "highly empowered and resourceful operative") can provide creative and innovative solutions for brand risks and as a counterpoint to customer power in the digital age.[23] HEROes are created when organizations allow employees to experiment with new media technologies within a safe space, with appropriate guidance, policies, and frameworks. Of course, this requires a change in mind-set and a cultural shift toward collaboration across functions and hierarchies.

So what can organizations do to facilitate use and embeddedness of ESM? As an example, when GE launched Colab, it focused on 'power users'—experimenters and champions across functional areas who drove use, gave feedback, and drew in more users. Feedback from users was integrated in subsequent updates.[24] Empowering employee champions and/or evangelists is a commonly used strategy but, overall, there is no single or best solution but a few options exist, each with their pros and cons. For example, organizations may adopt a bottom-up approach by harnessing the technology-savvy young experimenters, or begin with 'enlightened' executives who, by virtue of their stature in the organization, can ensure stakeholder buy-in.[25] It is not difficult to see the challenges in both cases: young champions may lack the credibility for organizational buy-in whereas seasoned executives may lack technological expertise. Organizations need to assess which strategies will work for their specific needs. With deeper embeddedness and more research, new and more comprehensive models will be available as starting points for the digital workplace.

Beyond the benefits and the how-tos of ESM, there is emerging concern that an 'always-on' world can take a toll on employees. In May 2016, France enacted a contested law that prohibits sending work email on holidays and weekends in an effort to alleviate burnout, spillover of work, and the pressures of a hyper-connected work environment. The law applies to companies with 50 or more employees, giving them 'the right to disconnect' and explains the people and health ramifications of unregulated information and communication technology use. The reform bill recounts the problems: "the burden of work and the informational overburden, the blurring of the borders between private life and professional life, are risks associated with the usage of digital technology."[26] One wonders if others will follow suit.

THE FUSS ABOUT SOCIAL MEDIA@WORK: KEY POINTS OF CONTENTION

LEARNING OBJECTIVES

- Understand the points of contention in social media@work.
- Appreciate the linkages between employee action and organizational reputation.
- Evaluate pros and cons of social media@work.

Following the discussion on the organizational benefits of ESM, we now turn our attention to the second part, looking at the more contested arguments about social media use in organizations or what we call social media@work. From a recent survey (Box 3.1), we can begin to see the substantive concerns (e.g., employee infractions) that prompt organizations to clamp down on social media and/or implement social media policies, all of which come with dilemmas as we note later. Thus, the question becomes how we might understand this other perspective on social media in the organizational context.

Box 3.1: Social Media@Work Trends

- Ninety percent of businesses in their study report using social media for business. But more businesses are taking measures to stop employees from using social media@work by blocking access (36%).
- Only 43 percent permit all of their employees to access social media sites, a fall of 10 percent since 2011, and over 40 percent monitor the use of social media at work.
- More than 70 percent of businesses report having to take disciplinary action against employees for misuse; current employees are responsible for most infractions (72.09%).
- The number of businesses with social media policies has increased significantly, from 60 to 80 percent.

Source: Proskauer (2014).[27]

To this end, we highlight three *interrelated* points of contention that, arguably, capture some of the complexities and uncertainties about social media@work. We briefly outline these arguments and then present key changes that illustrate their interlinkages and implications:

- Employees as reputation agents: To be or not to be?
- Blurring of the internal and external, the personal and the professional.
- 'Managing' the loss of control.

Thinking about the Role of Employees: To Be or Not to Be?

> In some ways, it seems obvious that it's not a question of what role employees play. They are the only ones who can build your corporate reputation.
>
> *Brian Walker*[28]

In the digital age, however, the role of employees in reputation building is perceived as a double-edged sword. On the one hand, employee alignment and identification with organizational goals and values is crucial for organizational success. By committing to and behaving in accordance with these beliefs and values, employees most closely represent and 'live the brand.' On the other hand, personal and organizational reputations, actions, and consequences are ever more entwined and with the near disappearance of personal and professional boundaries, a misguided tweet or Facebook post can spell trouble.[29] Indeed, there is no dearth of 'social media fails' on the Internet. While some make the headlines for a short time (such as when someone used the Chrysler Twitter account, @ChryslerAutos, for an expletive-ridden tweet, "I find it ironic that Detroit is known as the #motorcity and yet no one here knows how to f**king drive"),[30] others capture public imagination for a long time to come.

Case in point[31]: Justine Sacco, a former communication and PR consultant at a leading media and Internet firm IAC (NASDAQ: IAC), tweeted this (see below) as she boarded her flight from New York to South Africa in December 2013.

What she thought was an amusing tweet, that no one would take literally, ended up splashed across the Twitterverse by technology-blogger Sam Biddle. Along with the several thousand retweets, the hashtag #HasJustineLandedYet was trending worldwide as people waited in anticipation for Justine's reaction who was in flight and oblivious to the unfolding chaos.

Aside from the racist overtones, the fact that someone in a responsible and senior position would say something like this was fodder to fire, and her employer IAC was quick to distance itself, "This is an outrageous, offensive comment. Employee in question currently unreachable on an intl flight"; so did a colleague, "I'm an IAC employee and I don't want @JustineSacco doing any communications on our behalf ever again. Ever." Justine was eventually fired. She lost her job and reputation and reportedly continues to face public humiliation on social media well after the incident.

For digital reputation management, the role of employees is a fundamental point of contention. That employees shape corporate reputation is an understatement but this influence, both positive and negative, is increased manifold in the digital age. Just as consumers can express their pleasure and frustration, employee expression on social media "impacts not only that person, but that person's circle of influence as well. The same holds true if they send out a positive experience."[32]

When it comes to social media and employees, Miles and Mangold ask, are employees "untapped resources" or "ticking time bombs"?[33] Arguably, this question is about the 'power' of employees and the affordances of that power. When viewed as a threat to an 'official' voice, organizations may clamp down on employee use of social media. By contrast, when employees are viewed as positive brand representatives especially in an organizational crisis, organizations will likely empower (and train) them to "harness their creativity as a strategic force."[34] Arguably, neither unbridled access nor complete censorship alleviates reputation risks that may arise nonetheless. Refer to the Dominos' prank video or the HMV employee hijacking the company's Twitter account (see Chapter 4), both of which posed reputational challenges triggered by employee (ab)use of social media.

On the positive side, a trusting network communication environment can empower employees to become advocates and evangelists for their organizations. Guy Kawasaki, the former chief evangelist at Apple, explains that evangelism—"explaining to the world how your product or service can improve people's lives"—is not the responsibility of a single department or function. Rather, he notes that "in the social age, evangelism is everyone's job."[35] Technology companies have been the frontrunners in encouraging employees to blog about new products, services, and technologies. At one point, the erstwhile Sun Microsystems was reportedly called a "blog haven" where one in every ten employees maintained a blog.[36] Ex CEO of Sun, Jonathan Schwartz was quoted in an interview promoting employee evangelism, "If you want to lead, blog… We talk about our successes—and our mistakes. That may seem risky. But it's riskier not to have a blog."[37]

Research also bears out the idea that negative employee blogs open to the public can actually increase readership and create positive views of an organization.[38] Where overly positive posts arouse skepticism, honest, if critical, blogs are seen as more credible because they supposedly violate readers' preconceived ideas and expectations that employees will only say positive things about their organization. For the audience, the 'unexpected' honesty comes across as helpful and genuine, and organizational "tolerance for critical messages" may signal "openness and trustworthiness towards stakeholders."[39] Of course, a preponderance of negative posts is also detrimental to reputation so organizations need to tread the fine line between transparency and employee empowerment, trust and control, in managing their online reputation.

Some have argued that social media are a highly emotional and functional "space where employees express both happiness and frustration, and force organizations to make decisions much more quickly and with less precise information."[40] The uncertain and unknown prompts organizations to find ways to 'manage' employee use of social media, as explained later in the chapter. So how does this translate to social media strategy? One way to think about this question is in terms of managerial sense-making; in other words, how does management think about the contribution of employees to reputation building. Where employees are trusted as online brand ambassadors and organizations encourage an open culture of communication, we might expect active social media (employee) involvement. Subtle forms of 'control' may exist here as well, in the form of usage guidelines or when the boss is friends on Facebook! In situations where employee use of social media is seen as amplifying reputation risks, organizations may limit or restrict access. Depending on the context, attitude toward social media, and the perception of employee influence, online reputation management is indeed "a balancing act":

> between active versus limited company social-media presence; encouraging versus restricting employees in online participation; centralising versus decentralising responsibility and leadership; emphasising employees work versus private social-media roles; as well as disseminating marketing content versus authentic and 'naturally' transpiring content in social media.[41]

Blurred Boundaries: The Water Cooler Moves to Social Media

> At Amazon, workers are encouraged to tear apart one another's ideas in meetings, toil long and late…and held to standards that the company boasts are "unreasonably high." The internal phone directory instructs colleagues on how to send secret feedback to one another's bosses. Employees say it is frequently used to sabotage others …
>
> *Jodi Kantor and David Streitfeld*[42]

On August 15, 2015, The New York Times published a scathing article on Amazon's work culture. The article, titled 'Inside Amazon: Wrestling Big Ideas in a Bruising Workplace,' alleged that Amazon's leadership principles created an ultra-competitive environment and a ruthless culture. This short excerpt and the now (in)famous quote from a former worker, "nearly every person I worked with, I saw cry at their desk,"[43] was no small matter for the world's largest retailer (US$247.6 billion by market value against Walmart's US$230.5 billion). The story sparked a debate about the culture and legitimacy of Amazon and a flurry of reactions ensued (see Appendix).

First, this case is fascinating for foregrounding the role of employee advocacy in managing reputation. Amazon employee Nick Ciubotariu took it upon himself to defend his organization when he penned a detailed response on his LinkedIn page (over a million views), countering the scenarios presented in the *NYT* article.[44] His 'unofficial' positive response made its way into the official communication (Jeff Bezos' email to employees). Second, the back and forth between different actors (Amazon employee, the *NYT* editor, and company PR) was played out on social media.[45] The "sparring" between the *NYT* editor and the PR executive, that might have taken place in private not long along, was very public indeed as "both men, who have access to huge audiences of their own, published their posts on *Medium*, a site for essays and storytelling that is open to the public."[46]

Thus, our second point of contention posits that social media@work present profound dilemmas for organizations as they "traverse both the *private sphere* and the *public sphere*" which have traditionally been seen as separate.[47] Employee use of social media makes an organization's culture and character increasingly transparent to other stakeholders, amplifying their reach as external communicators.

Consider the case of Golden Corral,[48] an all-you-can-eat buffet restaurant chain in the United States. Back in 2013, an employee of a Golden Corral location in Florida uploaded a video on YouTube showing mounds of raw meat lying open near a dumpster in the back of the restaurant. The narrator (employee) claimed that these ingredients would later be cooked and served in the restaurant. As flies hovered over the trays of raw meat, the employee explained that the restaurant was hiding the food during a health inspection ("this is what my company likes to do to get ready for inspection") and that he had unsuccessfully tried to bring this matter to his manager's attention on prior occasions. Golden Corral and the location manager denied wrongdoing, claimed that the food was never meant to be served, and accused the employee of attempting to use the video for personal financial gain by offering a US$5,000 price on eBay (see statement issued by the company).

golden corral

goldencorral 3 hours ago

"In regard to the video that is currently being circulated by an employee of Golden Corral of an isolated incident of improper food handling at our Port Orange, Florida location please note

1. The food in the video was never served to a single customer.
2. All of the food was thrown away immediately.
3. The employee in the video participated in disposing of the food.
4. The employee in the video – through his father – offered to sell the video.
5. The manager at the restaurant was terminated.

© Golden Corral Reply

Source: Nye *(2008).*

The cases above are illustrative of how digital technologies offer a window into the inner workings of organizations, forcing them to balance competing expectations of "openness for participation and interactivity" and the lack of "*control* that is the mainstay of one-way, top-down information distribution models."[49] Are these isolated cases or symptomatic of fundamental problems, and are they somehow unique to social media? Is there a grounded explanation for the proverbial airing of dirty laundry on social media?

One perspective is to think about social media as a counter-institutional channel of communication that provide employees (and consumers) a platform to express dissent and resistance when institutional mechanisms fail to do so.[50] Such platforms are beyond corporate control and offer opportunities to voice resistance to organizational practices, policies, and managerial interests. Notably, not all communication on such platforms may be negative, as research has found, or meant to sabotage the organization, but they could very well be a manifestation of weak or ineffective organizational/official communication channels. It is ever more critical that 'open-door policies' and channels of communication are authentic so that employees have a safe space to share ideas, opinions, and feedback. Providing an appropriate organizational context and mechanisms for addressing employee voice is necessary for the effective management of social media@work and its outcomes. In the absence of these resources, employees may turn to alternative avenues of communication. As a final point, instances of online venting are a fitting illustration that such counter-institutional channels "blur the physical and temporal boundaries between organizational insiders and outsiders; this allows a wide variety of organizational stakeholders to come together and make their concerns public."[51]

With employer reviews on Glassdoor, CareerBuilder, and LinkedIn, among other social media, it may appear futile for companies to attempt to censor negative feedback. No doubt, negative employee reviews hurt the corporate brand as a Glassdoor survey found: 11 percent of job seekers would decline an offer from a company with a bad reputation, even if they were unemployed.[52] Reportedly, job seekers on Glassdoor are most deterred by negative reviews on compensation and benefits followed by senior management and work–life balance.[53]

Communication professionals recommend that instead of fearing and censoring employee reviews, companies should use platforms like Glassdoor to enhance employee engagement by encouraging and responding to reviews but also setting internal mechanisms to resolve conflicts and grievances before they are publicly shared.[54]

Negotiating the Loss of Control: Social Media Governance

The final point of contention relates to how organizations 'manage' digital reputation with employees. Arguably, organizations can never fully control employee use of social media@work, which explains their unease with digital employee advocacy. In India, for example, organizations are putting measures in place to discourage online venting by banning social media use at the workplace, formulating social media policies, and introducing legal clauses in employment contracts. In some cases, these codes and policies allow for disciplinary action and even oblige ex-employees to not engage in action that could result in defamation of the company.[55] In a hyper-connected world, some regard such censorship mechanisms as an exercise in futility,[56] but we do not know how employees respond, negotiate, and resist such policies and how does it impact their engagement and identification with the organization.

Since there are no legal standards, organizations rely on guidelines as governance mechanisms. Defined as "the formal or informal frameworks which regulate the actions of the members of an organization within the social web"[57] the social media policy along with training programs are currently the de facto form of governance. A quick Internet search will dole out mountains of advice on the why, what, and how of designing social media guidelines. Simply put, policies are a way to discipline (employee use of) social media and to mitigate risks—reputational, legal, and operational—by delineating a set of rules/guidelines for use. Given that much ESM use is employee-driven and bottom-up, it precludes organizations from relying on traditional mechanisms of technology governance.

Despite appearances, social media policies are not value-neutral documents. Rather, they need to negotiate the dilemmas we identified before, that is, participation and control, individual and organizational goals, and open/transparent and strategic communication. The number of voices that speak for and on behalf of the organization implies that organizations have to walk the tightrope between the participatory culture of Web 2.0 and strategic business interest. This paradox emerges as social media practitioners argue the need to integrate social media communication with the corporate communication function to ensure consistent and coherent brand messages. While the integrated approach is often advanced as part of 'social media strategy,' it also risks being "'colonized' for traditional organization-centric forms of strategic communication" and to the detriment of openness, democracy, and participation philosophy of social media.[58]

So how do organizations make sense of the social media policy and what do they include in these documents? A study sheds light on what organizations concern themselves with in these documents. The majority highlights the affordances (see Box 3.2) of visibility and persistence, reminding employees of the public nature of contributions and the availability of information for extended periods, respectively. Both these aspects are seen as "contributing to a loss of control and over the use and dissemination of content published through social media"[59] and, by implication, over image and reputation. The concern with mitigating risks explains why policies are more emphatic and specific about 'what not to post' as opposed to 'what to post.' Even editability is interpreted not in terms of employee ability to correct their contributions but in terms of others' ability to manipulate and edit content, again illustrative of employer concern with risk. Policies also illuminate the tension between personal and professional identities in their need for a statement of affiliation and identification (e.g., identify yourself) or disclaimers (e.g., your views are your own and do not reflect those of the organization). With regard to governance, this study found that most organizations rely on a combination of mechanisms—already established rules, new rules specific to social, encourage employees to rely on hierarchy in cases of ambiguity, and/or exercise personal responsibility/accountability—in the use of social media. However, there is also a temporal dimension in that newer policies focused less on risk reduction while recognizing the positive benefits of employee use of social media, suggesting a shift in employer attitude toward social media@work.

Box 3.2: Four Affordances of Social Media in the Organizational Context

Visibility: Ability to make known previously invisible information, behaviors, knowledge, preferences, and communication network connections.

Persistence: Akin to permanence, this implies that information, conversations, and communication are accessible in the same form as originally displayed.

Editability: Ability to craft and recraft a communicative act before others can view and/or to edit or revise content that has already been communicated.

Association: Ability to foster connections between individuals (i.e., social ties), between individual and information (e.g., a wiki contribution), and content to content (e.g., recommendations made by Facebook).

Source: Treem and Leonardi (2012).[60]

From a critical perspective, though, we might ask if the monitoring of employees' social media use is tantamount to surveillance, "the focused systematic and routine attention to personal details for purposes of influence, management, protection or direction."[61] Efforts to monitor employee use of social media have apparently birthed a US$200 million monitoring industry, expected to reach US$500 million in the next four years. Overall, the social business application market (including marketing automation, social media monitoring, web experience management, and enterprise collaboration tools) is expected to be worth US$37 billion by 2019 (currently, US$13.9 billion).[62] Needless to say, the ethical issues are profound, especially when surveillance is framed in business friendly terms such as 'time management' or 'productivity monitoring.' In fact, evidence is inconclusive if not contradictory: Only seven percent of working online adults report that their productivity dropped because of the Internet, email and cellphones, while 46 percent feel more productive.[63]

Some scholars offer a more nuanced perspective on the topic noting that surveillance is multi-faceted and can manifest as both 'care' and 'control'. While control mechanisms are usually articulated in negative terms, care is framed as safeguarding employees from problematic consequences (e.g., the possibility of a social media post being misused or abused). In a routinized way, of course, 'care' for employees is as much about "'care' for the organization, protecting the brand from potentially detrimental acts by employees."[64] Thus, social media monitoring may serve dual functions and cannot be oversimplified:

> although the formal and informal monitoring of employees may be intended to control practices, routine use also includes the acknowledgement of birthdays, special events, personal circumstances, and more importantly, contributing to personal well-being and promoting positive social relationships within the workplace.[65]

In sum, we can argue that as social media become more firmly embedded, organizations and scholars need to be mindful of ethical challenges, unintended consequences, and inherent tensions. Digital reputation management will require an understanding and evaluation of extant and emergent challenges, some of which include:[66]

1. **Power and transparency:** Social media can be a source of employee empowerment but they can also be a source of risk by making organizations and their culture more transparent online. Although the enactment of social media policies is meant to limit inappropriate usage, the attempt to control employee actions may instill "a sense of continual oversight" and lead to resistance. Therefore, organizations need to balance the need for employee empowerment and reputation management.
2. **Normalization:** Generally, organizations expect employees to participate in social media; however, the expectations and norms of participation are ambiguous, and these (unstated) expectations of engagement may disadvantage less engaged personnel.
3. **Function creep:** The unintended possibility that social media policies may go beyond brand protection and reputation management to infringe in the domain of personal performance and/or beyond creating a positive work culture to becoming a promotional tool for the organization. In other words, organizations need to be cognizant that social media monitoring may shift from the original intention, from "the identified and intended frame of practice."

PEOPLE, ORGANIZATIONS, AND ETHICS?

> The most pressing is to remember that nothing posted online ever truly goes away. The way to decide what to post requires a shift in thinking. You should not be living your life through social media, you must be curating it instead.
>
> *David Lahey*[67]

LEARNING OBJECTIVES

- Understand the people implication of new organizational practices.
- Reflect on the associated ethical dilemmas and consequences.

Good advice but easier said than done? Speaking of ethics and organizational reputation, social media also have personal reputation implications. If you have heard about www.crystalknows.com, you have already experienced the shock, awe, and strange discomfort from knowing that everyone has a digital persona, like it or not, that is constructed by pooling all publicly available information. Note that if you complete your personal profile on this website, the report can be uncomfortably accurate but even if you do not, your personality profile can be accessed on the basis of what is known about you (e.g., on LinkedIn, institutional or personal websites, etcetera). So, when one of us was told (without completing the personal profile) that she is "relationship-focused, expressive, and open, and prefers a predictable plan over immediate action," and more (e.g., how to communicate with her, win her trust), any illusion of 'private' information was cast away.

Along these lines, the expectation and normalization of social media use in work contexts has generated new practices such as cybervetting, the growing reliance on social media for assessing employee–organization fit. The normalization of cybervetting poses ethical dilemmas and necessitates a reexamination of personal branding, online identity management, and social media presence. Let us look at these developments in more detail.

Cybervetting refers to the process by which employers use the Internet (and social media) "to acquire informal, non-institutional, other-sourced, and/or aggregated information [...] that job candidates did not share or necessarily intend for employers' use."[68] In the not-so-distant past, employers relied on information furnished by candidates and/or institutional sources for job hires. Now, those searches have moved to social media. Monster uses Twitter as the primary network for 'social hiring'. With 60,000 jobs are tweeted each day, and an engaged professional audience, Twitter is increasingly used as a source for finding talent.[69]

Cybervetting goes beyond social hiring in its scope and consequences. It assumes a distrust of conventional sources of information and/or false or misleading credentials from candidates that could result in bad hiring decisions. Because online information mitigates worker control over information (and its manipulation), it is assumed to be more reliable in making personnel selection, "it implicitly promises access to the real person."[70] Although cybervetting is not illegal per se, the implications for privacy and for how candidates present themselves online are palpable (see Box 3.3).

Box 3.3: Realities of Cybervetting

CareerBuilder's 2015 survey finds that 52 percent of employers use social networking sites to research job candidates, up from 43 percent in 2014 and 39 percent in 2013. Fifty-one percent of hiring managers use search engines to research candidates. On the flip side, job seekers are also leveraging social networks to vet hiring managers.

What do recruiters look for?

- Job-related qualifications such as a professional portfolio
- Digital presence/online persona
- What other people are posting about the candidate
- Reasons not to hire the candidate

By industry, recruiters in Information Technology, Financial Services, Sales, and Professional and Business Services are reportedly more likely to cybervet.

How do they do it?

- By requesting to 'friend' a candidate or follow candidates that have private accounts. A majority (80%) of such requests were granted.

Content that rewards or punishes

- Digital content that corroborates a candidate's application, demonstrates candidate fit with job qualifications and the company, showcases creativity, professionalism, and communication skills is deemed positive. Provocative or inappropriate photographs, bad-mouthing peers or previous employers, and discriminatory comments are detrimental and may result in disqualifying a candidate from consideration.

Source: CareerBuilder survey (2015).[71]

Surveys confirm that more and more recruiters are turning to social media to research applicants.

Ironically, research finds that employers expect candidates to proactively make information available without being asked. This expectation of information transparency stems from the assumption that unsolicited information permitted access to 'the real person' such that the absence of a digital presence is viewed with skepticism and suspicion. Thus, employers evaluate workers not just on the presence but also on the absence of online information.[72]

Communication scholar Brenda Berkelaar's (2014, 2015) research examines *why* employers engage in cybervetting (how they make sense of it), and with *what* consequences. She conducted interviews with employers to investigate how they use online information for personnel selection and most employers reported the use of cybervetting to form early impressions of candidates. Aside from visual and textual content typically highlighted in survey reports (see Box 3.3), employers in her research report use relational cues (e.g., size of professional network) to assess candidate reputation, social capital, and trustworthiness. Likewise, technological information is deemed useful to judge professional qualifications and (lack of) job-fit.[73]

But how do candidates make sense of employer use of cybervetting? Berkelaar (2014) finds that although candidates perceive cybervetting to be problematic (e.g., no opportunity to clarify or explain possible misunderstandings; invasion of privacy) and *want* employers to be transparent about its use, they do not *expect* employers to be transparent. What explains this apparent paradox is that both parties have accepted the inevitability of cybervetting as the new way of technology-assisted information seeking.

The assumption of cybervetting as inevitable results in legitimating and normalizing self-management online. Berkelaar notes that managing one's professional identity and presence is considered necessary and "a fact of life," with the burden of proof resting on the candidates' discretion and assessment of what information to include (or exclude). Such a practice, then, stretches conventional career boundaries as workers are expected to curate their digital presence "across times, contexts, and roles not conventionally considered for career advancement."[74]

A direct consequence of online recruiting is a new look at professional identity management and personal branding. Job seekers are advised to pay attention to the profile picture, often the first point of contact, as part of their efforts to manage and appropriately present themselves on social networks. Why? Because in the absence of social cues about a candidate (e.g., non-verbal communication), available cues (such as gender and visible physical characteristics) are magnified, and decisions about initial credibility may be based on these cues. For example, research has found that women wearing spectacles and men with beards are perceived as more credible than their non-spectacled/bearded counterparts, especially for expertise jobs (e.g., architect in an architectural firm). Not surprisingly, candidates with higher perceived credibility are more likely to be invited for job interviews.[75]

As with the issue of surveillance, cybervetting may be viewed as unethical (though not illegal), an invasion of privacy, and hurt employee relationship with the organization. Considering the engagement imperative we discussed before, this distrust may actually cause disengagement.

(RE)KINDLING THE ROMANCE: THE ROLE OF LEADERSHIP AND CULTURE

> Winners in the digital age do much more than complete a technology checklist. They know their success hinges on people […] the real deciding factor in the digital era will be the ability to evolve corporate culture.
>
> *Accenture Technology Vision 2016*[76]

LEARNING OBJECTIVES

- Appreciate the relevance of leadership in the digital workplace.
- Examine the links between organizational culture, leadership, and social media technologies.

Success of social media in organizational contexts centers on enabling employees, a supportive culture, skilled leadership, and an integrated approach to social strategy. Creating a culture of social media goes beyond the tools and technologies. In her book, *Open Leadership*, author and social media expert Charlene Li outlines open leadership as the new paradigm that leaders have to embrace in the digital age. She defines open leadership as "having the confidence and humility to give up the need to be in control while inspiring commitment from people to accomplish goals."[77] Indeed, the fear of losing control is daunting for many organizations but Li argues that it is not a choice, and the question confronting leaders is not "whether you will be transparent, authentic and real, but rather, *how much will you let go* and be open in the face of these new technologies."[78] For leaders to succeed in the digital age and create cultures of trusted relationships, support, dialogue, and innovation, she offers the following rules:

1. Respect that customers and employees have significant power.
2. Share constantly to build trust.
3. Nurture curiosity and humility.
4. Hold openness accountable.
5. Forgive failure.

The need for a new kind of leader is echoed by others and rests on active leader involvement. Of course, new forms of leadership do not emerge overnight and organizations have to overcome inertia of legacy systems, attitudes, and cultures. Leaders that are able to overcome shortcomings of conventional organizational design and develop an enabling ecosystem for the strategic use of social technologies can better capitalize on the promise of social media.[79]

The logical question to ask, then, is how are leaders performing on social media? Weber Shandwick's 2015 survey *Socializing Your CEO III*[80] reports a 'dramatic' shift in CEO presence on social media. In contrast with 36 percent in previous years, 80 percent of the top 50 Fortune 500 CEOs now have a social presence in a combination of social networks, the company website, YouTube, or company blog. Social networks like Facebook and Twitter, however, lag behind the corporate website (68%) and YouTube (54%). Although optimistic, these results are confined to a few. A more extensive survey of Fortune 500 CEOs by DOMO and CEO.com[81] Social CEO Report finds that only 39 percent of CEOs are active on social networks. By implication, 61 percent have no social presence. This inertia is attributed to the lack of time, no demonstrable return on investment, lack of know-how and skills, and even the risk of missteps. Saying the wrong thing could endanger the company's reputation (recall Mike Jeffries, former CEO of Abercrombie & Fitch).

Aside from the expectations of transformed leadership, CEO social presence has reputational benefits as it offers an opportunity to "transparently tell the company's story and join the conversation."[82] With CEO reputation intimately tied to overall corporate reputation, employees with social CEOs reportedly feel more inspired, technologically advanced, and proud.

So where does this bring us: To reaffirming that employee relationships and organizational culture is the crux of social media@work. Scholars Huy and Shipilov (2012) argue that ESM or internal social media should focus on developing emotional capital or "the aggregate feelings of goodwill toward a company and the way it operates"[83] by encouraging feelings of authenticity, pride, attachment, and fun among employees. Their research flips conventional thinking about ESM by arguing that employers should first build emotional capital before they can extract benefits from ESM. They observe that in the absence of efforts to build community, organizations "may be tempted to compensate by making extensive investments in technological platforms to create communities. Yet such actions create cold communities without heart and spirit".[84]

Huy and Shipilov (2012) propose a five-step roadmap to deploy social media in organizations:

1. Identify leaders who are authentic and trusted by employees.
2. Help those people develop social media skills.
3. Ask them to build social media communities characterized by authenticity, pride, attachment, and fun—the components of emotional capital.
4. Sequentially deploy social media tools in line with the goal of emotional capital.
5. Only after emotional capital is developed should organizations expect to reap instrumental benefits (such as improved information exchange, motivation, morale, and reduced turnover).

In closing, this chapter has looked at social media and their influence on organizational practices, on employee relations, and organizational culture. We have addressed the central points of contention (e.g., employees as brand advocates, the paradoxes of social media participation) and the opportunities and challenges that confront organizations in the digital age. As with other phenomena, there is no fixed formula for success, and experiences may be drastically different based on the perceived affordances of social media. Finally, it is important to reiterate the focus on people, relationships, and engagement in organizations and create enabling cultures in which technologies become facilitators.

It is only appropriate to end the chapter with the different metaphors that have been used to make sense of the opportunities, challenges, and paradoxes of social media in the organizational content. These metaphors simultaneously reinforce the dynamic, even unpredictable, current as well as the optimism driving its proliferation (Box 3.4).

Box 3.4: Metaphors of Social Media in the Organizational Context

Leaky pipe: The metaphor implies that "the directionality of a particular communication (to whom it is directed) and the content of that communication (what the parties involved actually said to each other) is visible to people who were not involved in it." Although this has benefits (e.g., more transparency and knowledge of others' work), it may also result in more defensive self-presentation.

Echo chamber: Recognizes that "various types of communities within organizations can emerge and be supported." Yet, the potential benefits of the echo chamber (facilitating like-minded communities of practice) could also simultaneously have "balkanizing effects" and create differences.

Social lubricant: Supports the social fabric of organizations by enabling connections and cultivating a sense of belonging in the workplace. As with the other metaphors, there are benefits (e.g., ability to

(Box 3.4 Continued)

(Box 3.4 Continued)

create new connections and relationships) and challenges (e.g., may create false impressions of social connections where none exist).

What are the advantages and disadvantages of these metaphors for organizational communication? Can you think of other metaphors to describe the role of social media in the organizational context? What are the implications for organizations, their members, and reputation management?

Source: Leonardi, Huysman, and Steinfield (2013).[85]

Chapter Highlights

1. In the digital age, organizations have to adapt to new ways of working that profoundly affect corporate reputation management.
2. Social media offers news of organization–employee engagement, interactivity, and relationships. Yet they come with their share of challenges.
3. People, not technologies, are the starting point for a digital ecosystem.
4. Organizations may use commercial platforms or develop their own proprietary social networks for internal communication.
5. Although organizations are accepting ESM for internal collaboration, engagement, and innovation, they are as yet wary of employees advocating and speaking on behalf of the organization.
6. Social media@work is characterized with several paradoxes whereby employees are encouraged to live the brand but are constrained in their ability to represent the organization on social media. Hence, the role of employees as reputation agents is very much a balancing act.
7. Perhaps the most pronounced fear of social media@work comes from the blurring of public and private boundaries. Employees can easily share the 'inner workings' of their organizations and express professional (or personal) frustrations on social media, rendering the personal–professional distinction obsolete.
8. The perceived risks and incidences of employee infractions prompt many organizations to monitor, restrict, and censor employee use of social media@work.
9. In the absence of traditional mechanisms of control, social media policies are currently the main form of governance. These policies, combined with media training, arguably give organizations a sense of 'control' that they perceive to be losing with social media.
10. New organizational practices (e.g., cybervetting) pose significant ethical dilemmas for how current and prospective organizational members present themselves online. Digital presence, and lack thereof, can impact evaluations of credibility, worthiness, and competence, leading to more emphasis on impression management.
11. The role of organizational leaders is critical in inducing a sense of trust in employees and in creating an enabling ecosystem for social media@work. However, CEOs are still lagging behind in embracing digital.
12. Open and transparent cultures are the bedrock for organizations that wish to leverage social media. Building emotional capital prior to deploying social media in organizations is one way to embed new ways of working in organizational culture.

Activities

1. Based on your understanding of the chapter and additional research on 'best practices' and 'dos and don'ts' of social media use in organizations, create small role plays/skits with your group. Each skit should simulate a potential situation (positive or negative) that could create challenges for employee communication and engagement. Make the situation as realistic as possible and craft key messages, think about the social network in use, and use the role play for further discussion about possible solutions.
2. Talk with professionals (in your network) who work in virtual teams. Share in class the kinds of (digital) communication channels they use most often and why. What are the perceived benefits and challenges of using these channels? What do they see as hindrances and facilitators in the effective integration of digital communication in their team?
3. Imagine that a member of your team posts a negative comment on his/her Facebook/Twitter account about team dynamics and makes serious allegations about favoritism, unfair treatment, and a lack of empathy in the workplace. As the manager, the negative post (or Tweet) comes to your attention. In an effort to show openness to feedback and understand if the feeling is isolated or widespread, you ask human resource to poll your team (proximate and distributed). The results are disconcerting and you need to address the feedback both at the level of team culture and on social media. What possible approaches could you use to do so? What are the challenges you anticipate and how do you plan to overcome those?
4. Follow any one corporate (or organizational) blog for a few weeks. Assess the quality and quantity of activity on the blog? Who is the author, who is interacting, what kinds of comments you can find, what the frequency of updates is, what kind of information is posted, and so on. How would you assess the purpose of this blog? The class can pool collective knowledge to assess whether blogs serve different purposes and to what the differences are attributed (e.g., industry/business sector, culture, leader/CEO, etcetera).
5. Individually or in collaboration, conduct a comparative case study of social media policies. How do organizations frame the motivations and need for such a policy? How prominent is their placement on corporate communication channels (i.e., accessibility and prominence on corporate website, social networks, etcetera)? What are the main clauses of the policies? What is missing?
6. Analyze these policies from an affordance perspective and evaluate how they permit or constrain the agency of employees.
7. Conduct an informal interview with working professionals to learn how their organization uses new media in the workplace, learn about the management's approach to employee use of social media, and examine the perceived challenges and opportunities. How do participants make sense of these practices for their membership in the organization? Compare to discern differences across industry, type of organization, and so on.
8. You are an external consultant brought in to address organizational resistance to ESM. The problem is the client organization expected to have more employees using and collaborating on the new platform it developed and rolled out over six months ago. What will your approach be? Who are the stakeholders you need to speak with, and what information do you need? Based on this, think about creative ways in which you can build momentum for adoption.
9. You have recently been hired by a mid-sized IT company to help them lay down corporate social media guidelines for internal consumption. Prepare a stringent 10-point document that emphasizes integrity and honesty in approach.
10. In a recent blog post, one of the employees of your company has made an unwarranted remark which has damaged the reputation of your company. The cyber space is abuzz with dialogue on what has been stated. Discuss in your groups and present the strategy to be used to contain the damage and prevent a repeat of similar incidents in the future.

Discussion Questions

1. There is a lot of trust in employees as organization representatives but there is also debate on whether employers can or should trust other employees with the use of social media. Debate and discuss this paradox about the role of employees in reputation management. Support your position with appropriate examples.
2. Under what conditions are employees able to fulfill their roles as brand ambassadors? What is the role of organizational leaders in this process? Explain and illustrate with an example.
3. "Creating corporate guidelines for use of social media is of no significance. Employees do and will flout the same for multiple reasons." Discuss the same in light of any example that you have studied. Are there any 'rogue' employees on social media or are social media outbursts indicative of systemic problems? Why or why not? Discuss your position with appropriate examples.
4. Related to question 3, how can organizations manage rogue employees on social media and/or anticipate and prepare for situations of employee (mis)use of social media? Can there be 'foolproof' mechanisms?
5. What are factors/considerations that organizations need to take into account to integrate social media into their way of working? Can you classify these factors into specific categories?
6. Using a specific example/case, argue your position on the following statement:
   Social media policies are merely a modified form of organizational control and surveillance.
   What does your argument imply about organizational culture and leadership?
7. What are the pros and cons of monitoring social media@work? Discuss and reflect on the reputation implications of both perspectives.
8. Reflecting on your own or anecdotal experiences, how do you make sense of cybervetting? What are the practical lessons you can take from this research in managing your own professional profile? How might cultural contexts influence attitudes and behaviors toward cybervetting? What are the ethical challenges you can think of? What could be some unintended consequences of this practice?

APPENDIX

CASE

AMAZON: NOWHERE TO HIDE

August 15, 2015: *The New York Times* published a scathing article on Amazon's work culture that triggered a media frenzy and debate about Amazon's leadership philosophy encapsulated in the company's 14 leadership principles.[86] The aftermath was a public battle waged on social media.

August 16: In a LinkedIn post, Amazon employee Nick Ciubotariu defended his employer against the *NYT* accusations.[87] Drawing on his 18-month experience at Amazon, he presented counter-arguments for each of the allegations made by the journalists.

August 17: CEO Jeff Bezos sent an internal memo to Amazonians emphatically noting that he did not recognize the Amazon quoted in the article and the "shockingly callous management practices" it described. In his memo, he encouraged employees to report any practices or stories that looked like what was quoted in the article. His short memo also included a link to Ciubotariu's post for "very different take by a current Amazonian."[88]

October 19: Jay Carney, Senior Vice President for Global Corporate Affairs at Amazon, wrote a piece on *Medium* titled "What The New York Times Didn't Tell You" blaming the authors for misrepresenting Amazon, not meeting journalistic standards by fact-checking, and being sensationalistic. The opinion piece shared verbatim email correspondence with one of the authors (Jodi Kantor) to argue that Amazon was misled about the purpose of her investigation. As for quote about people crying at their desk, Carney explained at the very top of his writing (para 2):

> Here's what the story didn't tell you about Mr. Olson: his brief tenure at Amazon ended after an investigation revealed he had attempted to defraud vendors and conceal it by falsifying business records. When confronted with the evidence, he admitted it and resigned immediately.[89]

The fact that the first response from Jay Carney came two months after the *NYT* story was confounding as it "prompted a fresh flood of readers to the original article."[90]

October 19: The same day, Dean Baquet, *NYT* Executive Editor, responded to Jay Carney's post on the same channel. Reiterating support for the *NYT* story, he explained the methodology used to arrive at patterns of employee experience documented in the story and highlighted specific instances in response to Carney's piece (including Bo Olson's testimony that "he said he was never confronted with allegations of personally fraudulent conduct or falsifying records, nor did he admit to that"). As a final point, he noted that the journalists did their due diligence and that Amazon's surprise was unwarranted given that questions about company reputation and critical culture were always an explicit focus: "I should point out that you said to me that you always assumed this was going to be a tough story, so it is hard to accept that Amazon was expecting otherwise."[91]

October 19: Jay Carney posts follow-up response reinforcing his claim about fact-checking.[92]

Overall media coverage on the *NYT* story significantly overshadowed the announcement of Amazon's £160m Top Gear deal. Interestingly, *The Guardian* called the *NYT* story a win for traditional media noting that a long and thorough research process such as the one undertaken by the *NYT* authors "was simply not a luxury you get in today's fast-moving world of digital journalism, where the pressure on editors to get quick hits is as relentless as Amazon's thirst for sales."[93]

Voices from the Field

by Akanksha Singh (AS) and Kristian Andaker (KA)

1. **Reflecting on your organizational experience, how have social/new media influenced the way you communicate with internal stakeholders (employees)?**

   AS: Technology has rapidly changed the way we live—how people buy, interact with peers or engage with a company, how someone taps into a wide variety of insight and expertise, and how we can get work done from anywhere at any time. People are empowered like never before, with the instant ability to find and share information, the rise of social networking and mobile devices, and the proliferation of social media tools in the enterprise. According to Prescient Digital, 41 percent of GenY say social media is important to them in the workplace.

   Social media has radically transformed the way organizations communicate with all the key stakeholders, both external and internal (employees). It has created an environment of collaborative communication within the organization. IBM has been using social media platforms for employee engagement since social media was in its early stages of development. We launched one of our internal social media platforms, Media Library, as early as 2003–2004, and introduced our first IBM Blogging Guidelines in 2005.

   KA: It makes a huge difference. Before we had an enterprise social solution, wide employee communications were exclusively email, which is a top-down communications mechanism without a good way for employees to respond and discuss announcements among themselves.

   With Yammer in place, executives often announce things on Yammer directly, or send an email and include a link to a Yammer discussion for the announcement. It is not uncommon that we get hundreds of employee responses to such announcements in Yammer, with questions, encouragement, and ideas.

2. **What was/is the compelling need to integrate new media in the workplace? What are the benefits of doing so?**

   AS: While social media may sound revolutionary or groundbreaking to many, for the Millennial generation, it's probably the most natural way of engagement, as they have grown up in this environment. Increasingly, employees are self-forming teams around fast-moving opportunities. Barriers between people are disappearing, so it's important that organizations learn how to tap into this collective intelligence and distributed talent to drive business results. It is critical for any organization to adapt to this broader social–cultural change and be part of it. Social media creates an environment of openness, transparency, and collaboration within the organization, enabling employees to contribute to the broader organizational imperatives in a more engaging way.

   KA: The biggest benefit is how it connects people from across the organization in a way that promotes much more efficient cross-organization problem solving, than the communications paths that follow the organizational chart.

   Another big benefit is that when offering an internal company outlet for open and free discussions on company topics, employees no longer feel a need to spend time discussing company topics on external blogs or anonymous discussion forums. The amount of internal company topics which were discussed in external forums went down dramatically once Yammer was in place.

3. **How would you describe your enterprise social media strategy, especially as it relates to employee engagement?**

   AS: IBM has been open and inclusive toward social media since the beginning and we are using social media for employee engagement for a very long time. At IBM, we believe engaged employees drive client experience, which in turn drives business results. IBMers are the most important influencers for the organization and social media is an important instrument for enabling IBMers in new and agile ways of working. We leverage social media in designing experiences and building platforms for more personal engagements.

   We believe IBM is a social business, an organization whose culture of participation and systems of engagement encourage networks of people to create business outcomes. Using social tools inside of IBM, employees can connect to undiscovered information and experts, discover new relationships, capture and reuse user-created content, and execute better business decisions.

   KA: The number one aspect of our strategy in this area is that we avoid locking down and overly controlling the enterprise social environment. It's a place where employees can freely create groups and collaborate as they see fit, without a need for executives, managers, or IT to be involved in approving how the collaboration tool is used.

   Second, we ensure that executives and managers stay engaged in Yammer, to show employees both that this is the place where we expect company topics to be discussed widely, and to show employees that they really can reach executives and managers with feedback or ideas through Yammer.

   Third, our internal IT department and HR are always prepared with policies in place to deal with any insensitive or uncomfortable situations which show up in a wide forum like Yammer.

4. **How do you evangelize more employees to build momentum and support for social? Please provide an example of an initiative.**

   AS: Today, most employees use some form of social media in their daily life so they are familiar with the platform. We encourage our employees to extensively use social media both internally and externally to engage with all the relevant stakeholders, clients, influencers, or peers. Some people have a natural aptitude, like in any other field, to use this medium efficiently, whereas others take time to build that skill. We facilitate social media adoption for our employees by creating necessary enablement program and engagement platforms.

   Just five years ago, only 38 percent of IBM employees used IBM Connections (enterprise social networking tool) or an external social networking tool. Today, 98 percent of the company uses both internal and external social tools.

   KA: Through

   - Having Yammer show up in various contexts, such as next to the video broadcasts of large company all-hands meetings (to source questions for the Q&A, and so employees can discuss what is said during the meeting).
   - Having executives and managers engage on Yammer, answering questions and responding to ideas from employees.
   - Moving existing internal processes to happen through Yammer Groups. For example, Yammer Groups is where employees go to get help with many things related to IT at Microsoft.

5. **How do you mitigate possible risks (and inertia) through social media? Please share an example.**

   AS: The biggest risk associated with social media is employees disclosing company's sensitive information, advertently or inadvertently. In 2006, IBM penned its Social Computing Guidelines which provide both permission and direction for engaging on social networks. Hence, IBM has social media guidelines, as part of our business conduct guidelines and our employees must follow them.

   KA: Companies which deploy an enterprise social solution do need to have processes in place to mitigate the associated risks.

   The main risks are oversharing of sensitive information and people making insensitive or legally challenging statements in the company–public network.

   Oversharing is best addressed by educating employees and ensuring everybody understands that the social network is a public forum available to everybody in the company. Insensitive or even legally challenging statements made in the public network must be handled by IT and HR, having good preparedness to step in to delete content and to talk with users who are not behaving as expected.

6. **What, if any, is the role of leadership and corporate culture when we speak of organizational use of social media?**

   AS: The leaders can be role models, being active on social media and enabling others to use this important engagement channel. They can be the biggest internal influencers.

   KA: Without leadership engagement in an enterprise social forum, there will be much less employee engagement. One of the strongest ways to start illustrating to employees that an open enterprise social forum can be beneficial is to make it clear that this is a place where employees can engage with executives.

   Another aspect which is a prerequisite for an enterprise social solution to take-off within a company is that the company promotes and supports an open, collaborative culture. If employees are worried about losing their jobs if they say something stupid in the social forum, there won't be much sharing.

7. **How do you assess 'success' or 'effectiveness' of your efforts?**

   AS: At IBM, using social technologies is a part of the fabric of how we work. Social is integrated into our strategy, we have coaching and training available for employees who want to become more proficient using social, and we know social drives advocacy. For example, 200 IBM executives were coached on how to improve their social prowess over a two-year period. We found that executives who received coaching had four times as many network contacts and created six times as much helpful content as compared to un-coached executives.

   KA: By measuring the number of users who engage either as readers or contributors in the social network.

8. **What do these developments mean for corporate reputation?**

   AS: Social technologies can help leaders build reputation and build relationships inside and outside the company firewall. These authentic relationships result in trust, and trust is the new currency.

   KA: Offering modern collaboration tools and fostering an open, collaborative culture are great recruiting tools, and carry over to a company being perceived as modern and innovative in the industry.

9. **Best practices and advice for other organizations (including specific tools you have found useful) on how to effectively use enterprise social media?**

AS: Look beyond social media to see how social technologies can drive real business value. From marketing and sales to product and service innovation, social is changing the way employees connect, share expertise, and engage with each other and clients.

KA: Tools which can be useful, in addition to Yammer itself, are third-party apps which go beyond Yammer capabilities (e.g., for eDiscovery searches, gamification of Yammer collaboration, or deeper usage analytics).

10. **How do you envision the future of enterprise social media? What are the biggest opportunities and pitfalls going forward?**

AS: We see cognitive collaboration in the near horizon. We want to help our customers become better informed, to understand who should they be engaged with, who are the experts, what conversations they should be involved in, and so on. We're helping our clients figure out how to best use collaboration to improve the individual workplace experience today. There is no one single tool for social collaboration that will meet every scenario and business need, so we are increasingly looking at light-weight apps for collaboration and engagement.

KA: We see a future where the Yammer user experience will become better and better at helping users automatically find the collaboration groups they would benefit from being part of, and having the right context from past conversations in the network at their fingertips when they're reading up on something or writing a post or response. The integration of Yammer with the artificial intelligence on top of what we refer to as the 'Office Graph for Office 365' is going to be a huge area of investment for us over the coming years.

The biggest pitfall for specific companies which deploy enterprise social solutions is that their executives have to be prepared to not only get the benefits of having a direct communications channel with employees but also be ready to accept the sometimes time-consuming aspects of this. With a company–public forum like this, employees will ask uncomfortable questions, and executives will be required to engage on such uncomfortable topics, or the employee perception will be the opposite of the open, collaborative culture which the tool is deployed to help with.

11. **Any other comments and/or pressing questions about this issue?**

AS: Enterprise social platforms help flatten the organization, build agility at workplace with quick real-time interactions, add to productivity improvements, go a long way in improving employee experience. Text analytics of social content can provide insights to the organization on what is uppermost in the minds of the employees and thus enabling management to make interventions as appropriate.

Question that needs study over a period of time is to determine whether the content on enterprise social media platform can be leveraged for some predictive work relating to people subjects. Can it reveal the culture of the organization as it is evolving? Is it good enough to measure employee engagement levels in a stand-alone way?

KA: Enterprise social was the hot new thing in the technology world some 4–5 years ago. But it hasn't stopped growing since. It doesn't get the same news coverage it once did, but it is gradually being deployed at more and more companies.

NOTES

1 The original YouTube video is blocked on grounds of copyright but it can be viewed on several news sites such as this one: http://www.telegraph.co.uk/news/newsvideo/viral-video/10344179/Is-this-the-best-way-ever-to-quit-your-job-Marina-Shifrin-resigns-with-Kanye-West-dance-video.html

2 Shifrin, M. (2015, March 10). Don't quit your day job: Advice from a famous(ish) quitter. Retrieved May 15, 2016, from https://www.linkedin.com/pulse/dont-quit-your-day-job-advice-from-famousish-quitter-marina-shifrin

3 Lopez, J. (2014). Digital business is everyone's business. *Forbes*. Retrieved May 1, 2016, from http://www.forbes.com/sites/gartnergroup/2014/05/07/digital-business-is-everyones-business/#4a42cb622d66

4 Accenture Technology Vision. (2016). Retrieved May 14, 2016, from https://www.accenture.com/t20160314T114936__w__/us-en/_acnmedia/Accenture/Omobono/TechnologyVision/pdf/IT-Tech-Trends-Technology-Vision-Exec-Summary-2016.pdf - zoom=50

5 Ibid.

6 Leonardi, P. M., Huysman, M., & Steinfield, C. (2013). Enterprise social media: Definition, history, and prospects for the study of social technologies in organizations. *Journal of Computer-Mediated Communication, 19*, 1–19. doi:10.1111/jcc4.12029

7 Brown, N. (2015, January 6). The future of internal communications. Social Media Week (Infographic). Retrieved April 2, 2016, from http://socialmediaweek.org/blog/2015/01/future-internal-communications/

8 Ivanisov, Z., & West, J. A. (2012). *Communicating in organizations in the digital age* (Case Study No. UV6408). Darden Business Publishing.

9 Chaudhri, V., & Kaul, A. (2014). *IBM India: 'Localizing' a global model of corporate citizenship* (Case Study No. 9B14C020). Ivey Publishing, Richard Ivey School of Business and Harvard Business Publishing.

10 King, R. (2012, December 3). GE Colab tool brings good 'peeps' to life. *The Wall Street Journal*. Retrieved April 12, 2016, from http://blogs.wsj.com/cio/2012/12/03/ge-colab-tool-brings-good-peeps-to-life/

11 Ibid.

12 Cardon, P. W., & Marshall, B. (2015). The hype and reality of social media use for work collaboration and team communication. *International of Business Communication, 52*, 273–293. doi:10.1177/2329488414525446

13 IBM. (n.d.). Bring your own device. Retrieved June 3, 2016, from http://www.ibm.com/mobilefirst/us/en/bringyour-own-device/byod.html

14 Hamblen, M. (2015, July 15). The bring-your-own-device fad is fading. *Computer world.* Retrieved June 7, 2016, from http://www.computerworld.com/article/2948470/byod/the-bring-your-own-device-fad-is-fading.html

15 Weber Shandwick. (n.d.). Employees rising: Seizing the opportunity in employee activism. A Weber Shandwick study. Retrieved April 14, 2016, from https://www.webershandwick.com/uploads/news/files/employeesrising-seizing-the-opportunity-in-employee-activism.pdf

16 Brown (2015).

17 Weber Shandwick (n.d.).

18 Li, C., Cifuentes, J., & Solis, B. (2014, December 16). Strengthening employee relationships in the digital era: How digital employee engagement and advocacy transform organizations. Altimeter Group. Retrieved May 29, 2016, from http://www.altimetergroup.com/2014/12/strengthening-employee-relationships-in-the-digital-era/

19 Ibid.

20 Baer, J. (n.d.). 7 Ingredients for employee social advocacy. *Convince & Convert*. Retrieved June 5, 2016, from http://www.convinceandconvert.com/social-business/7-ingredients-for-employee-social-advocacy/

21 Li, Cifuentes, and Solis (2014).

22 Azyan, L. (2015, April 28). How to turn employees into social media advocates: Case examples. Retrieved June 5, 2016, from http://www.socialmediaexaminer.com/turn-employees-into-social-media-advocates/

23 Bernoff, J., & Schadler, T. (2010). Empowered. *Harvard Business Review, 88* (July–August), 95–101.

24 King (2012).

25 Guinan, P. J., Parise, S., & Rollag, K. (2014). Jump starting the use of social technologies in your organization. *Business Horizons, 57*, 337–47. doi:10.1016/j.bushor.2013.12.005

26 Mosbergen, D. (2016, May 25). French legislation suggests employees deserve the right to disconnect. *The Huffington Post.* Retrieved May 26, 2016, from http://www.huffingtonpost.com/entry/work-emails-francelabor-law_us_57455130e4b03ede4413515a

27 Proskauer. (2014). Social media in the workplace around the world 3.0. Retrieved May 14, 2016, from http://www.proskauer.com/files/uploads/social-media-in-the-workplace-2014.pdf

28 Greatplacetowork. (n.d.). Retrieved April 27, 2016, from http://www.greatplacetowork.com/storage/documents/Publications_Documents/Herman_Miller_-_Inspiring_Employees_to_Act_as_Brand_Advocates.pdf

29 Rokka, J., Karlsson, K., & Tienari, J. (2014). Balancing acts: Managing employees and reputation in social media. *Journal of Marketing Management, 30*, 802–27. doi:10.1080/0267257X.2013.813577

30 Kessler, S. (2011, March 9). Chrysler's Twitter account accidentally drops the f-bomb (updated). Retrieved June 7, 2016, from http://mashable.com/2011/03/09/chrysler-drops-the-f-bomb-on-twitter/#fIImYAI42iqy

31 Case based on information from the following sources: Waterlow, L. (2015, February 16). 'I lost my job, my reputation and I'm not able to date anymore': Former PR worker reveals how she destroyed her life one year after sending 'racist' tweet before trip to Africa. Retrieved April 5, 2016, from http://www.dailymail.co.uk/femail/article-2955322/Justine-Sacco-reveals-destroyed-liferacist-tweet-trip-Africa.html; Ronson, J. (2015, February 12). How one stupid tweet blew up Justine Sacco's life. *The New York Times Magazine.* Retrieved April 5, 2016, from http://www.nytimes.com/2015/02/15/magazine/how-one-stupid-tweet-ruinedjustine-saccos-life.html?_r=0

32 Biddle, S. (2014, December 20). Justine Sacco is good at her job, and how I came to peace with her. Retrieved April 5, 2016, from http://gawker.com/justine-sacco-is-good-at-her-job-and-how-i-came-to-pea-1653022326

33 Miles, S. J., & Mangold, W. G. (2014). Employee voice: Untapped resource or social media time bomb? *Business Horizons, 57*, 401–11. doi:10.1016/j.bushor.2013.12.011

34 Ibid.

35 Kawasaki, G. (2015). The art of evangelism. *Harvard Business Review* (June). Retrieved May 13, 2016, from https://hbr.org/2015/05/the-art-of-evangelism

36 Roush, W. (2005, April 1). Sun Microsystems: Blog heaven. Retrieved May 3, 2016, from https://www.technologyreview.com/s/403929/sun-microsystems-blog-heaven/

37 *The Economic Times*. (2011). Employee blogs can provide honest perspective on workings of a company: Jonathan Schwartz, ex-CEO, Sun Microsystems. *The Economic Times*. Retrieved May 5, 2016, from http://articles.economictimes.indiatimes.com/2011-12-02/news/30468114_1_bloggers-employee-sun-microsystems

38 Ibid.

39 Rokka et al. (2014).

40 Dreher, S. (2014). Social media and the world of work: A strategic approach to employees' participation in social media. *Corporate Communications: An International Journal*, *19*, 344–356. doi:10.1108/CCIJ-10-2013-0087

41 Rokka et al. (2014).

42 Kantor, J., & Streitfeld, D. (2015, August 15). Inside Amazon: Wrestling big ideas in a bruising workplace. *The New York Times*. Retrieved April 13, 2016, from http://www.nytimes.com/2015/08/16/technology/inside-amazonwrestling-big-ideas-in-a-bruising-workplace.html

43 Ibid.

44 Ciubotariu, N. (2015, August 16). An Amazonian's response to "Inside Amazon: Wrestling Big Ideas in a Bruising Workplace." Retrieved April 13, 2016, from https://www.linkedin.com/pulse/amazonians-responseinside-amazon-wrestling-big-ideas-nick-ciubotariu

45 Zipkin, N. (2015, August 17). Amazon's Jeff Bezos opens line of communication with employees in wake of damning article about company culture. *Entrepreneur*. Retrieved April 13, 2016, from https://www.entrepreneur.com/article/249654

46 Wingfield, N., & Somaiya, R. (2015, October 19). Amazon Spars with the times over investigative article. *The New York Times*. Retrieved April 13, 2016, from http://www.nytimes.com/2015/10/20/business/amazon-spars-withthe-times-over-investigative-article.html?_r=0

47 Macnamara, J., & Zerfass, A. (2012). Social media communication in organizations: The challenges of balancing openness, strategy, and management. *International Journal of Strategic Communication, 6*, 287–308. doi: 10.1080/1553118X.2012.711402

48 Case informed by the following sources (retrieved May 29, 2016): Nye, J. (2013, July 9). The restaurant where they keep the ribs next to the DUMPSTER: Golden Corral employee puts shocking video online. *MailOnline*. Retrieved from http://www.dailymail.co.uk/news/article-2358615/Fast-food-restaurant-Golden-Corral-video-shows-raw-ribs-kept-dumpster.html; Stuart, H. (2013, July 9). Golden corral dumpster food? Video shows trays of meat stored near trash. *The Huffington Post*. Retrieved from http://www.huffingtonpost.com/entry/golden-corral-dumpster_n_3560786.html?section=india; Waxman, O. B. (2013, July 8). Watch: Golden corral's dumpster ribs. *Time*. Retrieved from http://newsfeed.time.com/2013/07/08/watch-golden-corrals-dumpster-ribs/

49 Macnamara and Zerfass (2012).

50 Gossett, L. M., & Kilker, J. (2006). My job sucks: Examining counter institutional websites as locations for organizational member voice, dissent, and resistance. *Management Communication Quarterly, 20*, 63–90.

51 Ibid.
52 Careerarc. (n.d.). 13 Recruiting Stats HR Pros Must Know in 2016. Retrieved June 4, 2016, from http://www.careerarc.com/blog/2016/01/13-recruiting-stats-hr-pro-must-know-2016/
53 Osterhaus, E. (2014, January 8). How job seekers use Glassdoor reviews. *The New Talent Times*. Retrieved June 4, 2016, from http://new-talent-times.softwareadvice.com/how-job-seekers-use-glassdoor-0114/
54 Hannegan, C. (2014, December 4). Five ways to use Glassdoor as an employee engagement tool. Retrieved June 4, 2016, from http://edelman.com/post/five-ways-use-glassdoor-employee-engagement-tool/
55 Kably, L. (2014, March 13). India Inc tightens screws on quitters venting online. *The Times of India*. Retrieved May 28, 2016, from http://timesofindia.indiatimes.com/tech/social/India-Inc-tightens-screws-on-quitters-ventingonline/articleshow/31911505.cms
56 Holtz, S. (n.d.). The debate about blocking social media in the workplace. Retrieved May 8, 2016, from http://hiring.monster.com/hr/hr-best-practices/workforce-management/employee-performance-management/blockingsocial-media-us.aspx
57 Macnamara and Zerfass (2012).
58 Ibid.
59 Vaast, E., & Kaganer, E. (2013). Social media affordances and governance in the workplace: An examination of organizational policies. *Journal of Computer-Mediated Communication, 19*, 78–101. doi:10.1111/jcc4.12032
60 Treem, J. W., & Leonardi, P. M. (2012). Social media use in organizations: Exploring the affordances of visibility, editability, persistence, and association. *Communication Yearbook, 36*, 143–189.
61 Pridmore, J. (2015). Employee social media monitoring: Corporate reputation and new workplace surveillance practices. *VIKALPA: The Journal for Decision Makers, 40*, 472–75. doi:10.1177/0256090915618029
62 Chris, W. (2015, May 12). Social business apps are a $37 billion market in the making. Retrieved May 8, 2016, from http://www.mycustomer.com/experience/voice-of-the-customer/social-business-apps-are-a-37-billionmarket-in-the-making
63 Purcell, K., & Rainie, L. (2014, December 30). Technology's impact on workers. *Pew Research Center*. Retrieved May 8, 2016, from http://www.pewinternet.org/2014/12/30/technologys-impact-on-workers/
64 Pridmore (2015).
65 Ibid.
66 Ibid.
67 Rodionova, Z. (2015, September 30). One-third of employers use social media to recruit. Retrieved May 13, 2016, from http://www.independent.co.uk/news/business/one-third-of-employers-use-social-media-to-recruit-a6673541.html
68 Berkelaar, B. L., & Buzzanell, P. M. (2015). Online employment screening and digital career capital: Exploring employers use of online information for personnel selection. *Management Communication Quarterly, 29*, 84–113. doi:10.1177/0893318914554657
69 Budzienski, J. (2015, April 23). 3 Ways to be constantly recruiting star talent through social media. Retrieved May 13, 2016, from https://www.entrepreneur.com/article/245295
70 Berkelaar, B. L. (2014). Cybervetting, online information, and personnel selection: New transparency expectations and the emergence of a digital social contract. *Management Communication Quarterly, 28*, 479–506. doi:10.1177/0893318914541966
71 CareerBuilder survey (2015). 35 Percent of employers less likely to interview applicants they can't find online, according to annual CareerBuilder social media recruitment survey. Retrieved May 13, 2016, from http://www.careerbuilder.com/share/aboutus/pressreleasesdetail.aspx?sd=5/14/2015&id=pr893&ed=12/31/2015
72 Berkelaar (2014).
73 Berkelaar and Buzzanell (2015).
74 Ibid.
75 Van der Land, S. F., Willemsen, L. M., & Unkel, S. A. J. (2015). Are spectacles the female equivalent of beards for men? How wearing spectacles in a LinkedIn profile picture influences impressions of perceived credibility and job interview likelihood. *HCI in Business: Lecture Notes in Computer Science*, 175–84.; Van der Land, S., & Muntinga, D. G. (2014). To shave or not to shave? How beardedness in a LinkedIn profile picture influences perceived expertise and job interview prospects. *HCI in Business: Lecture Notes in Computer Science, 8527*, 257–65.
76 Accenture Technology Vision (2016).
77 Christensen, K. (2012). Open leadership: A new paradigm emerges. Interview with Charlene Li. *Rotman Winter Magazine*, 22–26. HBR case ROT156-PDF-ENG.
78 Ibid.

79 Deiser, R., & Newton, S. (2013, February). Six social-media skills every leader needs. *McKinsey Quarterly.* Retrieved May 15, 2016, from http://www.mckinsey.com/industries/high-tech/our-insights/six-social-mediaskills-every-leader-needs

80 Weber Shandwick. (n.d.). Socializing your CEO III: From marginal to mainstream. Retrieved May 15, 2016, from http://www.webershandwick.com/uploads/news/files/socializing-your-ceo-iii-exec-summary.pdf

81 Nusca, A. (2016, January 25). Social media use by CEOs is increasing—Slowly. *Fortune*. Retrieved May 15, 2016, from http://fortune.com/2016/01/25/social-media-ceo/

82 Ross, L. G. (2015, May 18). What CEOs have learned about social media. *Harvard Business Review*. Retrieved May 15, 2016, from https://hbr.org/2015/05/what-ceos-have-learned-about-social-media

83 Huy, Q., & Shipilov, A. (2012). The key to social media success within organizations. *MIT Sloan Management Review*, *54*(1), 73–81.

84 Ibid.

85 Leonardi et al. (2013).

86 Retrieved June 2, 2017, from https://www.amazon.jobs/principles

87 Ciubotariu (2015).

88 Zipkin (2015).

89 Carney, J. (2015, October 19). What the New York Times didn't tell you. Retrieved April 13, 2016, from https://medium.com/@jaycarney/what-the-new-york-times-didn-t-tell-you-a1128aa78931#.ycpx5n4dp

90 Chariton, J. (2015, August 19). New York Times' takedown of Amazon breaks site's comments record. *The Wrap*. Retrieved April 13, 2016, from http://www.thewrap.com/new-york-times-takedown-of-amazon-breaks-comments-record/

91 Medium (2015). Dean Baquet responds to Jay Carney's Medium post. Retrieved April 13, 2016, from https://medium.com/@NYTimesComm/dean-baquet-responds-to-jay-carney-s-medium-post-6af794c7a7c6#.psn3mqjuu

92 Medium (2015, October 20). Jay Carney's response to Dean Baquet. Retrieved May 24, 2017, from https://medium.com/@jaycarney/jay-carney-s-response-to-dean-baquet-c0407042e893#.86h6vmssn

93 Benigson, D. (2015, August 19). Brand damage for Amazon and a triumph for old media. *The Guardian*. Retrieved April 13, 2015, from http://www.theguardian.com/media-network/2015/aug/19/brand-amazon-media-jeff-bezos-times

CHAPTER 4

Influence of Social Media on Crisis Communication

CHAPTER OBJECTIVES

- Understand the role of social media in crisis management.
- Reflect on social media influences on crisis communication.
- Appreciate the reputational implications of crises in the digital age.
- Review crisis response strategies and recommendations from research and practice.
- Enable the application of acquired knowledge to case studies of organizational crisis.

Keywords

Anti-brand
Apology
Crisis communication
Crisis management
Crisis planning
Crisis response
Crisis type
Customers
Digital age
Hoax
Paracrisis
Pranks
Opportunity
Reputation
Reputation management
Reputation capital
Risk
Rumor
Social media
Stakeholder
Threat
Troll
Vigilantism

INTRODUCTION

> There is no crisis management today without a full understanding of how to use new media to listen to conversations around your brand in real-time, and understand what you do and don't need to respond to.
>
> *Chris Syme*[1]

How might we understand the role of new and social media in crisis communication and crisis management, more generally? Are social media decisively changing the way crises originate, spread, and are managed? Have new media revolutionized crisis management? What do these developments mean for corporate reputation? Are practitioners prepared for these changes? What constitutes successful/unsuccessful or effective/ineffective crisis management in a new media environment?

If there is one conclusion we would like to offer even before we begin, it is that perspectives on the questions above will vary, as they should. However, without sounding alarmist or proclaiming a 'do or die' situation, we also argue that not acknowledging the influence of social media in crisis communication and online reputation management is naive and amounts to sticking one's head in the sand!

Although crisis communication is a prolific area of research and practice, there is no single definition of a crisis. Likewise, there is no 'one-size-fits-all' approach in managing crises, whether traditional or socially mediated. In reviewing the select definitions (see Box 4.1), it is possible to identify some salient characteristics.

Box 4.1: Select Definitions of Crisis

- An incident that is *unexpected, negative,* and *overwhelming* (Barton, 2001).
- A specific, unexpected, and *non-routine* organizationally based event or series of events which creates *high levels of uncertainty* and *threat* or *perceived threat* to an organization's high-priority goals (Seeger, Sellnow, & Ulmer, 1998).
- Revised: A specific, unexpected, and non-routine organizationally based event or series of events which creates high levels of uncertainty and *simultaneously present an organization with both opportunities* for and *threats* to its high-priority goals (Ulmer, Sellnow, & Seeger, 2015).
- The *perception* of an *unpredictable* event that *threatens* important *expectancies of stakeholders* and can seriously *impact an organization's performance* and generate negative outcomes (Coombs, 2007).

Source: Based on existing research.[2]

Based on these definitions, we can deduce the following: First, crises are unpredictable. Perhaps you are familiar with the axiom that crises are a permanent part of any organization's life cycle. Ironical as it may sound, organizations of all kinds, big and small, are susceptible to crises. Despite the inevitability of crises, it may be difficult for organizations to fully anticipate the exact time, manner, and form of a crisis. 'Intentional' and/or 'preventable' crises caused by unethical business practice may be an exception as they signal a brewing problem waiting to erupt into a crisis. Second, crises are non-routine and "unique moments in the history of organizations,"[3] implying that not every incident (negative) experience, or operational risk is/will constitute a crisis. Third, crises produce uncertainty and warrant a (quick) response. What are the possible communication strategies and tactics that organizations may employ in order to mitigate damage has been a subject of investigation across crisis situations—individual, organizational, political, etcetera?

A salient component that is at the heart of what makes crisis management a compelling phenomenon is the associated, usually negative, consequence, especially the threat to organizational reputation and image. Depending on the type and severity of crisis, the consequences could range from business disruption to financial damage, loss of life, property, environmental/ecological damage, etcetera. The threat to an organization's reputation has a dire effect, though, and could even jeopardize the legitimacy and survival of an organization.

Finally, an emerging perspective that we address later in the chapter views crises not as intrinsically negative events but as opportunities for organizational learning and positive change.

WHAT HAVE ORGANIZATIONS TO LOSE?

> Companies need to understand that their decisions are creating a record today that will serve as the basis for their story tomorrow.
>
> *Daniel Diermeier*[A]

LEARNING OBJECTIVES

- Analyze the relationship between crisis management and reputation.
- Reflect on the different phases and types of crises.
- Understand the need for ongoing reputation management.

A crisis is a trying time for any organization. With high uncertainty comes the need for clarity, information, and answers (recall the yet unexplained disappearance of Malaysia Airlines flight MH370 in March 2014); failure to respond is tantamount to ceding 'control' of the story; relationships may become fractured as stakeholders evaluate the seriousness of the crisis and attribute responsibility; reputations are at stake. How an organization plans for and responds to a crisis determines, to a large extent, the outcome of the crisis and the associated reputational impact.

Given the propensity for reputation loss, the adage 'prevention is better than cure' rings true and loud. The 'always-on' digital age has remarkably elevated the need to prepare and effectively respond to challenges in the hope of mitigating the negative impact. Proactively tracking issues online to identify warning signs and brewing troubles can assist in reducing reputation threat. Often, being prepared as is, if not more important, then what an organization does during a crisis (see Figure 4.1).

From an organization's standpoint, crisis management efforts aim to minimize reputation damage. Reputations are the most valuable, intangible asset for any organization; yet, they come with tangible benefits ranging from competitive differentiation, talent recruitment and retention, partnership with opinion leaders and policy-makers, and better crisis management. In the 'reputation economy,' a term coined by the Reputation Institute, stakeholders "make decisions about companies based more on who they

FIGURE 4.1 *Phases of Crisis Management*

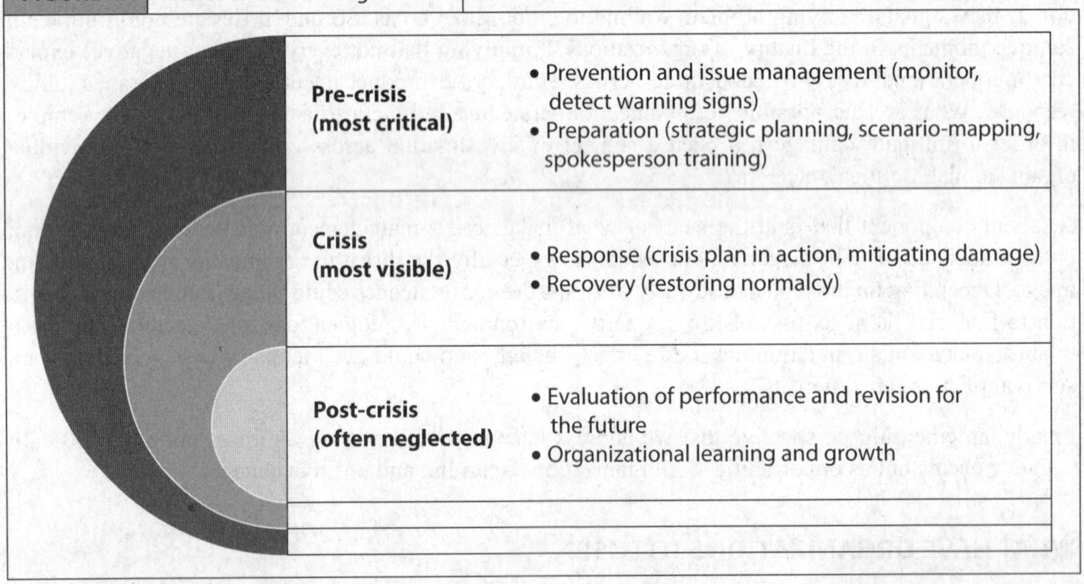

Source: Coombs (2011).[5]

are and what they stand for rather than focusing on what they sell."[6] Succeeding in a competitive situation, then, requires a collective reputation mind-set characterized by integration between reputation management and business planning and cross-functional collaboration. Likewise, reputation management needs to be an ongoing process, not something to be undertaken only in a moment of crisis.

The risk to reputation is the most critical business priority today. Reputation@Risk 2014,[7] Deloitte's global survey of business executives, found that managing reputation risk is an explicit focus area in many organizations. Incidents of ethical misconduct (e.g., fraud), security (e.g., cyber), and product/service (e.g., product safety) were perceived to be the most significant reputation threats. Those that experienced a negative reputation event in the past attested to the multidimensional consequences including financial impact (41%), loss in brand value (41%), and regulatory investigation (37%).

Prominent theories in crisis communication also underline the centrality of reputation in an organizational crisis. The Situational Crisis Communication Theory (SCCT) developed by Coombs (2007)[8] posits that crisis type (e.g., preventable, accidental, and victim), crisis history (if any), and prior relational reputation (past relationship with stakeholders) serve as guidelines to anticipate stakeholder reaction in a crisis situation. In other words, stakeholders will attribute higher responsibility to the organization if the crisis was preventable and the organization has a prior crisis history and an unfavorable prior reputation. Stronger attributions of crisis responsibility (e.g., relative to a victim cluster) will translate to higher reputational threat, negative emotions (e.g., anger), and behavior (e.g., negative word-of-mouth [WoM]). Communication in a crisis constitutes a big part of how stakeholder perceptions are formed, and understanding the crisis situation holistically is imperative to responding well (Box 4.2).

Box 4.2: Crisis Clusters and Subtypes Proposed in the SCCT

Preventable Crises: Strong Crisis Responsibility

- *Human-error accidents:* industrial accidents caused by human error
- *Human-error product harm:* product defect or harm caused by human error
- *Organizational misdeed:* management actions that are illegal and endanger stakeholders

Accident Crises: Low Crisis Responsibility

- *Challenges:* stakeholders may accuse the organization of behaving inappropriately or unethically
- *Technical error accidents:* equipment or technology failures
- *Technical error product harm:* equipment or technology failure that cause a product to be defective or potentially harmful

Victim Crises: Minimal Crisis Responsibility

- *Natural disasters:* natural acts such as earthquakes
- *Rumors:* false and damaging information about the organization
- *Workplace violence:* attack by former or current employee on current employees on-site
- *Product tampering/malevolence:* organizational damage caused by external agents

Source: Coombs (2007).[9]

While all crises have implications for reputation, some argue that a reputational crisis ought to be examined as a specific category of crisis in terms of magnitude of impact, causality, and responsibility of the organization in question. A reputation crisis is defined as "a major event that has the potential to threaten collective perceptions and estimations held by all relevant stakeholders of an organization and its relevant attributes."[10] Reputational crises may be based on either or both organizational dimensions: Corporate ability (CA; damage to reputation associated with quality product or service, technological innovation, and industry leadership) and corporate social responsibility (CSR; threat to reputation associated with stakeholder expectations of societal obligations). A CSR crisis is deemed more damaging for reputation than a CA crisis. According to this understanding, not all crises (e.g., natural disasters) are reputational crises, nor are reputational crises limited to social media.

However, building a reservoir of reputation capital can, to some extent, shield an organization (think of a *halo effect*) in a crisis when the stakes are high and time is of the essence. A case in point is the Nano crisis experienced by Tata Motors Ltd., a global conglomerate and India's third-largest automobile manufacturer. The Tata Group and its Chairman Emeritus, Ratan N. Tata, have been synonymous with integrity, trust, and corporate responsibility. One of the world's most powerful people according to *Forbes*, Ratan Tata had a dream of manufacturing the world's cheapest car at ₹100,000 (US$2,165) for 'the common man.' His dream turned into reality when Nano was launched in March 2009 in India. Unfortunately, immediately after its launch there were reported incidents of the car catching on fire. The media alleged poor design and assessed that the life of the common man behind the wheel was in danger. The company immediately called back the cars and promised a thorough investigation and addition of several safety devices. At this point, when stakes were high as customers were ranting and media was framing, Ratan Tata came on YouTube and addressed the customers, brushed aside all allegations, and reiterated his promise of Nano being safe for the customers. The public was forgiving and forgetting for the past reputation of the company and the legendary status of Ratan Tata lent credence to his statements. Although the sales plummeted, analysts were of the view that the drop cannot be attributed to the incident of fire but to changing market preferences.[11]

A CRISIS IS A CRISIS IS A CRISIS? (RE)THINKING CRISES IN THE NEW MEDIA ENVIRONMENT

> You need to be prepared for today's media culture, in which a tweet can become newsworthy and a news interview can become tweet-worthy.
>
> *Brad Phillips*[12]

LEARNING OBJECTIVES

- Understand the power and role of stakeholders in new media crises.
- Distinguish between different types of social media crises.
- Appreciate the importance of stakeholder feedback and suggestions for responding to grievances.

With this overview, the question becomes whether we should think differently about crisis management and communication in the digital age. *Are traditional crises different from social media crises?*

Think back to a time before Web 2.0. You reach out for a can of soup after a long workday only to find a layer of mold covering what would be delicious chicken noodle. You bought the sealed soup can a week ago, and it is well within the recommended expiration date. This was supposed to be your dinner and it is too late to order home delivery! What do you do? You might throw out the can and promise yourself to never purchase the specific brand of soup. You may share your experience with a few acquaintances the following day. You could, of course, decide to bring the can to the grocery store and get your money back. Assuming this has happened before, or if you feel so inclined, you may decide to complain by calling customer service. You could send a written compliant via post and wait for a response. In the age of Web 1.0, you could email the organization or submit feedback via the corporate website, should that option be available.

All of these options pale in comparison to the sound of a few deft moves on your smart device. Click a picture and post along with a comment to Twitter (#dinnerlastnight #moldysoup) or Facebook. Tag the organization, and chances are that you will be noticed. *Recall a time when you or someone you know expressed dissatisfaction with an organization on social media? How did the organization respond? What did that experience mean for your relationship with the organization in question?*

Now, we are not suggesting that every bad experience will escalate into a crisis. After all, there is always an element of risk in any business operation. One might even argue that a can of soup is too trivial an example. But what if other customers have had the same experience and start to weigh in, sharing your post, retweeting, and commenting?

Consider this incident: A group of young professionals went out for a Sunday brunch at Lemp Brewpub in Gurgaon, India. Unfortunately, the staff did not serve what was mentioned in the menu and reportedly even misbehaved with them. The menu was different, there was no open bar, and there was no supply of unlimited cocktails as promised in the brunch package. Repeated summons to the manager failed in getting any response. The group finally decided to walk out of the restaurant. At this juncture, the manager decided to step in and claimed the full bill, even for items that were not served. Altercations between the manager and the group were interrupted by bouncers and the police called by the customers. Even the payable fluctuated as the conflict progressed. Finally, authority and seniority won the day as the case moved to the police station and the customers were forced to pay. These young professionals posted a negative restaurant review as a blog post that went viral. Also referred to as the "Horrid Brunch Episode,"[13] the blog excited comments and extreme reactions from the online community that was both anti- and pro-Lemp.

The important point here is that new media give stakeholder groups (e.g., consumers, employees, and NGOs) the ability to make themselves heard. Much theorizing of online communication sees the Internet and now digital as an equalizer, a platform that allows stakeholder groups (including previously marginalized activist groups) to collectively organize and take coordinated action against an organization. Also, new media enable an 'echo chamber' effect that could amplify stakeholder concerns and turn a grievance into a crisis. What this implies is that crisis management and communication in the digital age are more visible and public.

The digital communication environment is also more vulnerable to "paracrises"[14] or incidents resembling a crisis that, if ignored, could potentially erupt into full-blown crises with serious reputational damage.[15] Paracrisis is defined as "a publicly visible crisis threat that charges an organization with irresponsible or unethical behavior."[16] The organization's response to a paracrisis is delivered in public view and subject to stakeholder evaluation. Viewing paracrisis as warning signals that warrant attention is recommended to avoid escalation, especially if the stakeholder group is powerful and the challenge(s) represents a legitimate concern, could alienate other stakeholders, and affect business operations. However, decisions to respond to the challenge also need to account for the cost of the change (as well as the reputational cost) and fit with the organizational strategy.[17]

FIGURE 4.2 *Types of Social Media Crises*

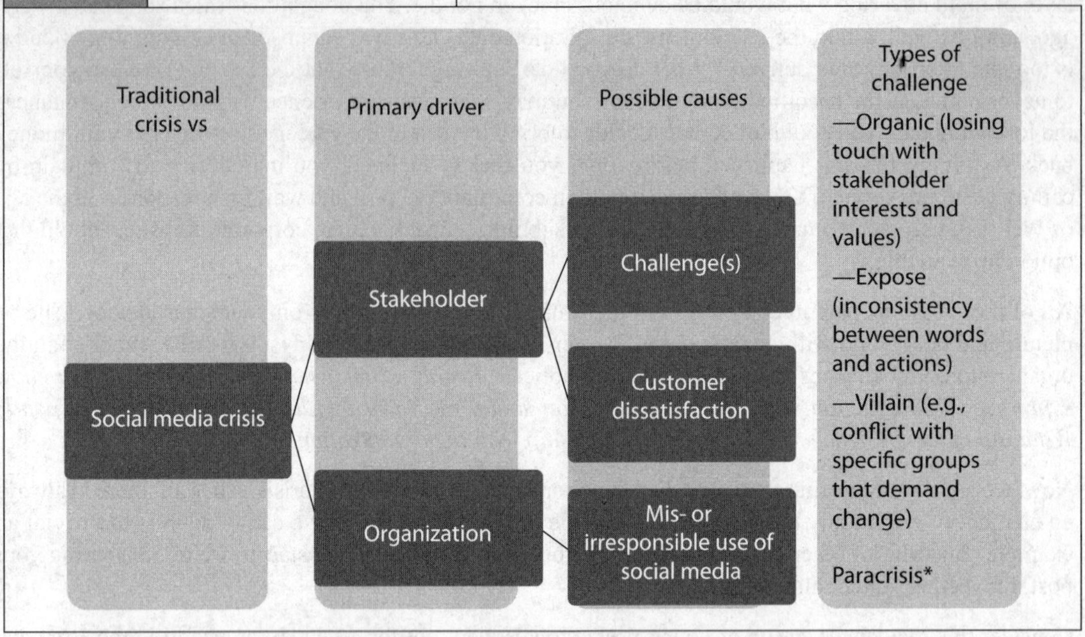

Source: Coombs (2015).[18]

Some scholars differentiate between traditional and social media crises noting that the reputational concerns are more pronounced in the latter, whereas the former typically concern issues of public safety and welfare. Using the origin/source of crisis as a point of departure Coombs (2015)[19] further categorizes social media crises into stakeholder-driven or organization-led crises (Figure 4.2).

After the all-important first step, determining the primary driver/source of the crisis, the question many would ask is what can I/we do? How can we assess the risks and what are the options available? One model[20] (Figure 4.3) offers a typology of social media crises based on two key dimensions: *controllability* (a social media crisis is controllable if responses to limit or eliminate the crisis by influencing its causes are known as well as executable) and *shock value of trigger* (the degree to which an incident that is embedded in the context and time offends members of the social media community). According to this matrix, organizations can categorize crises into one of four types and respond appropriately. One might question, however, whether organizations really have 'control' in a crisis situation.

GAINING TRACTION WITH DIGITAL

In our quest to unpack the confounding nature of new media crises and online reputation management, let us look at a few classic as well as contemporary cases of organizational crisis. Reflect on what these cases illustrate about new media influences on crisis management and communication (Box 4.3).

The Domino's case highlights, among others, the vulnerabilities of social media and illustrates how a prank, perpetrated via YouTube, posed a potential threat, driving even loyal Domino's customers to second-guess their relationship with the organization.[21] Tim McIntyre, VP Communication at Domino's,

FIGURE 4.3 *Typology of Social Media Crises*

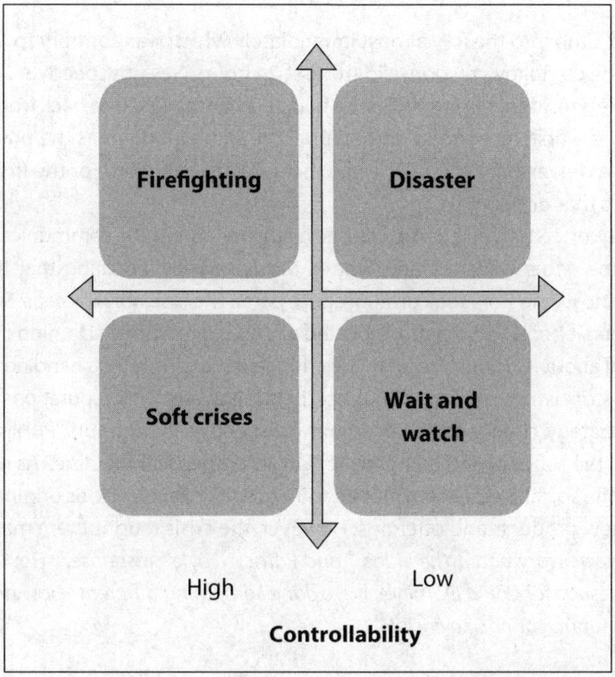

Source: Malshe (n.d.).[22]

Box 4.3: Domino's Pizza Gets a Taste of Social Media

On Easter Sunday in 2009, two Domino's Pizza employees in Conover, NC created and posted a prank video on YouTube that violated health standards. The clips showed one of the employees engaging in unsanitary acts (e.g., sticking cheese up his nose) on sandwiches soon to be delivered. Although the duo later claimed that the video was a prank and none of the food was meant to be delivered, the damage was done.

Tim McIntyre, vice president, communications, and the entire Domino's corporate team went into a shock when they heard of the antics of the employees through the consumer affairs blog, *The Consumerist*. Domino's got wind of the incident within 45 minutes of it being posted on YouTube. Soon the video went viral and social media were abuzz with the latest on Domino's. By the end of Tuesday, the hits and views had touched 250,000. Then began the chatter on Twitter. The initial chatter was, "Oh, my gosh. Look at this horrible thing."[24] Fortunately, the tweets tried to figure out if Domino's was familiar with what was happening and why was no action being taken. Domino's responded on Twitter, "Yeah, we know. Domino's has found them. It's a hoax." Domino's already had a crisis communication strategy in place which was to be implemented a week later. However, the current crisis

(Box 4.3: Continued)

(Box 4.3: Continued)

forced them to jump into the fray almost immediately which was contrary to their plan. Yet, there was criticism that the company's response in the first 24 hours was not speedy.

Patrick Doyle, President of Domino's who had been on leave, came back from Florida on Wednesday and, in what was a first, responded on YouTube, the same medium as the prank video. By midday on Wednesday, the viewership on YouTube had increased to a million. For the first time, Domino's search word surpassed that of Paris Hilton.

The intensity of communication increased with the corporate communication team reaching out through YouTube, other websites, and Twitter. McIntyre kept repeating that the prank had not been played by Domino's. "The story took on almost five parts. The first story line was: Somebody's tainting food at Domino's. Then it became: Somebody posted a hoax video starring Domino's. Then it became: What is Domino's doing about it? Then it became the critique of how Domino's handled these rogue employees. And today, the story is: How do brands protect themselves and their reputations in the YouTube era?"

Domino's strategy changed the consumer perspective in 48 hours. Public perspectives changed from shunning the product and company to "Oh, it happens all the time." As responses began to cool and fizzle out, the social media team moved to Twitter and Facebook, as originally planned, and began to talk about new products and offerings. However, the crisis taught them many lessons.

Watch the news story about the video[25] *and Patrick Doyle's response.*[26] *How would you evaluate the organization's response? Could Domino's have done something different? How do new media change the dynamics of communicating in a crisis?*

Source: Compiled from available information.[23]

reflected on what makes social media crises, especially hoaxes and rumors, so compelling in the digital age: "The opportunities and freedom of the internet is wonderful [sic]. But it also comes with the risk of anyone with a camera and an internet link to cause a lot of damage."[27] Noting the possibility of an issue escalating quickly and amplifying in social media, McIntyre and his team learned that although "you may not need the fire hose to put out the candle … in the social media realm, you might want to have the garden hose handy."[28]

Herein comes the issue of perception, also addressed in some of the definitions earlier in the chapter. The perceptual nature of crises implies that crises are socially constructed and stakeholder perception is central to what constitutes a crisis. In other words, if stakeholders perceive a specific event to be a crisis, then it is a crisis. Arguably, the hoax threatened Domino's legitimacy and created a paradoxical communication challenge forcing the organization to offer "a *substantial* response to an *unsubstantiated* claim" (emphasis in original).[29] The case confirms the power of perception such that even false and misleading claims that gain traction via social media, require an appropriate response. In the end, it is instructive to remember, "if the threat made in the hoax is plausible, the organization's ability to address the threat may be called into question."[30]

Pranks and parodies on social media pose a particularly novel challenge. In some cases, scholars question if it is indeed desirable to respond to an online parody as it may worsen the situation for the affected organization. No two cases are alike and assessing the potential impact on organizational goals can assist the decision about whether (and how) to respond and/or to "take the mocking in stride."[31]

There are several examples and cases (see Appendix A) which highlight, among others, the need for organizations to be aware of the possibilities that emerge from the inability to control information, the pressing need to actively listen to conversations about the brand/organization, and to be cognizant of what stakeholders believe and think about them. Doing so is critical to the (successful) outcome of social media efforts.

Know Thy Stakeholder

A specific stakeholder group that has garnered the most attention in research and practice is the consumer in all its facets—perpetrator, victim, target audience. Customer dissatisfaction has been a focal point of numerous social media examples, prompting the observation that "social media is customer service and a customer complaint line all in one, and we all get to watch."[32] And watch we did when Dave Carroll wrote his now famous lyrics "I should have flown with someone else or gone by car … cause United breaks Guitars"[33] hoping to receive a million views. Since 2009, his original version (the first in a trilogy) has close to 15 million views and, acknowledging United's role in propelling his career, Carroll has since leveraged YouTube to document his experience with the airline. The crisis cost United Airlines above US$180 million, and their share price plunged by 10 percent.[34]

The classic example of United Airlines clearly shows that what could be once controlled by the organization is no longer the case. The strategies of denying, obfuscating, or stalling have changed in the age of social media. For instance, the statement, "there is no such thing as bad PR"[35] was negated in this case. As Jeff Bezos, Founder of Amazon, aptly stated, "if you make customers unhappy in the physical world, they might each tell 6 friends. If you make customers unhappy on the Internet, they can each tell 6000 friends."[36]

Another recent example of an unhappy customer at Flipkart has created ripples in the market. The customer purchased a pair of Keen shoes at a discounted price. However, when he opened the box, the shoes were soiled with "shit and pebbles."[37] He posted the picture on Facebook and before Flipkart could realize, the post went viral with the online community sharing similar experiences and advising that the customer go to the court of law. The example demonstrates that while social media can make an organization more visible, there can also be negative reverberations.

Addressing a customer complaint before it juggernauts into a social crisis is recommended. But the truth is that new media make complaining much easier and much more visible. Not all complaints are created equal, though, and distinguishing among them is important (see Table 4.1).

Digital also open up the space to express (anti-)brand sentiment. When McDonald's initiated its campaigns (#McDStories and #Meetthefarmers) to collaborate and engage with customers, gather positive stories, and raise awareness about the supplier stores, the effort boomeranged. The hashtags soon turned into bashtags with consumers ranting about unsavory and unwanted items, as finger nails, food poisoning, and more,[38] reiterating the need for the fast food giant to do its groundwork to understand customer sentiment.

Further, a semiotic analysis (the study of how meaning is created in texts, signs, and symbols) of consumer-generated anti-brand advertisements for the world's most valuable brands illuminates the multipronged nature of online threats that represent deep-seated (and often legitimate) stakeholder concerns. Anti-branding efforts are most frequently communicated by altering the corporate logo (see illustrative examples below), subverting the corporate message (e.g., from McDonald's I'm lovin it to *I'm hatin it, I'm destroyin it*), brand name (from Google to *Greedle* positioning Google as a greedy company), and using hate language (*IBM sucks* or *Stop McKiller*).[39]

In addition to customers, social media also provide a platform to NGOs and advocacy groups to influence changes in business practices. As a case in point, Greenpeace International has leveraged new media in its campaigns against major corporations (e.g., Shell over Arctic drilling; Nestle over the use of palm oil

TABLE 4.1 *Classifying Customer Complaints on Social Media*

When	What	Assessment of Risk and Key Recommendations
Following initial service failure	Direct complaint (to request resolution of problem)	"Good": source of opportunity Acknowledge, prompt response, post outcome online
	Boasting (positive WoM after successful resolution)	Good Acknowledge customer appreciation but not overpublicize (e.g., by retweeting)
	Badmouthing (negative WoM through social networks, without contacting the firm)	"Bad": represents risk for the organization Identify and acknowledge complaint, propose private dialogue, post outcomes online
After repeated service failure/ failure to resolve	Tattling (complaining to third-party)	Bad Explore possibility for negotiation and reparation, seek third-party support/ counsel
	Spite (spreading negative WoM to get revenge)	"Ugly": poses serious crisis threat Acknowledge the situation, announce corrective action, initiate crisis communication
	Feeding the vultures (competitors' opportunistic response to benefit from or amplify the situation)	Ugly Attempt to diffuse by using wit and humor, be gracious

Source: Gregoire, Salle, and Tripp (2015).[40]

from unsustainable sources; major fashion retailers over the use of chemicals in apparel). We elaborate on these cases and their implications for CSR and reputation in a later chapter.

Organizations can choose to ignore (can they?), wait and watch, fight back (e.g., Nestle cited copyright infringement of the KitKat logo), and/or use these forums as expressions of stakeholder feedback. As customers publicly voice their experiences online, corporations need to "talk about and renegotiate their semiotic meaning systems"[41] lest they risk losing control of their brand image and positioning.

Dealing with negativity on social media and using it as an opportunity is still challenging for many organizations that would rather censor or ignore negative criticism.[42]

However, some situations are like zero-sum games, for example, trolling or the act of posting "inflammatory or inappropriate messages or comments … for the purpose of upsetting other users and provoking a response."[43] *How best to respond in these difficult situations becomes the critical question, and one that is very much dependent on context.*

On August 24, 2012, after 200 years of military defeat of America and burning of the White House, the British Embassy trolls the United States. The Americans were reminded of the event when a tweet accompanying a photograph of a cake with a perfect miniature reproduction of the White House flanked by the American and British flags carried the caption: "Commemorating the 200th anniversary of burning the White House. Only sparklers this time!"[44] The British Embassy in Washington, DC was forced to apologize when many American Twitter users described the tweet as lacking tact and diplomacy and being in "extremely poor taste." Soon the British Embassy retweeted, "Apologies for earlier Tweet. We meant to mark an event in history & celebrate our strong friendship today."

These cases help to highlight the myriad ways in which social, best described as a double-edged sword, complicate the nature of risks. This also means that all kinds of information and news, good or bad, accurate or misleading, have an equal chance of finding an audience. In the aftermath of the 2013 Boston Marathon bombing, the Boston division of the Federal Bureau of Investigation (FBI) posted carefully selected photos of the two suspects and solicited the help of the public in the search process. On the one hand, this form of crowd-sourced investigation helped speed up the identification and capture of the suspects; on the other, it revealed the dark side when some Reddit users misidentified a missing Indian American college student as being one of the two suspects in the picture and posted his name and picture. His name ended up trending nationally on Twitter, creating a spiral of speculation that some likened to "vigilantism."[45] Although Reddit had a policy against posting personal information, the website acknowledged that it had not pre-empted such an aftermath and issued an apology on its blog:

> Though started with noble intentions, some of the activity on reddit fueled online witch hunts and dangerous speculation which spiraled into very negative consequences for innocent parties. The reddit staff and the millions of people on reddit around the world deeply regret that this happened. We have apologized privately to the family of missing college student […].[46]

Interesting to note is how citizen journalists (Reddit users) assumed the role conventionally associated with traditional media, sans the censorship or filtering, and engaged in the instantaneous and widespread dissemination of (incorrect) information.

Reflecting on the preceding discussion, if we have to summarize the pivotal change in crisis management, it would have to be visibility. The examples amply demonstrate the blurring (perhaps non-existent) boundaries between private and public spheres; what was previously invisible is now visible, thanks to social media. This does not mean that traditional media are redundant, and many organizations recognize the need to adopt an integrated approach combing mainstream and social media. As a predictor of social media visibility, mainstream media are a powerful medium for sharing news and messages that provide pointers for social media conversation and vice versa.

A visual summary (Table 4.2) captures the main developments that have implications for crisis communication and online reputation management.

TABLE 4.2 *Summary of Changes in the Media Environment*

Traditional Media	New Media
• Journalistic gatekeepers	• Citizen journalism
• 'Objectivity' and attempt to 'tell all sides of the story'; censorship	• Personal and/or emotional influence; uncensored
• One-way communication	• Participatory and interactive
• Perishability	• Permanence
• Space/follow-up constraints	• Unlimited space/possibility for updates
• Boundaries, circulation/reach	• Boundaryless, instant, widespread

Source: Mei, Bansal, and Pang (2010).[47]

ADAPT OR REINVENT? MANAGING DIGITAL CRISES

We don't have a choice on whether we do social media, the question is how well we do it.

Erik Qualman[48]

LEARNING OBJECTIVES

- Introduce practitioner perspectives toward new media.
- Understand how practitioners are (not) using social for crisis management.
- Assess relevance of accumulated knowledge/crisis communication theories.

The risk of crisis is always palpable. So what do these developments mean for the way organizations practice crisis management now or in the future? Are social media being used in crisis management today, and for what purpose? If not, what are the challenges? What do we know about organizations' use of social media in a crisis?

There are no easy answers. Studies advance a diverse array of perspectives that preclude any definitive conclusions; rather, they underpin the need for dialogue, research, and a grounded understanding of new media influences and usage.

Grappling with the information explosion in its numerous forms remains a decisive challenge for communication professionals and business leaders. For public relations executives, dealing with the speed and volume of info flow (23%), managing the rise of social media (15.3%), measuring communication effectiveness (12.2%), and preparing for crises (11.9%) are the most important issues facing the profession.[49]

The outlook toward social media is heavily dependent on how professionals assess the 'value' of social media in terms of both risks and benefits. Perceived risks include reputational threat, false/misinformation, cybercrime/information security, lack of control, employee concerns (e.g., threat from disgruntled employees, leak of sensitive information), slow response time, lack of dedicated personnel, preponderance of negative commentary on new media, and ambiguity about who influences opinion online.[50] Survey results from Continuity Insights (2014)[51] confirm that opinions about the use of social media in a crisis are divided, although efforts are being made to integrate digital into crisis planning. More organizations now use social media to gather information during a crisis (62% in 2014; 52% in 2012), and Twitter trumps Facebook as the preferred medium in a crisis (82 to 78% respectively).

With the exponential growth in online, mobile, and social media communication, professionals are cognizant or at least have ideas of what stakeholders expect from such communication. The 2014 European Communication Monitor results show that information about crises (70.1%), new products and services (66.2%), and CSR (64.2%), are perceived to be the (social media) content categories that most concern stakeholders. Further, professionals believe that interaction with stakeholders (e.g., consumers; 86.6%) and enabling two-way communication (e.g., ability to comment; 72.5%) are expected company behaviors.[52]

Yet, organizations have a long way to go in translating these expectations. Most Fortune 500 companies have an official Facebook page, but only a few use this network to communicate during a crisis. A study[53] found limited organizational effort to engage stakeholders and partake in Facebook conversations, and the selection of inappropriate response strategies resulted in a bevy of mostly negative or neutral audience responses to official crisis communication from the organization. Where the organization had responded to user messages, stakeholders responded positively to official crisis messages. Even when organizations engage in dialogic communication in a social media crisis, they seek to uphold and create consensus around organizational interests (e.g., take control of the crisis discourse, clarifying/sharing the organization's position on the issue, or attempting to divert attention away from the crisis). Fewer organizations encourage participant-centered dialogue, aimed at finding collective solutions to resolve the situation.[54]

One thing we can say with surety is that effectively harnessing digital (in good times and bad) requires a holistic understanding, a mind-set change that goes beyond the technological features to an integrated communication approach that situates organizations and stakeholders in an interdependent relationship.

Do these developments necessitate a complete overhaul, new capabilities, new knowledge, and new strategies? Partly, yes. For instance, crisis professionals profess that it is no longer sufficient to appropriately *act* and *react* in a crisis; organizations also need to *interact* with stakeholders and media in an ongoing effort to improve reputation and perception.[55] However, we may not need to reinvent the wheel. Coombs (2015) purports that it is a myth to assume that our accumulated knowledge of crisis communication is now redundant, and that speed and tactics supersede the need for strategic planning. He argues that the basics of crisis communication continue to be relevant and therefore it is more realistic to treat these developments not as a revolution but as an evolution in the field of crisis communication. He explains that:

> Crisis managers still face the same needs to identify warning signs, confront the same basic communication demands utilize the same concepts, and must enact effective strategic responses.... What has changed is how the information is collected and, in some cases, how that information is processed.[56]

Indeed, crisis communication has a rich theoretical tradition that continues to be adapted and extended to include social media. For example, Image Restoration Theory (IRT) and SCCT have been the dominant perspectives in crisis communication research. Practitioners and scholars stand to benefit from this repertoire of knowledge to formulate informed crisis communication strategies (Appendix B).

ARE THERE ONLY RISKS OR ALSO OPPORTUNITIES?

> Never let a good crisis go to waste.
>
> *Winston Churchill*[57]

LEARNING OBJECTIVES

- Reflect on the opportunity potential of a crisis.
- Examine ways of strategically leveraging a crisis situation.
- Apply learning to crisis case studies with risks and opportunities.

A 'good crisis' is no longer an oxymoron. Indeed, scholars and professionals affirm that emerging strong from a crisis can have positive benefits. As a lead food giant, Domino's had planned to enter into the social media in a big way. However, the incident of employees indulging in unhygienic games forced them to cut short their original plan. Their forced entry, experimentation with YouTube after the first 24 hours, was applauded by customers and industry analysts. Domino's took this learning to heart and began talking about its new products, addressing consumer queries and issues and inviting consumers to track their orders and check different news items posted by the company. With this tracking of consumers and events, the company gained knowledge about what was happening and being talked about in the social media. The senior management team began Twitter feeds, and the company hired a media specialist with the specific objective of listening to conversations in the cyberspace and assessed the messages in the context.[58]

Although image and reputation repair via strategic messaging in the immediate aftermath of the crisis have been the predominant lenses in crisis communication, a focus on the opportunity potential of crises offers an important complementary perspective.[59] By focusing on renewal in the aftermath of a crisis, organizations and their leaders can use the crisis as an opportunity to learn, grow, and rebuild, to motivate employees and inspire a new future. Instead of solely dwelling on the problem and who was to blame, scholars contend that organizational leaders must also focus on the future (as opposed to the past), communicate ethically in all stages of the crisis, and substantiate their crisis response with demonstrable action and behavior change, as necessary. Here, organizations stand to benefit from prior positive stakeholder relationships, although the crisis may also generate new opportunities to create goodwill.

A well-known example of strategically leveraging a crisis situation comes from KLM Royal Dutch Airline, often cited as a social media exemplar (Appendix C). Especially notable is the organization's handling of an industry crisis and turning it into an opportunity that marked its leadership in and commitment to social strategy.

On April 14, 2010, the eruption of the Eyjafjallajökull volcano triggered an Icelandic ash cloud that engulfed most of Western and Northern Europe causing thousands of flight disruptions for six days. Airlines reportedly lost revenues in excess of US$1.7 billion in this period, with losses amounting to US$400 million per day at the peak of the crisis (April 17–19, 2010). Further, 29 percent of global aviation and 1.2 million passengers a day were affected.[60] Although KLM was already present on Twitter and Facebook since late 2009, the influx of customer queries and rebooking requests resulting from the ash cloud threatened their ability to provide high-quality customer service. By mobilizing an internal network of volunteers, KLM, as well as other airlines (e.g., Lufthansa, SAS Scandinavian Airlines), turned to social media to provide status updates and respond to user requests. Although KLM was applauded for its efforts, the "trial-by-ash-cloud"[61] marked the organization's transition to becoming a social business (see Appendix C for details).

Just as social media present challenges, they also provide opportunities to enhance risk and crisis communication. Following the 2015 Nepal earthquake, Facebook galvanized its technological prowess to help people connect with their loved ones. Social media are being actively used to tap volunteers as in the case of the Red Cross and to create awareness, provide instructions, and share information and safety updates in case of natural disaster or health emergencies. The Centers for Disease Control and Prevention (CDC) used social media (Twitter, Flickr) to educate US citizens about the Ebola outbreak.[62] The CDC's most recent tweet provides US citizens a checklist to prepare for the hurricane season.[63]

The exponential growth of digital and the potential for social media crises also necessitates an understanding of how publics or stakeholders make sense of organizational crises. Historically, crisis communication, as a field of practice and scholarship, has privileged organizational interests. How publics consume different (social) media, how they evaluate organizations' crisis communication efforts, whether some mediums are more credible than others, how a crisis may be differentially framed across media types, and so on, are becoming important questions. Listening to stakeholders on social media offers meaningful insight about their sentiments and reactions toward an organization and/or specific issues. Case in point: Analysis of 300,000 Greek and English-language tweets surrounding the Greek referendum in July 2015 revealed largely a negative outlook toward Greek Prime Minister Alexis Tsipras.[64]

From a research perspective, an untapped opportunity relates to internal communication during a crisis. As stakeholders that are most proximate to an organization, employees' sense-making, response, and reactions in/to a crisis merit attention and should be integrated in the crisis communication plan. A survey of Danish organizations confirmed that crises generate insecurity and frustration among employees, intensifying the need for information and informal communication. Employees were reported to be communicatively active at the workplace in times of crisis (66%) and were involved as organizational ambassadors (as 47% internal and 40% external ambassadors) in a crisis. Apart from the finding that internal social media and internal blogs lag way behind meetings, intranet, and email as the preferred channels of crisis communication, the study does not address new media but it paves the way for future research. As a final point, organizations are getting better at formal/formalized contingency plans and crisis-preparedness mechanisms while the internal communication dimension in a crisis presents an emergent opportunity.[65]

MAKING SENSE OF THE MANY VOICES

> The match is struck. Now what that match has to light makes all the difference in the world.
>
> *David Krejci*[66]

LEARNING OBJECTIVES

- Review evidence-based best practices for crisis management.
- Understand the importance of caring for stakeholders in a crisis.
- Reflect on the importance of company and leader character on crisis response.

Crises lead to a difficult and dynamic situation that warrants efforts at managing reputation and demonstrating leadership. There is no universal formula for what constitutes 'successful' or 'effective' crisis communication in the digital age, and strategies are context-dependent. Knowing your stakeholders and listening to what they think/say about you, devising and regularly reviewing crisis plans, and developing a presence in social media to engage with influential stakeholders constitute the fundamentals of crisis preparedness. Tracking online customer sentiment can also provide important cues about stakeholder reaction to organizational crisis messages. The assumption is that organizations can benefit from prior positive relationships with stakeholders and their response to organizational messages in a crisis, in particular, can signal the (in)effectivess of crisis management efforts. The need for crisis planning, both online and offline, cannot be overstated, and as the fate of reputations is being decided in the public sphere, organizations can no longer afford to be bystanders in the digital age.

Guidelines on how to use social media in a crisis are mushrooming. For example, the International Air Transport Association (IATA) provides a comprehensive checklist of dos and don'ts for the aviation industry across a variety of scenarios which could be equally applicable for other business sectors.[67] How should organizations prepare for crises and respond during and after a crisis? Scholarly and professional sources agree on the need for pre-crisis prevention as the decisive first step, from scenario planning, having ready crisis plans, and identifying and training designated organizational spokespersons.[68] In the digital age, the pre-crisis phase involves an integration of new media in crisis management plan, actively scanning online conversations to assess potential risks, and devising strategies for engagement in the event of a crisis.

As we have seen before, crises can and will occur and prepared organizations are better able to respond in a crisis. Responding quickly, accurately, and consistently, using the right messaging and tone of voice with a view for public concern and stakeholder safety, are best practices for crisis response. Finally, after the worst is over, there is still work to be done. Here, organizations ought to deliver on their commitment to stakeholders (e.g., information promised, corrective action taken) and using the crisis as a point of reflection for future crisis management efforts.

Time is of the essence in a crisis that has originated or amplified in social media. Being the first to report, the crisis situation can provide reputational benefit to an organization. By "stealing thunder,"[69] organizations suffer lower reputation loss than if the crisis was reported by another source, or worse, if the organization knowingly chose to cover up the crisis. Concealing information for fear of reprisal is counterproductive because it "creates the impression they do not care about the safety of their stakeholders."[70]

As organizations make sense of the multifold influence of new media on corporate communication, it is reasonable to expect roadblocks along the way, some more serious than others. Responding to a (potential) crisis in an informed and appropriate manner can have a decisive effect on relational reputation. So when former BP CEO, Tony Hayward said in an interview, "I'd like my life back,"[71] he worsened an already precarious situation. In the midst of the worst environmental disaster in recent history that resulted in the loss of life, livelihoods, and ecological damage, this proclamation signaled the complete lack of empathy for the affected publics.

In the end, showing care and sensitivity toward stakeholders says a lot about organizational character and leadership. Although an organization's attitude toward stakeholders should be part of everyday business conduct, it is subject to greater scrutiny and evaluation in times of crisis. Malaysia Airlines lacked empathy when they sent a text message to the family members of the missing passengers on MH370, even though the airline claimed that the text was only an additional channel, beside personal and telephonic communication. The airline has also been severely criticized for not helping the families cope with the aftermath and reportedly accused of withholding information and for lack of transparency in post-crisis communication. The process of recovery, rebuilding, and renewal rests on the leadership capabilities of the organization; the reputation, strength, and vision of the leader; and the potential to see the opportunity in a crisis.[72]

In contrast, following the crash of Airbus A320 flight on March 24, 2015, carrying 150 people, Germanwings, discount carrier of Lufthansa, made an emotional connect with the people through social media. The very same day as the crash, both Lufthansa and Germanwings changed the color of their logo on Twitter and Facebook to grey and black. The next day, they posted a video statement of their CEO C. Sophr with a hashtag #indeepsorrow. Statements demonstrating deep sentiment and sorrow were posted on their websites and repeated in the social media. "Everyone at Germanwings and Lufthansa is deeply shocked and saddened by these events,"[73] the companies said, offering a telephone hotline to all families of the passengers involved. "Our thoughts and prayers are with the families and friends of the passengers and crew members."[74]

Chapter Highlights

1. Crises are unpredictable, non-routine, and unique events in the history of an organization that produce uncertainty and warrant a quick response.
2. A crisis is usually associated with negative consequences, especially the threat to organizational reputation and image. However, they may also present opportunities for an organization.
3. Communication in a crisis constitutes a big part of how stakeholder perceptions are formed and reputation is built. Online reputation management is an ongoing process, not just to be undertaken in a crisis.
4. A reputation threat can be reduced by proactively tracking issues online to identify warning signs and brewing troubles.
5. The digital communication environment is vulnerable to "paracrises" or incidents resembling a crisis that, if ignored, could potentially erupt into full-blown crises with serious reputational damage.
6. New media provide stakeholder groups the ability to make themselves heard and enable an 'echo chamber,' implying that crises in the digital age are more visible and public.
7. A hoax on social media can threaten organizational legitimacy and create a communication challenge.
8. Pranks and parodies on social media pose a particularly novel challenge. No two cases are alike and assessing the trade-off can assist the decision about whether to respond or not.
9. Customer dissatisfaction, grievances, and complaints should be addressed immediately with care and sensitivity. Organizations can choose to ignore, wait and watch, fight back, and/or use online forums as expressions of stakeholder feedback.
10. Perceived risks in social media include reputational threat, false/misinformation, cybercrime/information security, lack of control, employee concerns, slow response time, lack of dedicated personnel, preponderance of negative commentary on new media, and ambiguity about who influences opinion online.
11. Effectively harnessing digital requires a holistic understanding, a mind-set change that situates organizations and stakeholders in an interdependent relationship.
12. Crisis management strategies are context-dependent and time is of essence in a crisis that has originated or amplified in social media.
13. The process of recovery, rebuilding, and renewal rests on the leadership capabilities of the organization; the reputation, strength, and vision of the leader; and the potential to see the opportunity in a crisis.

Activities

1. Research the web and select an example each from the preventable, victim, and accident clusters. Study the strategies used by the companies embroiled in a crisis for image restoration and prepare a matrix with similarities and dissimilarities in approach.
2. Search the web and find 10 instances of customer complaints. Classify them on the basis of the "what" in the message. What are your recommendations for the company? What should be the company's response to customer grievance?
3. Prepare a list of post-crisis strategies employed in a few recent or well-known crises. What kinds of organizational learning opportunities did these crises offer? How did the respective organizations use these opportunities?

4. In your groups, select 10–15 crisis situations, preferably across social media networks (e.g., Twitter, Facebook, and YouTube). Examine the details of the crisis and crisis communication strategies used. Based on your understanding of the differences among social networks, suggest if the strategies adopted by the companies were appropriate. Can you identify 'best practices' of crisis communication across the different platforms?
5. Select some situations in which pranks, hoaxes, or rumors triggered a (potential) organizational crisis. What lessons can you draw from the cases about (variations in) addressing ambiguous situations and deciding how to respond? What role did social media have in these cases?
6. Until recently, crisis communication research has been corporate-centric, serving to uphold company interests over all else. How stakeholders make sense of a crisis, how they are affected, and how they (can) contribute to crisis discourse is underexplored. Select an organizational crisis or a crisis issue on social media and conduct an analysis of stakeholder comments. What is the tone of these comments; what are the topics being discussed; how are the organizations interacting with stakeholders on these platforms; and how is a negative feedback handled by the organization/s in question?
7. You are an entrepreneur and have recently opened a restaurant in front of a famous Business school. In less than a month, students have begun to flock in and outside the restaurant. You have also provided for Internet facilities. However, this was not a very wise move as students sit for hours surfing the net. One day, your partner happens to chance upon the restaurant with a group of 30 friends. He is unable to find any empty table as almost all are occupied by students. In a loud voice, he makes a caustic remark about the younger generation and how they while away their time. One of the young boys takes offense and enters into a dialogue which converts to a heated exchange of words. This boy then takes upon himself the onus of rapping the restaurant owners with misconduct using #knowthycustomer. Soon the conversation gains momentum and other students join in to rally against you. How would you respond on social media? How will you address the wrath of the younger generation? Craft a first response with a focus on the messaging content and tone of voice.
8. You are a member of the marketing communication team of an FMCG company with a stellar reputation. The recent debacle of worms being found in the soup packets manufactured by your company has left the customers in a state of shock. The incident has attracted huge attention in social media with almost a million hits in the last five days. Customers are commenting on the breach of trust and expressing their concerns over the spate of activities. Sales have dropped dramatically with competitors gaining ground. You have been asked by the management to design a social media crisis management and communication plan.
9. You are the corporate communication manager at a lead pharmaceutical company. The R&D department of your company has come up with a drug to fight cancer. The NGOs are claiming that it contains animal fat. They have gone on Facebook and have excited a debate where fanatics and non-fanatics are discussing the merits of the drug. Within a week, the share price of the company has dipped by 10 percent. Prepare an online crisis community strategy.
10. You are the corporate communication manager at an oil exploration company. Much of your interaction has been with the Petroleum Ministry and the local (tribal) communities where you have your rigs. The recent spate of social media activism and crises in this industry have forced you to review the current communication patterns in this space. Your CMD wishes you to prepare a Social Media Crisis Communication Plan that helps prepare in advance for any untoward incident. Draft a plan that includes a comprehensive situation analysis, the types of crisis that could occur, the stakeholders that could be involved, steps that should be taken by the company to address the issues, and time line of action. Think about the possible ramifications of your recommendations for corporate reputation and stakeholder relations.

the post and apologized on Twitter, "The image was re-blogged in error by one of our international social media employees who was born after the tragedy and was unaware of the event. We sincerely regret the insensitivity of that selection and the post has been deleted" (American Apparel).[79]

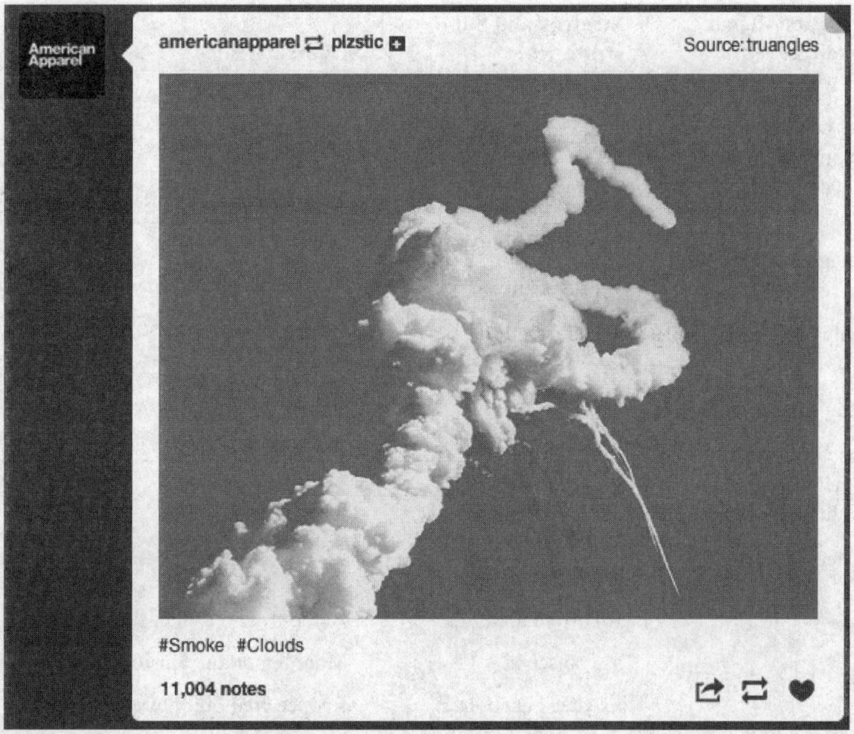

In another instance, in 2013, an HMV employee hijacked the company's official account to tweet about the "Mass execution, of loyal employees who love the brand. #hmvXFactorFiring."[80] The tweet instantly reached 70,000 Twitter followers of HMV, was reported by mainstream media, and retweeted about 1,300 times just in the first 30 minutes.[81] HMV quickly deleted the tweets but the damage was already done. A similar situation at the American Red Cross did not produce negative ramifications illuminating the importance of context in assessing a risky situation and the possibilities for response. A rogue tweet sent by one of its employees ("Ryan found two more 4 bottle packs of Dogfish Head's Midas Touch beer … when we drink we do it right #gettngslizzerd") could have spiraled into a crisis but the organization handled the situation using a bit of humor ("We've deleted the rogue tweet but rest assured the Red Cross is sober and we've confiscated the keys") accompanied by the employee's personal apology.[82] A combination of factors (the tweet was deemed unprofessional but not quite controversial), the legacy of the organization, and the 'humility' of response on the corporate blog ("While we're a 130 year old humanitarian organization, we're also made of up human beings. Thanks for not only getting that but for turning our faux pas into something good")[83] served the organization well in the face of an impending crisis.

These cases highlight, among others, the need for organizations to be aware of the possibilities that emerge from the inability to control information and the pressing need to actively listen to conversations about the brand/organization and to be cognizant of what stakeholders believe and think about them. Doing so is critical to the (successful) outcome of social media efforts.

APPENDIX B

SELECT CRISIS COMMUNICATION THEORIES/MODELS

Image Restoration/Repair Theory (Benoit, 1995)[84]	**Strategy and Sub-strategies**	**Characteristics**
Image is essential to organizations and individuals. An attack on image necessitates a communicative response. Attack on image involves two components: • the accused is held responsible for the act • act is portrayed as offensive In the absence of the two conditions, there is no reputational threat Five (5) master strategies	**Denial**	
	• Simple denial	Did not do act (or act did not occur, or act is not harmful)
	• Shift blame	Another did act
	Evade Responsibility	
	• Provocation	Act was response to another's offense
	• Defeasibility	Act happened because of lack of information or ability
	• Accident	Act was a mishap
	• Good intentions	Act was meant well
	Reduce Offensiveness	
	• Bolster	Stress good traits
	• Minimize	Act not serious
	• Differentiate	Act less serious than similar ones
	• Transcend	More important considerations
	• Attack accuser	Reduce credibility of attacker
	• Compensate	Reimburse victims
	Corrective Action	Plan to solve or prevent recurrence of problem
	Mortification	Apology
Situational Crisis Communication Theory (Coombs, 2007)[85]	**Strategy**	**Subtype and Recommended Use**
Audience-oriented perspective Stakeholders make attributions about *crisis responsibility* which affect how stakeholders interact with the organization in crisis. Two-step process: • Assess crisis type/level of responsibility (see Box 4.2) • Assess "intensifying factors" of crisis history and prior reputation Match response strategies to reputational threat	• Denial May be used in a rumor crisis	Deny crisis exists Attack the accuser Scapegoat/shift the blame (avoid)
	• Diminish Appropriate in crises with low levels of responsibility	Excuse: Minimize responsibility by denying intent to do harm and/or claiming inability to control the events that triggered the crisis. Justification: Minimize perceived seriousness or damage
	• Rebuild	Compensation (a crisis has visible victims) Apology (the organization is responsible)
	• Reinforce (supplemental strategy)	Highlighting positive information about the organization through Ingratiation: Thanking/praising others Bolstering: Emphasizing past good works

(Appendix B Continued)

(Appendix B Continued)

Social-mediated Crisis Communication (SMCC) Model (Austin, Liu, & Yin, 2012)[86] *Information form* (traditional media, social media, or offline WoM) can impact public's crisis communication behaviors	Albeit not a theory, the SMCC model describes interaction between an organization in crisis and three types of public who produce and consume information in a crisis: 1. influential social media creators—create crisis information for others to consume 2. social media followers—consume the influential social media creators' crisis information 3. social media inactives—may consume influential social media creators' crisis information indirectly through WoM with social media followers and/or traditional media who follow influential social media creators and/or social media followers This model also looks at information flow, how information is distributed by social media directly (e.g., from creators to followers) and indirectly (e.g., from followers to inactives)

APPENDIX C

CASE: TRIAL-BY-ASH CLOUD: A SOCIAL MEDIA OPPORTUNITY FOR KLM

Koninklijke Luchtvaart Maatschappij N. V., better known as KLM Royal Dutch Airline, is often cited as a social media exemplar.

Encouraged by its successful handling of the 2010 ash cloud crisis, KLM established a social media hub at its headquarters in the Netherlands, to facilitate open dialogue with consumers and listen and respond to suggestions and complaints. A marriage of KLM's corporate communication and e-commerce departments, and staffed by specialists from different functions, the social hub was envisioned as the pivot for all things social (the beating heart of our social spider web).[87] On July 18, 2011, KLM became one of the world's first companies to go 24/7 in social media.[88]

Still, KLM is not immune to social media crisis or negative feedback, and the learning continues. Following Holland's victory over Mexico in the 2014 FIFA world cup, KLM issued this tweet that quickly caused immense outrage and was seen as racist and culturally offensive (note the moustache, sombrero, and serape blanket with the message 'Adios Amigos!'). Mexican actor Gael Garcia Bernal, with a fan following of two million, responded emphatically (@KLM I'm never flying your shitty airline again. Fuck you big time).

Source: The Guardian.[89]

In an interesting play on the incident, Aero Mexico, Mexico's national carrier, issued a welcome message for the returning Mexican team:

Gracias por este gran campeonato, estamos orgullosos y los esperamos en casa #VivaMéxico

["Thank you for the championship. You have made us proud and we are waiting for you at home."][90]

The image contrast drove the point home:

Source: AeroMexico.[91]

KLM responded that their tweet was meant to be a joke, and the airline did not intend to be offensive. The tweet was quickly deleted and KLM later issued a formal apology.

KLM blogposts and interviews emphasize the importance of "learning by doing wrong" to acknowledge mistakes but simultaneously use them as learning opportunities.

Voices from the Field

by Henjo Guitjens and Erik Martens (HG/EM) and Vikram Menon (VM)

1. **When you hear 'crises in the digital age,' what are the first thoughts that come to your mind? Has the practice of and approach toward crisis management really changed dramatically now? Please highlight the most significant developments from your perspective.**

   HG/EM: Any crisis can start with a single tweet. Hence, 'the crowd' frames the way a crisis is being perceived. In practically all situations, 'victim organizations' and authorities (due to bureaucracy and checks and balances) become reactive, most of the times eager to counter emotion with facts. Like it or not: 'perception rules' and 'established facts' appear to be of subaltern importance. You need to bridge these two worlds by displaying an emphatic attitude.

   Speed has increased. News is spread within minutes, even live video, while in the 'old age' even TV and radio were not able to report within an hour. And everybody is a reporter. News is no longer the domain of professionals. Consequence is that news is unfiltered. In crises, it therefore is even more of the utmost importance to take control of messaging and take a proactive attitude.

   VM: My first thought would be 'is it really a crisis?' In the current digital era, we do have a tendency to overreact as people and as brands. Identifying what is and what isn't a crisis is becoming critical. Having said that, it's not the easiest thing to do.

   Crises in the digital age are not as uncommon or as unusual as they used to be. Traditionally, there was a certain predictability of where crises emerged from. Today, anyone, anywhere, has the capability to create a crisis and impact the brands reputation with little provocation and minimal effort.

   And that is what has impacted how we deal with crises. Crisis management now needs to start with seriously evaluating the scale and importance of a crisis. Most importantly, 99 percent of potential crises can be resolved with timeliness and appropriateness of response. Timing is of essence. Unlike crises that used to occur earlier, in the predigital, presocial media age where there was a predictable way to address them using predictable channels of communication and specific individuals/influencers, digital crises can be a lot more unpredictable and sudden. More than solving for the crisis eventually, how you react to it is equally important since people start expecting a response almost immediately and then change their perceptions based on that response.

2. **Although no two cases are alike, what may be some criteria that organizations should consider in using social media for crisis communication?**

   HG/EM: Be prepared and be 24/7 alert. Prepare stopping statements. Authorize specialists to address those without consulting the hierarchy. Respect 'the golden minute.' Conduct 24/7 monitoring and assessing intelligence. Take careful consideration where to respond and how. Use owned/shared media to come with the right facts. Total integration of all social/digital using departments is very important.

   VM: Given the nature of social media and the fact that anyone can tag anyone on any issue—without a clear idea of an issue/problem owner—here are a few things that come to mind:

   - A response is important. Setting expectations on your social channels on how soon one can expect to hear back from the brand is a good way. Take a look at this example: https://www.klm.com/travel/et_en/plan_and_book/klm_on_social_media/24_7_service_and_assistance/index.htm

- When a question is directed to a specific individual, some sort of a response must go. You cannot afford to be non-responsive or seem to 'pass the buck.' So in consultation with the PR/social team, address the issue and redirect to the correct response handle (corporate communication/social agency, etc.)
- Basic social media training for all employees, with clear dos and don'ts is critical.
- In many cases, a direct call to the crisis 'creator' offline also solves the problem, without prolonging engagement on the issue on the brand social channel.

3. **What constitutes 'successful' or 'effective' crisis communication in the digital age? Has the definition of 'success' or 'successful' crisis communication changed now? Please explain your response.**

   HG/EM: Success looks like when an organization 'under fire' is able to bridge and connect with its audience. It should be noted that this requires also in times of peace active stakeholders' engagement, also via online and social media.

   VM: In terms of output or result, the definition of success has not changed. The metrics may have changed—how soon the issue got resolved, how did you restrict the 'reach' of the crisis, how smoothly you addressed the key issues, etc.

4. **Are there some ground rules for how organizations should (not) communicate in a social-mediated crisis?**

   HG/EM: Firstly, any organization should be out there in the digital and social space. Implicitly, that presence confirms that it listens to 'sounds from outer spaces' and wishes to engage in a (social) dialogue with its stakeholders.

   Don'ts are clear: don't be offensive, don't display a paternalistic attitude. Acknowledge any stakeholder. Don't be judgmental. Be careful with humor (could easily backfire).

   Do's: Only communicate confirmed facts and validated data. Explain why that is important to you: you want process communications is always a lifeline.

   VM: To ignore or belittle an issue that someone thinks is important is the worst way of making a social-mediated crisis more serious. So it's important that the words we use are carefully chosen to communicate that the brand takes every issue raised seriously and will respond/address appropriately.

   For example, a biscuit brand once had a situation where a customer had put a picture of a worm infested cookie and tagged the brand. From the look (ridges on the cookie), it was discovered to be of a competitive brand. The team was able to call immediately, explain the situation, and address the issue. But ignoring the situation would not have been an option.

   A couple of other things to keep in mind:

   - Have a process. This is like the fire drill in the offline world. It's a chore and will showcase its value only during the crisis but this needs to be done. The process usually identifies a designated spokesperson: his/her backups two levels down, a first response protocol, and activating an ongoing monitoring and internal information sharing system.
   - In typical social media-driven crises where everybody has a voice, more than the brand's own voice, it helps to get other third-party voices of support to combat an online mob. This involves building a list of pro-influencers long before a crisis hits. This would come particularly helpful in cases where the crisis stems on a social platform where the brand/company has no/inadequate presence.

5. **What do these developments mean for reputation management? What is your foremost advice for managing reputation in the digital environment?**

   HG/EM: Be on the ball, be transparent, constantly 'read' your audiences, and engage in active dialogue. Listen to what is being talked about considering your brand, organization, and market. Look for upcoming issues online (see it as a long-range radar) and prepare. Exercise how to respond. Set up an integrated team.

   VM: Serious social listening is a must combined with an empowered, agile response management system.

   Reputation management is about perception management. In digital environments, perceptions are more fluid and fickle and can change based on multiple sources of information, credible or not. So, the most critical thing to do is to build a system to listen/hear online—a few random tweets or messages do not make a reputation. Companies should invest in social command centers to be truly aware of the scale and nature of crises that impact perception and then act accordingly. Knee-jerk reactions on something small can balloon into larger crises owing the company's own misconceptions.

6. **Many scholars and practitioners agree that crises are instructive moments and offer valuable learning opportunities. How does this translate in the digital age? Beyond a select few (e.g., KLM), how can organizations use a social media crisis as an opportunity? Please share an example.**

   HG/EM: Indeed, learn from other crises. What worked best, what not? Describe useful and effective ways of social engagement/response and share it internally. Organize monthly discussions on what happened, what can be improved. Ikea does that well.

   VM: I believe this is less true today than it was earlier. If you look at the big crises cases of the past, there were genuine opportunities for the brands to accept the challenge and take the brand reputation and conversation to the next level. Today, several crises are manufactured, and therefore part of the challenge is to know what a real situation is and what is not.

   Communicators know this instinctively, but it is worth reiterating—words, or choice of words, make or break things. A pertinent area in crisis communications that words take on critical importance is communicating apology during a crisis. A recent example of how it is done can be seen in this blog post by CEO of Buffer. It is honest, doesn't shift blame, and explains a follow-up process.[1]

7. **In the social media landscape, is culture more or less relevant for crisis communication and reputation strategy?**

   HG/EM: Talking about internal cultures: yes. It works best if the corporate communications culture is collaborative, open, and transparent. There must be the will to learn from each other. It's all about trust. If we take a look at international differences, then we can see that in the western hemisphere, most social conversations are very direct and have a tendency to express disagreement, while in the eastern part conversations are still more political polite. This asks for different responses.

   VM: A culture of transparency is critical. Being completely honest is vital to resolving issues. Half-truths and opaque responses lead to a deepening of the crisis. In addition, a few select employees

[1] Tough News. (June 16, 2016). Retrieved from https://open.buffer.com/layoffs-and-moving-forward/

need to be trained and empowered to act confidently as spokespeople for a brand without having to go through several levels of approvals to respond to a crisis.

8. **What are the skills that practitioners need to develop or acquire to effectively do their job now?**

HG/EM: All have to be digital savvy to a certain basic level. They must know how to find their way in the social/digital landscape and to interpret data and must be able to make a quick first analysis. More experienced, 'older' practitioners must learn to work closely with the (very) young social and digital experts. This is a challenge in traditional hierarchical organized corporates.

VM: I think the core marketing/communication skills stay the same. Additionally, practitioners need to demonstrate agility in thinking and execution to meet the real-time needs of the social landscape. One thing to keep in mind is that conventional communication skills, while a basic necessity, may be found lacking when you're responding not to a select set of well-meaning people but to anyone, anywhere, who are sometimes completely anonymous.

9. **Any other comments?**

HG/EM: Any organization, be it a corporate, an NGO, or a governmental body, should appreciate that online and social media have become an integral part of the way we digest, evaluate, and spread news. They should be willing to engage in an ongoing conversation in order to explain themselves constantly.

NOTES

1 Mireles, A. (2014, May 15). Where does social fit in crisis communications planning? Retrieved June 1, 2015, from http://www.cision.com/us/2014/05/where-does-social-fit-in-crisis-communications-planning/

2 References for Box 1.1: Barton, L. (2001). *Crisis in organizations II* (2nd ed.). Cincinnati: College-Divisions South—Western; Seeger, M. W., Sellnow, T. L., & Ulmer, R. R. (1998). Communication, organization, and crisis. In M. E. Roloff (Ed.), *Communication yearbook* (Vol. 21, pp. 231–275). Thousand Oaks, CA: SAGE Publications; Ulmer, R. R., Sellnow, T. L., & Seeger, M. W. (2015). *Effective crisis communication: Moving from crisis to opportunity* (3rd ed.). Thousand Oaks, CA: SAGE Publications; Coombs, W. T. (2007). Protecting organization reputations during a crisis: The development and application of Situational Crisis Communication Theory. *Corporate Reputation Review, 10*, 163–176. doi:10.1057/palgrave.crr.1550049

3 Ulmer et al. (2015).

4 ChangeThis. (n.d.). Retrieved May 18, 2015, from http://changethis.com/manifesto/83.03.ReputationRules/pdf/83.03.ReputationRules.pdf

5 Coombs, W. T. (2011). Crisis management and communications. Retrieved July 1, 2015, from http://www.instituteforpr.org/crisis-management-and-communications/

6 Report retrieved May 22, 2015, from http://www.reputationinstitute.com/research/Reputation-Leaders-Study

7 Survey retrieved May 12, 2015, from http://www.deloittereputationrisksurvey.com/#

8 Coombs, W. T. (2011). Crisis management and communications. Retrieved July 1, 2015, from http://www.instituteforpr.org/crisis-management-and-communications/

9 Ibid.

10 Sohn, Y. J., & Lariscy, R. W. (2014). Understanding reputational crisis: Definition, properties, and consequences. *Journal of Public Relations Research, 26*, 23–43. doi:10.1080/1062726X.2013.795865

11 *Indian Express*. (2011, March 3). Tata Nano catches fire, again. Retrieved May 22, 2015, from http://archive.indianexpress.com/news/tata-nano-catches-fire-again/757099/

12 Mireles (2014).

13 *Indiatimes*. (2013, June 11). The most controversial Sunday brunch. Retrieved May 29, 2015, from http://www.indiatimes.com/news/india/lemp-brew-pub-curious-case-of-a-hawaiian-brunch-in-gurgaon-82716.html

14 Coombs, W. T., & Holladay, S. J. (2012). The paracrisis: The challenges created by publicly managing crisis prevention. *Public Relations Review, 38*, 408–415. http://dx.doi.org/10.1016/j.pubrev.2012.04.004

15 Ibid.

16 Coombs and Holladay (2012).

17 Coombs, W. T. (2015). Effects of the online world on crisis communication and crisis management. In W. T. Coombs (Ed.), *Ongoing crisis communication: Planning, managing, and responding* (pp. 17–30). Thousand Oaks, CA: SAGE Publications.

18 Ibid.

19 Ibid.

20 Malshe, A. (n.d.). A typology of social media crises (Unpublished manuscript). Retrieved May 21, 2015, from http://www.academia.edu/1476436/A_Typology_of_Social_Media_Crises

21 Clifford, S. (2009, April 15). Video prank at Domino's taints brand. *The New York Times*. Retrieved June 1, 2015, from http://www.nytimes.com/2009/04/16/business/media/16dominos.html?_r=0

22 Malshe, A. (n.d.). A typology of social media crises. Unpublished teaching note used with author permission.

23 Case based on information from the following sources: Jacques, A. (2009, August 17). Domino's delivers during crisis: The company's step-by-step response after a vulgar video goes viral. Retrieved May 24, 2017, from http://www.prsa.org/Intelligence/TheStrategist/Articles/view/8226/102/Domino_s_delivers_during_crisis_The_company_s_step#.Vfp2RSx961u; Domino moves ahead with speed and alacrity: Response to viral video. Retrieved June 1, 2015, from http://www.prsa.org/Intelligence/TheStrategist/Articles/view/8226/102/Domino_s_delivers_during_crisis_The_company_s_step#.VWQYt9Kqqko

24 Ibid.

25 Watch a news story about the video: https://www.youtube.com/watch?v=OhBmWxQpedI

26 Patrick Doyle's response video: https://www.youtube.com/watch?v=dem6eA7-A2I

27 Kiley, D. (2009, April 15). Domino's pizza Youtube video lesson: Focus on standards, and pack your own lunch. *Businessweek.com*. Retrieved June 1, 2015, from http://www.businessweek.com/the_thread/brandnewday/archives/2009/04/dominos_pizza_youtube_video_lesson_focus_on_standards_and_pack_your_own_lunch.html

28 Jacques (2009).

29 Veil, S. R., Sellnow, T. L., & Petrun, E. L. (2012). Hoaxes and the paradoxical challenges of restoring legitimacy: Dominos' response to its YouTube crisis. *Management Communication Quarterly*, *26*, 322–345. doi:10.1177/0893318911426685

30 Veil, S. R., Petrun, E. L., & Roberts, H. A. (2012). Issue management gone awry: When not to respond to an online reputation threat. *Corporate Reputation Review, 15*, 319–332.

31 Ibid.

32 Al-Khoury K. (2014, September 8). Al-Khoury K. Tweeters, hackers and trolls: How to handle a social media crisis–Part 2. Retrieved April 24, 2017, from http://www.webershandwickseattle.com/2014/09/tweeters-hackers-and-trolls-how-to-handle-a-social-media-crisis-part-2/

33 Video retrieved May 24, 2017, from http://www.davecarrollmusic.com/music/ubg/

34 *The Economist*. (2009, July 24). Did Dave Carroll lose United Airlines $180m? Retrieved May 24, 2017, from http://www.economist.com/blogs/gulliver/2009/07/did_dave_carroll_cost_united_1

35 Hendershot-Hurd, K. (2009). What to do when social media creates a shit storm. Retrieved May 26, 2015, from http://virtualimpax.com/2009/07/13/social-media-shit-storm/

36 Banks (n.d.). Jeff Bezos on customer service. Retrieved May 9, 2015, from http://blog.paylane.com/ jeff-bezos-on-customer-service/

37 Vora, V. (2015, May 25). Very long post (and a little depressing), but please read the entire thing. Retrieved May 24, 2017, from https://www.facebook.com/vishal.vora.927/posts/10153290124110409

38 Hill, K. (2012, Jan 24). #McDStories: When a hashtag becomes a bashtag. Retrieved June 20, 2016 from https://www.forbes.com/sites/kashmirhill/2012/01/24/mcdstories-when-a-hashtag-becomes-a-bashtag/#1cb97acfed25

39 Kucuk, S. (2014). A semiotic analysis of consumer-generated antibranding. *Marketing Theory* (Online First). doi:10.1177/1470593114540677

40 Grégoire, Y., Salle, A., & Tripp, T. M. (2015). Managing social media crises with your customers: The good, the bad, and the ugly. *Business Horizons, 58*, 173–182. http://dx.doi.org/10.1016/j.bushor.2014.11.001

41 Ibid.

42 Dekay, S. H. (2012). How large companies react to negative Facebook comments. *Corporate Communications: An International Journal*, *17*(3), 289–299. http://dx.doi.org/10.1108/13563281211253539

43 Definition retrieved May 20, 2015, from http://dictionary.reference.com/browse/trolling

44 Case based on Prince, R. (2014, August 25). British Embassy forced to apologise for tweet celebrating anniversary of burning of White House. Retrieved May 24, 2017, from http://www.telegraph.co.uk/news/worldnews/northamerica/usa/11054506/British-Embassy-forced-to-apologise-for-tweet-celebrating-anniversary-of-burning-of-White-House.html

45 Sanchez, R. (2013, April 19). Boston marathon bombings: How social media identified wrong suspects. *The Telegraph*. Retrieved May 19, 2015, from http://www.telegraph.co.uk/news/worldnews/northamerica/usa/10006028/Boston-marathon-bombings-how-social-media-identified-wrong-suspects.html

46 Reddit Originals. (2013, April 22). Reflections on the recent Boston crisis. Retrieved May 19, 2015, from http://www.redditblog.com/2013/04/reflections-on-recent-boston-crisis.html

47 Mei, J. S. A., Bansal, N., & Pang, A. (2010). New media: A new medium in escalating crises? *Corporate Communications: An International Journal*, *15*, 143–155. http://dx.doi.org/10.1108/13563281011037919

48 Qualman, E. (2015). Retrieved June 1, 2015, from http://www.goodreads.com/quotes/729544-we-don-t-havea-choice-on-whether-we-do-social

49 Berger, B. K. (2015). Conversations with PR leaders: Heading into a dynamic and uncertain future at warp speed. Retrieved May 10, 2015, from http://www.instituteforpr.org/wp-content/uploads/IPRRC-Paper-2015-Convoswith-PR-Leaders.pdf

50 Burson Masteller. (2013). Burson Masteller survey of crisis planning. Retrieved May 2, 2015, from http://www.burson-marsteller.com/what-we-do/our-thinking/crisis-survey-2013/

51 Continuity Insights. (2014). Crisis Communications 2014: Social media and notification systems. Retrieved May 5, 2015, from http://www.burson-marsteller.com/what-we-do/our-thinking/crisis-survey-2013/

52 Zerfass, A., Tench, R., Verčič, D., Verhoeven, P., & Moreno, A. (2014). European communication monitor 2014. Retrieved May 15, 2015, from http://www.zerfass.de/ECM-WEBSITE/media/ECM2014-Results-ChartVersion.pdf

53 Ki, E. J., & Nekmat, E. (2014). Situational crisis communication and interactivity: Usage and effectiveness of Facebook for crisis management by Fortune 500 companies. *Computers in Human Behavior*, *35*, 140–147. http://dx.doi.org/10.1016/j.chb.2014.02.039

54 Romenti, S., Murtarelli, G., & Valentini, C. (2014). Organisations' conversations in social media: Applying dialogue strategies in times of crises. *Corporate Communications: An International Journal*, *19*, 10–33. http://dx.doi.org/10.1108/CCIJ-05-2012-0041
55 MacDougall, A. (2015, May 13). How to manage a crisis in an 'always on' world. Retrieved May 22, 2015, from http://www.mslgroup.co.uk/blog/2015/may/how-to-manage-a-crisis-in-an-always-on-world.aspx
56 Coombs (2015).
57 Churchill, W. (2015). Retrieved May 15, 2015, from http://www.goodreads.com/quotes/717228-never-let-agood-crisis-go-to-waste
58 Jacques (2009).
59 Ulmer, R. R., Seeger, M. W., & Sellnow, T. L. (2007). Post-crisis communication and renewal: Expanding the parameters of post-crisis discourse. *Public Relations Review, 33*, 130–134.
60 IATA. (2010, April 21). Volcano crisis cost airlines $1.7 billion in revenue–IATA urges measures to mitigate impact. Retrieved April 24, 2017, from http://www.iata.org/pressroom/pr/Pages/2010-04-21-01.aspx
61 Think with Google. (2012, December). Out of the ashes. Retrieved September 18, 2015, from https://www.thinkwithgoogle.com/articles/out-of-the-ashes.html
62 Murphy, T. (2014, September 24). How the CDC uses social media to inform Americans about Ebola outbreak. Retrieved June 1, 2015, from http://www.humanosphere.org/global-health/2014/09/cdc-uses-social-media-informamericans-ebola-outbreak/
63 CDC Emergency. (n.d.). Retrieved September 18, 2015, from https://twitter.com/CDCemergency
64 Report retrieved May 24, 2017, from http://www.pewresearch.org/fact-tank/2015/07/15/twitter-users-turn-critical-eye-toward-greek-prime-minister-after-referendum/#comments
65 Johansen, W., Aggerholm, H., & Frandsen, F. (2012). Entering new territory: A study of internal crisis management and crisis communication in organizations. *Public Relations Review*, *38*(2), 270–279.
66 Al-Khoury, K. (2014a, July 25). Tweeters, hackers and trolls: How to handle a social media crisis–Part 1. Retrieved May 21, 2015, from http://www.webershandwickseattle.com/2014/07/tweeters-hackers-andtrolls-how-to-handle-a-social-media-crisis-part-1/
67 IATA. (2015). Guidelines—Crisis communications in the digital age. Retrieved May 21, 2015, from http://www.iata.org/publications/pages/crisis-communications-guidelines.aspx
68 References for best practice recommendations: Coombs, W. (2014, September 23). Crisis management and communications (updated September 2014). Retrieved March 6, 2015, from http://www.instituteforpr.org/crisis-management-communications/; Syme, C. (2015, April 8). Social media monitoring in 30 minutes a day. Retrieved May 27, 2015, from http://cksyme.com/social-media-monitoring-in-30-minutes-a-day/; IATA. (2014, December). Crisis communications and social media: A best practice guide to communicating in an emergency. Retrieved September 20, 2015, from http://www.iata.org/publications/Documents/social-mediacrisis-guidelines.pdf
69 Coombs (2014).
70 Ibid.
71 Lubin, G. (2010, June 2). BP CEO Tony Hayward apologizes for his idiotic statement: "I'd Like My Life Back." Retrieved August 25, 2015, from http://www.businessinsider.com/bp-ceo-tony-hayward-apologizes-for-sayingid-like-my-life-back-2010-6?IR=T
72 Ulmer, R. R., Seeger, M. W., & Sellnow, T. L. (2007). Post-crisis communication and renewal: Expanding the parameters of post-crisis discourse. *Public Relations Review, 33*, 130–134.
73 Bradley, D. (2015, March 24). Lufthansa, Germanwings darken logos on social media in mourning after crash. Retrieved May 28, 2015, from http://www.prweek.com/article/1339923/lufthansa-germanwings-darkenlogos-social-media-mourning-crash
74 Ibid.
75 All quotes in this example come from Ramsey, N. (2013). Pasta Barilla boycotted after CEO's "homophobic" remarks. Retrieved May 27, 2015, from http://www.msnbc.com/the-last-word/pasta-barilla-boycotted-after-ceos
76 All quotes in this example come from Porter, C. (2013, May 23). Abercrombie & Fitch CEO Mike Jeffries finally says sorry over comments. Retrieved May 27, 2015, from http://www.news.com.au/technology/abercrombie-fitch-ceo-mike-jeffriesslammed-over-comments/story-e6frfro0-1226644223630
77 All quotes in this example come from Saha, A. (2015, May 20). Twitter rage at Modi: Story of #ModiInsultsIndia and #ModiIndiasPride. Retrieved May 27, 2015, from http://www.hindustantimes.com/india-news/twitter-comes-down-on-pm-modi-for-sayingindians-were-ashamed-till-a-year-ago/article1-1348664.aspx

78 All quotes in this example come from Giammona, E. (2011, February 11). What not to do with Hashtags–The Kenneth Cole debacle. Retrieved May 27, 2015, from https://www.text100.com/articles/hypertext/what-not-to-do-with-hashtags-the-kenneth-cole-debacle/

79 All quotes in this example come from Plautz, J. (2014, July 4). American Apparel apologizes for using challenger disaster photo instead of fireworks. Retrieved May 29, 2015, from http://mashable.com/2014/07/04/american-apparel-challenger/#ytYtFb7DHkk0

80 Evans, N. (2013). "Someone had to speak": HMV employee who live tweeted firing of 60+ staff from chain's official Twitter revealed. Retrieved June 1, 2015, from http://www.mirror.co.uk/news/uk-news/hmvxfactorfiring-poppy-rose-cleere-behind-1568494

81 Immediatefuture. (n.d.). HMV: A social media crisis. Retrieved June 1, 2015, from http://immediatefuture.co.uk/blog/hmv-a-social-media-crisis/

82 Wasserman, T. (2011, February 16). Red Cross does PR disaster recovery on rogue tweet. Retrieved June 2, 2015, from http://mashable.com/2011/02/16/red-cross-tweet/

83 Praetorius, D. (2011, February 16). The Red Cross' rogue tweet: #gettngslizzerd on Dogfish Head's Midas Touch. Retrieved June 3, 2015, from http://www.huffingtonpost.com/2011/02/16/red-cross-rogue-tweet_n_824114.html

84 Benoit, W. L. (1995). *Accounts, excuses, and apologies: A theory of image restoration strategies*. Albany: State University of New York.

85 Coombs (2007).

86 Austin, L., Liu, B. F., & Yin, J. (2012). How audiences seek out crisis information: Exploring the social-mediated crisis communication model. *Journal of Applied Communication Research, 40*, 188–207. doi:10.1080/00909882.2012.654498

87 Drimmelen, J. (2012, July 25). KLM's social media strategy–Part 2. Retrieved July 29, 2015, from https://blog.klm.com/klms-social-media-strategy-part-2/

88 Ibid.

89 Image retrieved June 19, 2016 from http://www.theguardian.com/football/2014/jun/30/klm-sobrero-tweet mexico-world-cup-holland-gael-garcia-bernal#img-1.

90 Aero México. (n.d.). Retrieved September 18, 2015, from https://twitter.com/AeroMexico/stat

91 Image retrieved June 19, 2016 from http://twitter.com/AeroMexico/status/483333017901858816/photo/1

CHAPTER 5

UNDER THE MICROSCOPE

Corporate Responsibility in a Social-mediated Era

CHAPTER OBJECTIVES

- Review the importance of and developments in business–society relations.
- Examine how social media are influencing strategy and communication of corporate social responsibility (CSR) or sustainability.
- Reflect on the challenges and opportunities for corporate communication of CSR.
- Understand the interplay of ethics, leadership, and culture from current cases.

Keywords

Business practice
Co-creation
Collaboration
Consumer
Corporate social responsibility (CSR)
CSR communication
CSR reputation
Crowdsourcing
Culture
Dialogue
Digital Activism
Engagement
Ethics
Fraud
Greenwash(ing)
Leadership
Legitimacy
Non-government organization (NGO)
Purpose
Shared value
Social media
Stakeholder
Sustainability
Sustainable development
Reputation
Transparency
Trust
Values

INTRODUCTION

> We know that we have disappointed many people—people who have placed their trust in Volkswagen. We stand by our responsibility. And we are doing everything in our power to regain trust.
>
> *Matthias Mueller*[1]

> I am disappointed that some actions we have taken to fund scientific research and health and well-being programs have served only to create more confusion and mistrust. I know our company can do a better job engaging both the public-health and scientific communities—and we will.
>
> *Muhtar Kent*[2]

Through last year, we have seen a string of corporate apologies from large, global organizations across an array of issues. The one common thread: deliberate, unethical, and manipulative business practice. Arguably, we could redact the name of the respective organizations and the statements above could apply to many others. Another common denominator: Defaulting organizations have previously expressed deep commitment to corporate social responsibility (CSR) and enjoyed positive CSR reputations. Cases in point: Prior to the emissions scandal in 2015, Volkswagen ranked among the top 20 most reputed CSR firms globally, and Coca-Cola has been in the top 10 for six consecutive years in Fortune's ranking of the World's 50 Most Admired Companies.[3]

So what, we might ask? Aren't the instances above or others we know just one more reason to be skeptical of CSR claims? After the initial brouhaha, won't we simply return to 'business as usual'? Don't these developments merely illustrate the sham that is CSR and its inadequacy, perhaps failure, to even remotely challenge Milton Friedman's prophetic claim that "the business of business is business"?[4]

While the temptation to concur is indeed strong, let us pause a moment, and take a few steps back.

Our point of challenge in this chapter revolves around the need to revisit the relevance of CSR in today's business environment. No doubt, recurrence of corporate malfeasance undermines trust in business and reinforces skepticism that business only 'talks the talk.' This is indeed detrimental in an environment where transparency and reputation are at a premium. At the same time, and precisely because of the trust deficit, there is a compelling need to (re)focus on CSR. Indeed, there is a deepening conviction among a sizeable segment of firms that profit and purpose are not mutually exclusive and that business can contribute positively to societal development. The need to address changing and greater stakeholder expectations and reliably communicating CSR issues is also confirmed in recent CEO surveys.

In this chapter, we explore the developments in the realm of CSR and sustainability. Although CSR and sustainability have different connotations and roots,[5] our premise is that as organizations navigate a tumultuous business environment marked by societal problems, global inequities, and skeptical consumers, they need to re-assess their purpose and integrate CSR in business strategy. We also contend that the fast-paced and open-media environment elevates stakeholder scrutiny of CSR communication with high(er) potential to reward good practices and penalize offenders. Based on this overview, guiding questions include how is CSR or sustainability changing, evolving, or developing in the digital era? How have stakeholder expectations of and from business changed in contemporary times? What are the 'new' possibilities that social media offer for CSR communication, conversations, and engagement? What are the challenges and opportunities for organizations' CSR or sustainability (reputation) efforts in an always-on digital environment?

None of these questions has an easy answer; rather, they are the subject of complex conversations that cannot be oversimplified. Adding to the complexity is the ambiguity and diversity of definitions and understandings of what exactly constitutes CSR and whether businesses mean the same thing when they speak about CSR.

To lay the groundwork for discussion, we start by unpacking the case for renewing conversations about CSR and briefly outline the terminologies commonly used in CSR conversations. Then we weigh in on three broad topics aligned with current practice and research: a collaborative approach to CSR with dialogue at its core; stakeholder activism as a way to influence business practice; and the transparency imperative in the digital age. With each topic, we reflect on the underlying assumptions and points of contention about the potential of social media in re-defining the landscape of business–society relations.

CSR, SUSTAINABILITY, SHARED VALUE...: WHY NOW?

> Our philosophy is that corporate social responsibility is nothing but maximizing the value of your company over a long period of time, because in the long term, social and environmental issues become financial issues. There is really no hocus-pocus about this.
>
> *Lars Sørensen*[6]

The business world, it seems, is divided and on a precipice when it comes to CSR—the general belief that the purpose of business goes beyond profit maximization for shareholders to include a range of responsibilities toward a wider group of stakeholders, such as consumers, employees, the environment, and society at large. Proponents of CSR argue that business and society are interdependent and challenge traditional paradigms that solely privilege profit-making and shareholder value.

Having said this, support for CSR has waxed and waned over the years. Early conceptualizations of CSR designated it a discretionary practice, separate from business priorities.[7] Even activities deemed socially responsible cover a wide spectrum from providing good paying jobs and quality products to engaging in environmental preservation and community development. Differences still persist in how CSR is interpreted and framed which translates to limited agreement on what it means and whether those meanings translate across organizations and contexts. For example, India's Companies Act 2013 adopts a monetary lens on CSR by stipulating that companies with high net worth (₹500 crore/US$80 million), turnover (₹1,000 crore/US$160million) or net profit (₹5 crore or more/US$0.8 million) in any financial year spend at least two percent of their net profits for CSR.[8] Others look at CSR more broadly, for instance, The European Commission (EC) defines CSR as "the responsibility of enterprises for their impact on society."[9] The EC treats CSR as a company-led effort combining legal compliance and "integrating social, environmental, ethical, consumer, and human rights concerns into their business strategy and operations."[10] Although we recognize the need to be cognizant of differences in meaning, we work with a broader understanding of CSR, viewing it not as an 'add-on' to but as an integral part of business strategy.

CSR, it is argued, can give firms tangible and intangible benefits—a source of competitive differentiation and innovation, stakeholder trust and support, access to investment and new business opportunities, employee recruitment and retention, positive image and goodwill, and reputation capital. As a key driver of reputation, along with leadership, products and services, financial performance, workplace culture, governance, and innovation, CSR contributes roughly over 40 percent toward a firm's reputation.[11]

Although CSR has gained momentum over the years, its usefulness has been questioned in recent times. Already, the global financial recession dealt a severe blow to CSR and business legitimacy, more generally. Some even pronounced that CSR is dead, having failed to halt irresponsible business practice, for being mere 'spin,' and most important, disconnected from business. The OECD, for example, prefers the term 'responsible business conduct' (RBC) in its Guidelines for Multinationals Enterprises. The rallying cry of business seems to favor a common language around sustainability (aligned with the United Nations Sustainable Development Goals) and/or the concept of 'Shared Value' popularized by management scholars Porter and Kramer, not without debate (Box 5.1).[12] One perspective is that we should not summarily dismiss CSR especially as more companies, especially in developing and emerging economies, are "waking up to CSR."[13] Still others argue that, in principle, sustainability and responsible business are not contradictory but complementary,[14] and that is our position in this chapter.

Further, the optimism and belief in a broader societal purpose is reinforced by the magnitude and urgency of new 'grand challenges'—global inequality, political volatility, social instability, and climate change, to name a few—that confront business today. On September 25, 2015, all member countries of the

Box 5.1: What's in a Name?

CSR: As a construct about the role of business in society, CSR defies an easy definition, is differently interpreted, and often ambiguous. The first reference to CSR as "the obligations of businessmen to pursue those policies, make those decisions, or follow those lines of action which are desirable in terms of the objectives and values of our society" is attributed to Howard Bowen in 1953.[15] An analysis found that CSR definitions generally incorporate five common dimensions—stakeholder-orientation, voluntariness, and social, economic, and environmental concerns.[16] Organizations vary in how they define the scope of CSR, for example, the TATA group conceptualizes CSR in terms of "integrating environmental, social and ethical principles into the core business, thereby enhancing long-term stakeholder value."[17] TATA's 10 core CSR principles include sustainable development goals.

Sustainability is generally argued in terms of 'sustainable development' introduced in the Brundtland Report as "development that meets the needs of the present without compromising the ability of future generations to meet their own needs."[18] Sustainability (and often CSR) is defined in terms of triple bottom line (TBL) of people, profit, and planet (3Ps). Coined in 1994 by John Elkington, the 3Ps offer an integrated look at corporate impact in all spheres—social, economic, and environmental.

The Dow Jones Sustainability Index refers to corporate sustainability as "a business approach that creates long-term shareholder value by embracing opportunities and managing risks deriving from economic, environmental and social developments."[19] CSR and sustainability are often implicated such as when CSR is defined as "an integral vision of sustainable business practices."[20]

Creating Shared Value (CSV) is popularized by management scholars Michael E. Porter and Mark R. Kramer. They define CSV as "the policies and operating practices that enhance the competitiveness of a company while simultaneously advancing the economic and social conditions in the communities in which it operates."[21] According to them, CSV is fundamentally different from CSR whereby the latter is limited in its scope (the ability to fundamentally transform business processes and create joint value for companies and communities), processes (CSR budgets are limited), and outcomes (unlike CSR which they deem discretionary and separate from profit maximization, CSV is integral to competing and making profit).

United Nations adopted the 17 Sustainable Development Goals (SDGs) to tackle "wicked problems"[22] that demand multi-stakeholder solutions. With ambitions to tackle a wide range of issues until year 2030—poverty, hunger, sustainable cities, climate change, responsible consumption, etcetera—the SDGs provide a common platform around which firms may organize their sustainability goals.

Indeed, the assertion that business cannot exist in a society that fails rings louder as do the calls for a new kind of leadership that is resilient, creates business and societal value, and is future oriented. The need for a holistic and long-term view is aptly captured by Ajay Banga, CEO and president of MasterCard: "You've got to run a company for profit, you've got to run it for revenue growth, but you also have to run it to be around ten years from now doing the right things."[23] At its core, the leadership challenge for business leaders today is revitalizing trust in the institution.

In sum, emerging business scandals (from EpiPen's price manipulation to Volkswagen's emissions scandal to global tax evasion) and societal challenges confronting business, closing the trust gap and reflecting on the purpose of business, are of utmost importance and urgency. An authentic purpose that goes beyond short-term financial considerations gives organizations a competitive edge, provides a common vision around which stakeholders can align, and can even improve financial performance.[24] In this complex environment, a renewed commitment to CSR is both a necessity and an opportunity for business to make a meaningful contribution toward sustainable solutions for societal problems.

Clearly, the phenomenon, we address in this chapter comes in various hues and forms, is fundamentally about the role of business in society, and assumes—at least in principle—certain positive outcomes (e.g., value creation, legitimacy, reputation) for both business and society. A study by Accenture (2016) reports that 80 percent of CEOs believe that commitment to a societal purpose is a key differentiator, and a majority, therefore, sees sustainability as central to their strategic planning.[25] The business yields of sustainability are promising. Proof positive: Unilever's 'Sustainable Living' brands contribute to half of the company's total growth (twice as fast as the firm's other brands), making it one of the few global organizations to generate upward of a billion dollars in annual revenue from sustainable products or services.[26]

Organizations with favorable CSR reputations also enjoy positive stakeholder evaluation, support, and word-of-mouth. Consumer surveys report that social and environmental commitments now rank higher in inspiring brand loyalty and trust, per the 2015 Nielsen Global Corporate Sustainability Report.[27] According to the same report, a focus on sustainability also yields revenue returns (consumer brands that focus on sustainability reportedly grew more than 4% globally in 2014) and consumer willingness to pay more (up to 55%) for sustainable goods.

Of course, reputations are not static but created and modified over time, and efforts to use CSR as a smoke screen can severely undermine reputation. So, where and how do social media fit in business ambitions to communicate CSR in an effort to build and maintain CSR reputations?

CORPORATE COMMUNICATION OF CSR: THE DIGITAL AGE BECKONS

> Social media as the Wild West of CSR communications is a reality that calls for the use of imagination and creativity […] It requires unpicking, deconstructing, and to make sense of it, some repackaging of the CSR message is needed. The social media world of CSR is a communicative construct.
>
> *Ralph Tench and Brian Jones*[28]

LEARNING OBJECTIVES

- Understand the imperative for communicating CSR or sustainability.
- Examine new developments and changes in the media and communication landscape.

Paralleling the mainstreaming of CSR or sustainability or Triple Bottom Line (TBL) is the heightened importance of communication. Researchers have articulated the case for CSR communication in different ways, from generating awareness to reducing stakeholder skepticism, from information to dialogue, and encouraging stakeholder feedback to dialogue and participation in CSR.[29] Via CSR communication, firms can share information about CSR commitments and progress, engage and align stakeholders, and partner to find solutions to societal challenges with a goal to build relationships, trust, and reputation. Along with the functional and relational imperative, recent research focuses on how communication is central to creating (shared) meaning—what does CSR mean to/for an organization—and how are these meanings created, shared, managed, or altered in negotiation with stakeholders?[30] Seeing CSR as a co-created phenomenon situates communication at its core while regarding stakeholders as active participants in meaning construction as well as CSR design and implementation.

No surprise then that CSR communication has been on the rise. The KPMG survey of CSR reporting shows an upward trajectory with 90 percent of the world's most profitable firms (G250) reporting on CSR in 2015.[31] There is also a promising uptake of CSR or sustainability communication on social networks propelled by business interest to be where stakeholders are present, coupled with stakeholder interest in direct engagement with firms on relevant CSR issues (see Appendix A).

We can equally agree that social media have disrupted traditional ways of communicating about CSR and the unique characteristics of social media—reach, speed, low costs, unfiltered peer-to-peer communication, networked capability—are abundantly clear. Limited control over communication and the shift toward multi-directional communication signal a change in the way organizations and stakeholders engage. Not long ago, a plethora of research was looking at corporate website as central sources for CSR communication arguing, among others, the superiority of Web 1.0 over traditional channels of communication and web-based communication as a signal of proactivity and transparency.

Move over Web 1.0. Social media have flipped the equation and continue to demand communication flexibility, agility, transparency, authenticity, and uniqueness, all in one. Students in a graduate seminar at one of our institutions questioned the 'bulky' formats of CSR communication on websites (even blogs), message 'inconsistency' across social networks, and the lack of integration between the corporate (e.g., official company Facebook page) and CSR account. As representatives of the Millennial generation, this group was likely to make impressions about and evaluate CSR performance based on a few Facebook posts or Twitter feeds, which lends itself to the question: How are organizations to effectively communicate in a fragmented media environment?

Search the web and a lot of advice spills forth. The starting point for all is to ditch one-way communication in favor of two-way dialogue and engagement. From listening to stakeholders, crowdsourcing ideas and brainstorming solutions, co-creation, to building online communities, social media are seen as facilitators of long-term relationships as a source of reputational and relational capital.[32]

Let us look at an example. Hero MotoCorp Ltd, the largest manufacturer of two wheelers in the world, based in New Delhi, India, is actively integrating social media to realize its CSR vision of "a greener, safer and equitable world."[33] The firm's CSR program features four main pillars (Happy Earth, *Hamari Pari* [Our Fairy], Educate to Empower, and Ride Safe India) under the label 'We Care.' For much of its CSR strategy, the company relies on social media including YouTube, Twitter, Instagram, and Facebook.

For *Hamari Pari*, a collaborative initiative to empower underprivileged girls, the company website features an interactive story about *Pari* who is out to save young girls forced into employment or child marriage and to get them their 'right to education.' The initiative was launched via a short video film that created instant buzz on social platforms, with 28 lakh (2.8 million) views on the first day and became a trending topic on Twitter for 8 hours.[34] Bolstered by the initial success, a second video was launched with the promise that for every 10 shares, the company would support a girl child. In an interview, Vijay Sethi (chief information officer and CSR head) reported that the video had "more than 74 lakh (7.4 million) views and more than 50,000 shares," bringing 5,000 more girls under the *Hamari Pari* umbrella, and reported that "Facebook has also put up HamariPari as a custom cause under status activities of What's on your mind."[35]

For its road safety initiative #RideSafeIndia, Hero MotoCorp has a YouTube channel with a playlist of road safety videos containing practical information on riding gear and driving techniques.With almost 1.2 million fatal road accidents in the last decade, India has the highest number of traffic accidents in the world. The road safety initiative also aligns closely with the core business of the company. In addition to YouTube, Twitter has been an effective networking tool for real-time connection in the form of live chat sessions for youth awareness and engagement. Through combined digital and offline efforts (e.g., conducting 'Road Safety Awareness Program' for schools and colleges), the company hopes to reinforce impact on the ground with the support of a growing digital population.[36]

So far, the CSR strategies of Hero MotoCorp have been recognized, winning them awards for the *Hamari Pari* social media campaign, innovative programs in the automobile sector, and 'on-the-ground' impact of CSR initiatives. So, what was the digital imperative and how does the company reflect on the contribution of social media to the process? According to Vijay Sethi, the effective incorporation of technology serves multiple goals: raise awareness about the issues that matter, encourage other people throughout the country to support the cause, thereby creating a ripple effect, and transform silo efforts into holistic endeavors.[37] Specifically, social media allowed targeted communication for CSR campaigns, "…the right message is delivered to the right people using the most relevant medium. Targeted communication was done on a large scale helping in scaling up the awareness attempts."[38] The company is now looking into a CSR blog to allow more people to contribute to their efforts and conversations.

That social media will find a firm footing within CSR or sustainability communication seems inevitable. Current state of research suggests that few companies are fully utilizing the dialogic potential of social media, using them primarily as information dissemination platforms. Also, while it is tempting to dismiss all 'non-digital' forms of communication in an effort to be present where the stakeholders are, one might reflect on whether social media (and which ones, in particular) are an effective platform for conversations about CSR. Often these conversations can be complex, for example, how might a chemical company use social media to tell its sustainability story in an accessible and relatable manner? Is it just about mastering new channels of communication?

Then again, stakeholder groups are hardly homogenous in their expectations and behaviors, widely distributed, and assumedly want to collaborate with corporations in doing good for the world. From aligning expectations between organizations and their stakeholders to creating avenues for dialogues to working with stakeholders as partners in CSR, the spectrum of communication is indeed diverse. Further, as the opening quote indicates, organizations operate in an uncertain landscape with multiple, often conflicting, voices. They must contend with making sense of these voices while simultaneously strategizing ways to break out of the clutter and tell their sustainability stories in a credible and trustworthy manner. How firms can engage, listen, and involve stakeholders in a mutually reinforcing manner is a defining feature of contemporaneous CSR. In this 'new normal,' CSR is not something that organizations do *to* or *for* stakeholders but *with* stakeholders.

TAKING PEOPLE ALONG: THE 'NEW NORMAL' OF CSR

> Together with our customers, partners and communities, we help solve some of society's toughest challenges.
>
> *Xerox Global Citizenship Report*[39]

LEARNING OBJECTIVES

- Understand shifts toward CSR as a collaborative effort of stakeholder engagement.
- Review the ideal and pragmatic considerations for effective CSR dialogues.

Earlier in the chapter, we noted that organizations need to develop new capabilities to deal with global complexities and greater stakeholder expectations. Collectively, these changing are driving them to reflect on their own sense of purpose and to better align it with changing expectations. Open engagement and interaction can indeed strengthen relationships with stakeholders, allowing them greater understanding of the firm's CSR or sustainability efforts and possibilities to partake in these.

A company that has done well to take people along in its CSR journey is TOMS[40] (short for 'Tomorrow's Shoes'), best known for its founding mission of 'one for one'—for every pair of shoes bought, the company donates one pair to a child in need, donating over 60 million pairs of shoes globally since 2006. Inspired by his fateful trip to Argentina where he saw the overwhelming numbers of children without shoes unable to attend school and prone to disease, Blake Mycoskie founded TOMS as "a mission with a company" that has made customers integral to its purpose. In 2015, TOMS took its annual 'One Day Without Shoes' campaign social, inviting people—no purchase necessary—to go bare feet for a day and post a picture to Instagram with the hashtag #WithoutShoes. In return, the company would donate one million shoes at the end of the campaign period. Just three days after the start of the campaign, there were 99,000 submissions and, overall, the #WithoutShoes hashtag produced 17 million impressions across TOMS' social platforms and 62 million impressions in total. Fans of the brand also posted YouTube videos to the company account documenting their day without shoes. By integrating social media in their 'giving' tradition, TOMS created a groundswell of interest and support for the issue globally, reportedly engaging over 3.5 million people in 2016, and ranking in more than US$300 million in revenues. Inspired by TOMS' success, several 'one for one' enterprises have sprung up in the past decade.

Using social media, TOMS has actively engaged and empowered consumers to become involved in giving for various social causes (e.g., providing eyesight, promoting local artists, clean water) and furthered the brand ethos, something that Mycoskie believes is sound business strategy: "I think it's incredibly sustainable. Built into our cost structure is the intention to provide great benefit to our customers because they feel like they're getting to be part of something more than just a transaction [...] By doing that, we're able to form more loyal customers; we're attracting new customers."[41] Still the company has been criticized for its business model including the unintended consequence of disrupting local business and questionable ground-level social change.[42]

Like TOMS, other organizations are using creative ways to strengthen the linkages among social media, CSR strategy, and business strategy. Admittedly, purpose-driven CSR is not a direct consequence of social media although it is well aligned with the collaborative possibilities of social media. As in the case of TOMS, transforming "customers into benefactors"[43] has allowed the firm to sustain its efforts without relying on external fundraising.

Aside from consumers, CSR is a driver for employee identification, pride, advocacy, and commitment. Indeed, engaged employees are likely to go the extra mile (57 percent more effort on the job) and 87 percent less likely to resign, relative to disengaged employees.[44] Unilever's 'Heroes' program celebrates and recognizes employee initiative and commitment to the firm's sustainability mission via video case studies on social media and the company website. For its centenary in 2011, IBM India asked employees in a series of virtual JAM sessions, what they cared about and social initiatives they would like the organization to focus on. Input from 19,000 participants across India allowed IBM to tap into employee aspirations and create projects that combined IBMers' values with local priorities.[45] Crowdsourcing CSR can be a source of innovative and diverse perspectives, ideas, and opinions. Further, it deepens engagement by involving stakeholders in defining the norms of CSR and enabling them to become brand advocates. Employee advocacy can mitigate the skepticism that is often associated with CSR communication by firms.

Many organizations are looking toward collaborative problem-solving platforms to further their innovation efforts and sustainability goals by leveraging the power of ideas. General Electric (GE) Open Innovation is one such platform that regularly posts open challenges, invites creative ideas, and reward-winning entries. Organizations like Timberland strive to engage their extended community of suppliers, distributors, consumers, and local community members to contribute toward and enlarge the footprint of its Earthkeeper program. Non-profit organizations also rely on the power of the crowd for campaign ideas (e.g., Greenpeace regularly polls people to gather input for future action and priorities), fund-raising (especially during humanitarian and nature disasters), and volunteer recruitment.[46]

How can organizations fully leverage the support and involvement of stakeholders? To effectively mobilize collective action in favor of sustainability, Unilever's 'five levers of change' offer a systematic approach to design behavioral change interventions (see Figure 5.1).

FIGURE 5.1 *Unilever 'Five Levers for Change,' Inspiring Sustainable Living*

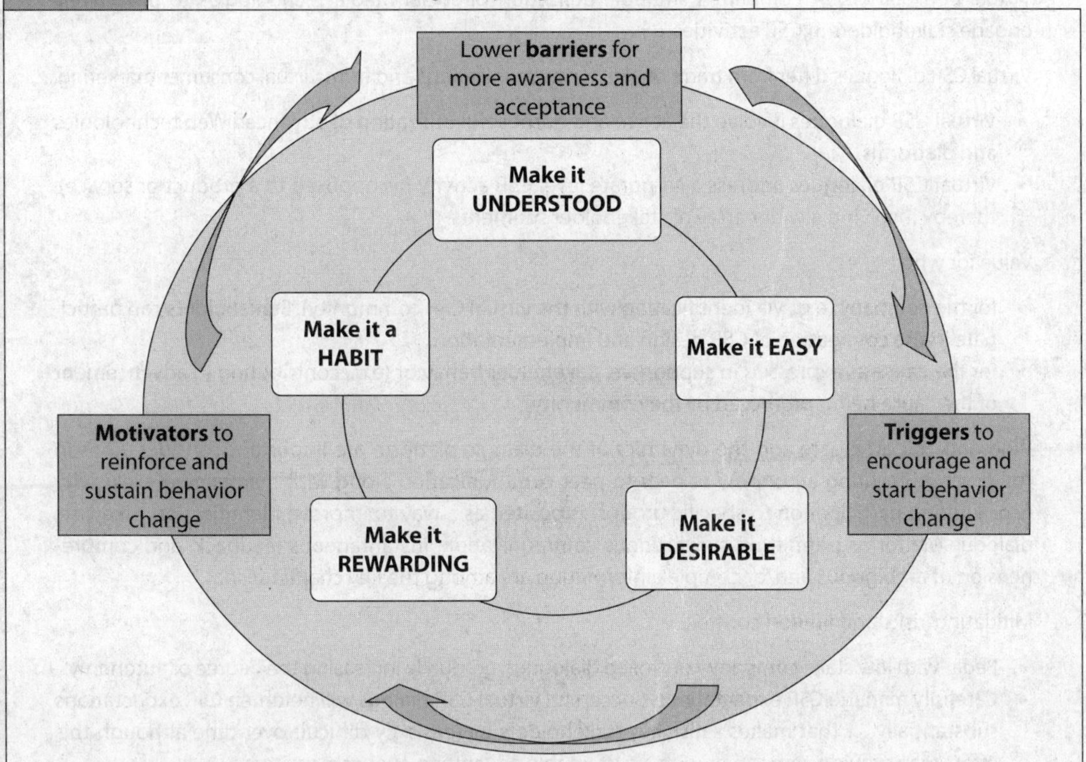

Source: Figure adapted from company document.[47]

A participatory approach to CSR demands a shift away from one-way communication/information dissemination, toward interactive and dialogic communication. From co-creation and co-construction of CSR to CSR crowdsourcing, dialogue facilitates and invites stakeholders to participate in CSR strategy and implementation, as opposed to just being recipients of CSR information. To this end, dialogue reigns supreme as the most prominent manifestation of the 'new normal.'

Dialogue, Dialogue Everywhere

Social-mediated CSR dialogue is purported to help organizations create social capital by strengthening stakeholder relationships, building trust, enabling stakeholder identification, and clarifying or establishing norms of behavior between organizations and their stakeholders. Through dialogue, organizations can better understand, incorporate, and respond to stakeholders, translating into possibly greater social support and legitimacy.

Scholars are weighing in on the why, what, and how of CSR dialogue on social media. Scholars Korschun and Du (2013) theorize that 'virtual CSR dialogues' can generate value for organizations (Box 5.2).

Box 5.2: Virtual CSR Dialogues: A Theoretical Conceptualization

Virtual CSR dialogs: "A company's strategic utilization of social media technologies to proactively engage stakeholders in CSR activities."

Virtual CSR dialogues differ from traditional CSR communications and from virtual consumer marketing:

- Virtual CSR dialogues involve the active and purposeful utilization of advanced Web technologies and platforms.
- Virtual CSR dialogues address a corporate level CSR activity (as opposed to a product or service), thereby involving a wider array of stakeholder segments.

Value for who:

- for the company (e.g., via identification with the virtual CSR community). Stakeholders can participate in the co-creation of CSR design and implementation.
- for the cause as expressed in supportive stakeholder behavior (e.g., contributing to advancement of the cause being promoted by the community).

Who gets to participate and the dynamics of the dialogic platform are important considerations in the process. Ensuring autonomy of peer-to-peer communication along with maintaining exclusivity (e.g., limiting participation to specific groups) is posited as a way to improve identification. Likewise, dialogue platforms permitting synchronous communication, instantaneous feedback, and comprehension of ambiguous and/or complex information are among the key characteristics.

Mitigating 'risks' and limited control:

- Begin with low stake company-controlled dialogues, gradually increasing the degree of autonomy.
- Carefully manage CSR expectations. Successful virtual CSR dialogs will heighten CSR expectations substantially … that makes satisfying stakeholders increasingly difficult over time although this effort may provide companies with a sustainable advantage over competitors.

Source: Korschun and Du (2013).[48]

Other scholars also confirm the reputational gains from an interactive communication strategy.[49] Higher interactivity is linked to increased message credibility (by placing a check on inaccurate corporate claims that users can denounce) and creating feelings of identification between stakeholders and organization. Identified individuals and groups are more likely to engage in positive word-of-mouth translating to reputation gain. Still, organizations need to watch out for 'ifs' and 'buts' and content specifics. For instance, when users see CSR messages with mostly positive evaluations, they are less likely to believe those messages. But a majority of negative evaluations is equally, if not more, problematic in that negative information is perceived to have more credence and could erode reputation.[50]

Beyond the instrumental benefits, however, dialogic CSR communication is seen by many as more ethical, "a relational and humanistic focus that sees people as inherently valuable."[51] Although compelling, such an invitation overlooks the infusion of power in most dialogue and its situated nature. Indeed, dialogue does not automatically preclude power, and to that extent, CSR communication may be seen as "a process of reciprocal influence,"[52] an interplay of power and resistance between organizations and their stakeholders. The questions we should be asking then are how should dialogue be operationalized; what does dialogue look like, and from whose perspective? Some caution that terms such as engagement, dialogue, and conversations are often used loosely and as surrogates for what merely amounts to providing more information. Are all dialogues equal? Prior CSR reputations can become a key differentiator, producing differential output for the same effort. Organizations with high(er) CSR ratings are more likely to proactively adopt social media for online presence and encourage user-driven communication as compared to firms with lower CSR reputations.[53]

One might also ask if all stakeholders want dialogue with corporations, or is it that an invitation to dialogue is an expression of goodwill and a way to build corporate credibility?[54] A study finds that stakeholders ideally expect three dialogic CSR spaces—for co-learning, co-innovating, and co-deciding. In comparison with learning and innovation, spaces for co-decision appear to be limited, fueling speculation that organizations "often set the confines of the dialogue too tightly, making real dialogue impossible."[55] Firms need to balance their need for control with the openness that stakeholders expect. Simply creating spaces for dialogue does not automatically generate dialogue and certain enabling conditions are necessary (see Table 5.1) to achieve the ideals of dialogic communication.

TABLE 5.1 *Dialogue Works IF and WHEN: Constraints and Facilitators*

	Facilitators	Constraints
Organizational level	Empathy for and value of stakeholders	Personal empathy may conflict with professional goal to advance organizational objectives 'Unreasonable' or 'illogical' arguments
	Understanding corporate–stakeholder interdependence	Stakeholders may use codependence as a bargaining chip; dialogue becomes an appeasement tool to avoid potential problems Previous history of trust may erode mutuality
	Recognize value of stakeholder input and collaboration for organizational activity (e.g., CSR)	Legal, technical considerations may put boundaries on what is up for deliberation Lack of time The 'risk' of sharing too much/disclosure of potentially sensitive information;
	Commitment to dialogue	Could be tempered by lack of: • Knowledge and familiarity with social media • Resources managerial skepticism about the value of dialogue Informing (and one-way communication) as opposed to engagement

(Table 5.1 Continued)

(Table 5.1 Continued)

	Facilitators	Constraints
Stakeholder perspective	Organizational willingness to invite input, and follow through	Organizational and/or industry-level considerations (e.g., legal); stakeholders may not appreciate corporate effort to control the agenda
	Choice of dialogue platform (to facilitate open discussion)	'Organization knows best' mind-set; attempt to control agenda
	Dialogue participation: what they do and who participates	Power play and/or relative power and standing that create inequities of voice and representation
		Exclusive focus on the positives at the exclusion of difficult and challenging issues

Source: Compiled by authors based on existing research.[56]

The preceding discussion suggests a mixed picture—a belief in the instrumental value and normative supremacy of dialogue and practical challenges in realizing this vision. The temptation to use dialogue only for consensus around organizational issues and interests is counterproductive to stakeholder engagement. Although many efforts are still experimental, thinking about the strategic objectives of dialogic engagement is a crucial first step, as in the case of purpose-driven CSR campaigns which can create authentic and long-lasting engagement with organizations and/or associated causes.

Consider the case of Marico's[57] Saffolalife campaign #ProtectHerHeart that started a dialogue on women's heart health in India, roping in celebrities and key influencers to spearhead the engagement. The goal of the 2015 #ProtectHerHeart campaign was simple: to build awareness amongst women and their loved ones on the connection between women's weight-to-heart risk. The urgency of the issue became apparent in a pan-India study which placed two of four Indian women at risk of heart disease and the World Health Organization confirmed that cardiovascular diseases among Indian women are under-recognized and remain undertreated.

The campaign followed a 360-degree outreach on World Heart Day, combining digital and television commercials, offline events, and online engagement led by key influencers. First, the campaign used the husband as an influencer to partner his wife in making changes to her lifestyle, to safeguard and improve her heart health. A one-minute television spot, "*Har kadam saath chalne ka jo vada kiya tha, aaj use nibhane ki bari hai,*" [Now is the time to keep the promise you made to be together at every step of the way] reminded the Indian husband to fulfill his wedding promise to protect, love, and care for his wife by sparing 30 minutes of his time to walk together with her on a daily basis. Second, celebrity couple Shilpa Shetty and Raj Kundra led by example and engaged 100 couples to take a pledge to walk together every day for 30 minutes to #ProtectHerHeart. For online engagement, key opinion leaders from the film fraternity (Bollywood) and sports (e.g., Sania Mirza) were enlisted. Nationwide, bloggers joined the initiative by taking the pledge to walk together with their spouse. Finally, women were encouraged to complete an online self-test to assess their current heart health.

Over 45,000 people took the Heart Fitness Tests on the website, and the topic of women's heart health and the pledge to walk together for 30 minutes resonated across media and social networks. Campaign results—60 million media impressions with India's top news outlets; earned media worth US$1.7 million, a 33 percent increase over the previous year; more than 76 blog posts with a reach of 7+ million; and 11 million Twitter impressions—attest to its success in starting a conversation with, by, and among individuals, prompting them to become mindful of the issue.

Reflecting on this and other initiatives, we can see that firms can leverage social media to shape CSR perceptions, frame specific issues as salient, and tell the CSR story in an engaging, authentic, and resonant manner. Notwithstanding the success of this campaign, one might ponder if social media have a 'positive bias' in being favorable to some points of view while obscuring others? This question is pertinent in light of some critique of the company's efforts to brand itself as 'heart healthy.' Research conducted by The Center for Science and Environment challenged the assertion of a "healthy oil" urging stronger regulatory measures along with lifestyle changes (more physical activity, lower fat intake, and healthy eating) to address the prevalence of heart disease.[58]

In this section, we have argued that CSR strategy and communication are becoming a collaborative enterprise, designed and implemented in partnership with stakeholders. If the success of this new face of CSR is contingent upon the active involvement of stakeholders, organizations also have to recognize that stakeholders are not passive recipients of corporate information nor are they reluctant to voice their discontent, to critique and to influence change in business practice.

THE TRANSFORMATION OF STAKEHOLDERS: SITTING DUCKS TO ROARING LIONS?

> Hold business to account. Reward those companies that are trying to do the right thing. And withhold your dollars from those who aren't.
>
> *Paul Polman*[59]

LEARNING OBJECTIVES

- Understand the changing roles of stakeholders as active participants in CSR.
- Focus on specific instances of stakeholder activism as a way to influence business practice.

Few firms can be so bold to invite stakeholders to hold them accountable. Like it or not, stakeholder voices are no longer confined to or by information gatekeepers in traditional media but can ring loud and clear with unfettered access to social media.[60] Social media create a level playing field in which aware and active stakeholder groups are willing and capable of expressing dissent. Instead of fuming alone, consumers find comfort in sharing their experiences and creating a support community that pressures organizations to listen and respond.

The potential benefits are not only available to formal stakeholders but can also create participatory opportunities for individual citizens to debate and organize matters of public good. As some scholars have noted, social media facilitate new "citizenship arenas"[61] whereby individuals can contribute to corporation-led efforts to engage (corporate arenas) and/or organize in more inclusive, "public arenas"[62] that address a broad spectrum of social concerns. These developments are important because they widen the scope of influence, interest, and participation in ethical and societal issues.

In 2015, more than 10,000 petitioners called on Dutch pension fund ABP to review the climate impact of its €336 billion portfolio and stop investments in coal, oil and gas.[63] An initiative of 350.org, Fossil Free is a global movement that encourages institutions (government, educational, religious) to cut ties with the fossil fuel industry for its detrimental contribution to climate change, to strip the "veneer of legitimacy" that the industry gets from "sponsor relationships."[64] ABP, one of the largest pension funds in the world with close to 3 million members, was recently petitioned to divest from fossil fuel (the pension fund currently invests more than €30 billion in fossil fuels compared to just about €1 billion in renewable energy) and invest more sustainably.

Just as stakeholder challenges are more visible, so are organizational responses to these challenges. The willingness to listen, engage, clarify, and, if appropriate, modify business practice can shape perceptions of CSR commitment and reflect transparency in communication. Referring to the petition, ABP Vice-Chair José Meijer was quoted as saying, "these kind of initiatives are good, they keep us sharp. We are going to take a critical look at the influence our investments have on climate change and better communicate what we do."[65] ABP's fossil fuels holdings are reportedly down by €5.3 billion, and the Fossil Free movement urges supporters to continue pressure to #DivestTheRest by tweeting @ABPpensoen or posting on the fund's Facebook page.

The ability to make opinions heard can result in significant changes as in the case of ABP or the Occupy movement or SeaWorld. Relenting to mounting pressure from activists, watchdog groups, and consumers, SeaWorld announced in 2016 that it would end its killer whale (orca) breeding programs. The issue first surfaced in 2010 when one of the killer whales dragged and drowned its trainer in the midst of a show, and amplified in 2013 with the release of the documentary *Blackfish.* SeaWorld's decision to end its captive breeding for entertainment purposes has been well received as the percentage of consumers who would consider visiting SeaWorld after this decision jumped from five to 17 percentage points and social-media sentiment about SeaWorld turned positive for the first time 2015.[66]

Who or what is driving these changes?

Light on the Horizon: Millennials Driving Corporate Conscience

An influential stakeholder group that dominates the headlines these days are the Millennials. Expected to constitute 50 percent of the workforce by 2020 with considerable spending power (estimated US$200 billion annually by 2017, only in the United States), Millennial influence on ethical business conduct is predicted to grow exponentially.[67] Aside from their commercial power, surveys[68] affirm that Millennials are positive about business potential to be responsible and receptive to such efforts but equally alienated by business preoccupation with its own agenda and the lack of ambition beyond profit. Given their interest in social issues, Millennials want to be heard and engaged (e.g., 69% want business to make it easier for consumers to get involved in social issues) and will not shy away from advocating their favorable or negative opinion on brands that are irresponsible.

Although Millennials are not a homogenous group and cultural differences could very well exist, their media habits tend to be similar. Tech-savvy and 'connected' by digital technologies, Millennials are unlikely to respond to traditional mechanisms of communication (one-way, advertising-based messages). As management scholar Paul Argenti puts it, Millennials' "'BS meters' are very finely tuned"![69] For the levels of engagement and trust they seek to fulfill their aspirations of ethical consumption, organizations need to turn to social media as an interactive space for CSR conversations, exchange of ideas, and real-time feedback. Argenti cites the case of Perdue Farms, one of the largest poultry companies in the United States that is working toward new standards in delivering cruelty-free meats. Among the "precedent-setting" changes are reducing the use of antibiotics and providing more humane conditions for chickens both in "life and death."[70] According to the Chairman, Jim Perdue, the changes are in response to growing consumer demand especially from Millennials, and signal the company's responsiveness to align business practices with consumer values.

Further, different stakeholder groups (e.g., NGOs and citizens) often work in tandem, mobilizing together to influence change in business practices. For NGOs, non-profit organizations (NPOs), and advocacy groups, social media are seen as 'potential equalizers' marking the shift of activism from the fringe to the center, from margins to the mainstream.[71] Of course, NPOs are using social media for many different goals—for example, UNICEF has effectively used Twitter, Facebook, Instagram, Tumblr, and Snapchat to bring attention to the international development and humanitarian issues such as the kidnapping of Chibok schoolgirls in Nigeria.[72] Here, we focus on how advocacy groups use social media to influence business practice and add strength to their campaigns. One of the early adopters of social media, Greenpeace campaigns are illustrative of both challenges and opportunities of digital advocacy (Box 5.3).

Box 5.3: Digital Activism to Influence Business Practice

Greenpeace's 2010 Kit-Kat campaign[73] targeting Nestle's unsustainable palm oil sourcing from the rainforests of Indonesia and endangering orangutan habitat is well known. A YouTube video that appropriated the brand's message shows a bored worker taking a break to devour his Kit-Kat only to bite into an orangutan finger. With blood dripping from the side of his mouth, the campaign delivered a clear message to Nestle, "give the oran-gutan a break" and urged viewers to stop Nestle from sourcing palm oil from unsustainable producers such as Indonesia's Sinar Mas. The video was named Best Viral 2010 at Viral Video Awards, Berlin International Short Film Festival. The pressure created by Greenpeace and Nestle's own mishandling the response forced the organization to reflect on its social media and business (sourcing) practices. Greenpeace's former International Director, Kumi Naidoo, was quoted in a blogpost acclaiming the "collective power of the Internet and social media" that offers "a powerful new way of speaking truth to power, of taking a stand and making a demand."[74]

Greenpeace made waves once again with its social media spoof in June 2012, curated in collaboration with Yes Men, to stop Shell from drilling in the Arctic. The three-part action involved a fake website (Arcticready.com) made to look exactly like Shell's website, a YouTube parody video showing a press conference gone wrong (#ShellFAIL: Private Arctic Launch Party Goes Wrong; published June 7, 2012; more than 8.5 million views till date), and a fake Twitter account (@ShellIsPrepared) that mimicked the corporate account. In particular, an Ad Generator option on the ArcticReady website allowed users to create parodies of Shell's advertisements using symbolic visual imagery (e.g., polar bears, melting ice, birds soaked in oil), irony, and corporate language.[75]

On the one hand, this Greenpeace campaign (Let's Go!) "empowered ordinary citizens by providing them with tools to create and disseminate their own anti-Shell messages"[76]; on the other, the hoax website itself had mixed responses as Greenpeace followers and critics questioned the ethics of such "brandjacking" (brand hijacking). Not ignoring ethical questions, if the goal of this social media parody was to undermine the legitimacy of Shell's claims of preparedness, safety, and contingency planning, Greenpeace was effective in doing so.

Even then, it is important to see these efforts in the larger context, that is, the social media action was one in a series of Greenpeace efforts from 2012 through 2015 that did not exclude offline action. In September 2015, after spending US$7 billion on the project, Shell announced that it was abandoning its Arctic plans citing a difficult regulatory environment and commercial (in)viability. Greenpeace claimed victory, giving credit to their supporters ("You did it!," "This is your victory") for forcing the company's withdrawal.[77] We might ask whether Shell's decision was a direct result of Greenpeace efforts. No easy answers, but the case is instructive for how we might understand the potential of social media in influencing Shell's decision. As noted above, large-scale campaigns demand integrated use of multiple media, offline and online protest actions, petitions, and lobbying. Social media supplement offline tactics, allowing NGOs to bypass traditional media and directly reach and mobilize

(Box 5.3 Continued)

(Box 5.3 Continued)

their target audiences, and enabling citizens to participate in varied forms of collective resistance to undermine corporate reputation and/or the legitimacy of corporate action.

Alas, nothing is without consequence and social media make everything—the good, the bad, and the ugly—highly visible. When Greenpeace activists took their climate change message to the historic landmark of Nazca in Peru, they were accused of desecrating the ancient Peruvian heritage site. With their message ahead of the 2014 UN Lima climate talks ("Time for Change: The Future is Renewable"), the group hoped to draw attention to the urgency of the problem; instead, it had to issue a formal apology.[78]

Source: Compiled from publicly available information.

Not only large and formally organized groups stand to gain from the 'equalizing' potential of social media but also smaller organizations that would otherwise struggle to make themselves heard. Jhatkaa.org is one such organization in India that took on Unilever to clean up the residual and lingering effects of mercury contamination caused by its now defunct factory in India.[79] In a YouTube video, reportedly costing under US$250, Chennai rapper Sofia Ashraf relayed the group's resolve to not give up (*Kodaikanal* Wont) until Unilever complied with all demands including environmental cleanup, adequate compensation, and long-term healthcare for former workers and residents who were exposed to mercury poisoning. Via the video, the group urged viewers to sign a petition and join a conversation on Twitter (#UnileverPollutes) and Facebook. A simple tweet ('Wow') by Nicki Minaj whose hit single 'Anaconda' was the musical inspiration for the rap video resulted in a spike in tweets and views.[80] In March 2016, Unilever agreed to pay compensation to 591 former workers although Jhatkaa and their supporters continue to pressure the global giant for a complete resolution involving cleanup. Ashraf is now using a similar format (*Dow v/s Bhopal|Toxic Rap Battle*) to seek justice for the Bhopal gas tragedy victims urging that Dow Chemicals be held accountable for their actions in 1984. The video directly calls on the US Department of Justice to stop shielding Dow Chemicals and for being unresponsive to India's calls for summoning Dow. Viewers could sign a (now closed) petition on the White House website which reached its target of 100,000 signatures (127,532 to date). In an indirect response to the petition is a White House factsheet outlining the outcome of US–India talks "to advance a strategic partnership on energy security, clean energy, and climate change and reaffirmed our two countries' cooperation on environmental stewardship."[81] Whether this issue gains as much traction (the video has just over 17,000 views in comparison to over 3 million for *Kodaikanal* Wont) is to be seen. However, the constraints on NGO influence due to the massive imbalance in institutional power are telling, and important for a realistic assessment of what NGOs can accomplish in different contexts.

From the discussion thus far, we can be sure about the digitally driven changes, challenges, and opportunities in stakeholder influence and organization–stakeholder communication approaches. As noted before, it is important to examine these developments contextually, accounting for ground-level experiences and challenges. Surely, there are other strategies (e.g., cross-sector partnerships) that are equally or more effective at influencing business practice. Likewise, Millennials are not a unitary whole so, at the very least, we need to learn more about their motivations, attitudes, involvement, and responses to social issues across cultures and contexts.

As a final topic, we turn our attention to the issue of transparency and the assumption that social media can clamp down on misleading or exaggerated claims (as in the case of greenwashing), and make business more accountable and transparent. Grounded in the growing importance of CSR reputations and stakeholder action on social media is the conviction that companies have nowhere to hide.

GREENWASHING: GOING, GOING, GONE?

> You take a little step, you don't get caught. So yeah, you take another little step…And then maybe you don't even realize how far over the line you are.
>
> *John German*[82]

LEARNING OBJECTIVES

- Understand the reputation implications of greenwashing.
- Reflect on the possibilities (and limitations) of social media to promote ethical business practice.
- Review the linkages among ethics, culture, and leadership in building CSR reputations.

Along with the interest in environmentally friendly products and practices and organizations seeking to optimize the reputation value of 'green' identities comes the possibility of incorrect, false, and misleading claims aka greenwashing. An 'old favorite' Enron has arguably been supplanted by recent incidents, increasing skepticism of corporate actions. First came the Gulf of Mexico oil spill in 2010 that sharply contradicted BP's major brand repositioning and greening project initiated in 2000. As the newest poster child of greenwashing, Volkswagen's outright deception while proclaiming the green benefits of its diesel vehicles (VW reportedly spent US$77 million in the United States in 2015 to advertise its diesel cars[83]) highlights the scale of greenwashing, the roots of which go deep into corporate culture and ethics (see Appendix B).

Also defined as "any communication that misleads people into adopting overly positive beliefs about an organization's environmental performance, practices, or products,"[84] greenwashing is arguably not just limited to corporations and can take various forms (Table 5.2). Other actors (politicians, NGOs, governmental, and transnational organizations) may actively undertake and/or be implicated in

TABLE 5.2 *The Many Faces of Greenwash*

Source	Forms and Practices of Greenwash
Greenpeace greenwash criteria (as listed on http://www.stopgreenwash.org/)	o **Dirty Business:** Touting an environmental program or product, while the corporation's product or core business is inherently polluting or unsustainable. o **Ad Bluster:** Using targeted advertising and public relations campaigns to exaggerate an environmental achievement in order to divert attention away from environmental problems or if it spends more money advertising an environmental achievement than actually doing it. o **Political Spin:** Advertising or speaking about corporate 'green' commitments while lobbying against pending or current environmental laws and regulations. o **It's the Law, Stupid! It's the Law, Stupid!** Advertising or branding a product with environmental achievements that are already required or mandated by existing laws.

(Table 5.2 Continued)

(Table 5.2 Continued)

Source	Forms and Practices of Greenwash
TerraChoice Seven sins of greenwashing (as listed on http://sinsofgreenwashing.com/findings/the-seven-sins/)	o **Hidden trade-off:** Highlighting narrow environmental qualities at the exclusion of other important issues o **No proof:** unsubstantiated claims o **Vagueness:** Broad and ambiguous claims (e.g., 'all-natural') o **Worshipping false labels:** Fake labels and endorsements o **Irrelevance:** An environmental claim that may be truthful but is unimportant or unhelpful for consumers seeking environmentally preferable products o **Lesser of two evils:** claim may be true but seeks to draw attention away from larger, paradoxical, impact (e.g., fuel-saving SUV) o **Fibbing:** making outright false claims
Gillespie (2008)[85] 10 signs of greenwash	o Fluffy language o Green products made by dirty companies o 'Suggestive pictures' Misleading visuals (green images) o Irrelevant claims o Best in class? o Just not credible (e.g., eco-friendly cigarettes) o Gobbledygook (using jargon and/or overly specialized/technical information) o Imaginary friends (a fictional 'third-party' endorsement) o No proof o Outright lying (fabricated claims or data)

greenwashing efforts. Institutional actors such as CSR accreditation organizations need to be cognizant of their own credibility. Forest Stewardship Council (FSC), a global leader in promoting responsible forest management and certification, has been criticized by several of its stakeholders (e.g., FSC-Watch) for weak implementation of its own principles.

In an always-on, highly transparent world with vigilant stakeholders, there is an assumption that social media can discourage false or misleading environmental claims. Could social media have stopped VW from greenwashing? Doubtful, because the magnitude of fraud points to systemic problems and a deep-rooted corporate–State nexus. But once revealed, the effects of greenwashing on reputation—because it cannot go on forever—are far more damaging. Volkswagen's reputation standing plummeted from number 14 in 2015 to 123 in 2016, enough to boot it out of the 2016 Global RepTrak 100. The biggest drops reflected the failings in VW's governance, citizenship, and leadership. VW sales in the US plummeted immediately after the revelation (down 25% in November 2015).

Overall, the demand and support for eco-friendly products is growing. Across the European Union (EU) member states, consumers overwhelmingly support eco-friendly products for ethical reasons ('the right thing to do') and would pay more for such products. However, the confidence tumbles down when evaluating the credibility of green claims. Further, given the low state of trust in corporate self-reports on environmental performance, many support mandatory reporting on environmental firm and product performance.[86]

Paradoxically, the growing demand for green and eco-friendly products and organizational ambition to get their share of the 'green pie' along with limited clarity on regulation and enforcement fuels firms' propensity to greenwash. Even where rules exist (e.g., International Environmental Product Declarations or EPDs), the specifications may differ across regions causing confusion among consumers and creating opportunities for companies to exploit loopholes. In the interim, there is optimism that social media can fill the current void (and even complement) the efforts to ensure transparency and limit greenwashing. Organized groups can call out organizations for misleading claims and pressure them to take action.

The belief that social media can put the brakes on greenwashing is predicated on the power of word-of-mouth, reach (because bad news travels fast), and the ability of civil society to collectively protest deceptive practices in a variety of ways (e.g., naming and shaming, mocking corporate speak, culture jamming, and tweetjacking). Others posit that social media make it easier to recognize and penalize incidents of greenwash. On a platform like ProjectJust, users can learn about the sustainability practices of clothing brands. Then there are groups like Brandalism that use 'subvertising' as a way to draw attention to corporate green advertising. The group made waves on social and traditional media during the December 2015 UN Climate summit in Paris when it installed over 600 artworks challenging what it perceived as the 'corporate takeover' of the climate talks and exposing the hypocrisy of sponsor claims. A statement issued by the group outlined the rationale for the project highlighting the power of civil society to take on resource-rich corporations "The multinationals responsible for climate change can keep greenwashing their destructive business models, but the communities directly impacted by them are silenced. It's now more important than ever to call out their lies and speak truth to power [...]."[87]

As organizations seek to build CSR reputations via social media, they need to contend with all kinds of possibilities—the potential for dialogue, engagement, and community on the one hand, and the expectation and demand for openness and transparency on the other. Stakeholders can question and challenge organizations on false promises and inconsistencies with societal norms and values, creating a CSR crisis that threatens corporate reputation and stakeholder trust. The cases of Volkswagen, BP oil spill in the Gulf of Mexico, Shell's Arctic drilling are but a few illustrations. Taken together, the gravity of greenwashing can induce high degrees of cynicism of green claims and reduced purchase intention to lowering investor confidence in green firms, and creating disincentives for firms making concerted effort to be green.

Combining research and practice perspectives, we can summarize the strategic considerations for credibly communicating CSR or sustainability in the digital age (Table 5.3).

TABLE 5.3 *Strategic Considerations for CSR Communication*

Media strategy	• A strategy for communication is important, and can guide customization and tailored messages for different audiences and stakeholder groups. • Engage in dialogue as opposed to one-way communication; share and not sell the CSR story. • Engage with the media to tell the story; however, only focusing on the positives (or a picture-perfect company) can arouse skepticism. • Social media are a valuable platform to engage and crowdsource ideas; In addition to company–consumer communication, organizations may network with their peers to seek information and ask for help with CSR efforts.
Stakeholder engagement strategy	• Don't underestimate the public in terms of their interest in CSR, demand for information, and ability to analyze knowledge and practices. • Demonstrate commitment to stakeholders by asking questions, listening, and responding to comments; Doing so will signal leadership, attentiveness, and assurance to work with stakeholders to address their concerns. • Balancing control with co-creation in a way that allows room for alternative points of view is important for dialog to be credible and effective.

(Table 5.3 Continued)

(Table 5.3 Continued)

Organizational strategy	• Instead of looking at CSR communication as the prerogative of a single department, organizations might leverage the whole organization to support CSR efforts. For instance, employees as CSR ambassadors might mitigate the skepticism of CSR communication. • In light of transparency expectations, organizations should not shy away from troublesome issues and challenges. Addressing these head-on and having the difficult conversations can demonstrate effort to be honest and balanced. • Follow through on expressed CSR commitments to avoid claims of greenwashing.

Source: Compiled by authors based on existing research.[88]

The preceding discussion reinforces the centrality of ethics, leadership, and culture—again, nothing new but oh so important as newer incidents and cases tumble out of corporate closets. If building trust, and strengthening stakeholder relationships and reputation are the hallmarks of CSR, repeated ethical missteps will bring these efforts to a grinding halt, more swiftly now than ever. Is leadership geared to meet the demands of the digital age, to be transparent? What are leadership challenges and skills in translating the ideals of CSR into everyday practices, of walking the walk, and taking genuine efforts to make a difference? Circling back to our opening provocation to re-establish the relevance of CSR or sustainability, we cannot underestimate the decisive role of leadership.

NOWHERE TO HIDE: TRANSPARENT LEADERSHIP?

> The currency of leadership is transparency.
>
> *Howard Schultz*[89]

Poignant words at a time when powerful corporations are being forced to reveal all by governments, NGOs, and investigative media. Global giants Starbucks, Google, and Apple have been investigated for tax evasion for having 'legally' avoided paying their taxes by funneling revenues to establishments in low tax countries. In 2014, Apple paid only €50 in taxes for every million euros in profit and has been ordered to repay 10 years of back taxes amounting to €13 billion. Similarly, Google paid €28.6 million tax in Ireland, only a miniscule 0.16 percent of its total 2014 revenues of €18 billion.[90] Such questionable practices deepen the lack of trust in business, raise ethical questions, and overshadow other achievements. Take Coca-Cola as an example.

In 2016, Coca-Cola announced that it had achieved its goal of 100 percent water replenishment globally, one important step toward fulfilling its sustainability commitment on Water Stewardship.[91] However, the same company was slammed for funding research to deflect criticism about the role of sugary beverages in contributing to obesity. To provide a scientific façade to its activities and to promote its message about the need for exercise as the solution, Coca-Cola 'donated' US$1.5 million to start a new non-profit group, Global Energy Balance Network, and funded research scientists (to the tune of US$4 million) who have been influential in formulation of US federal guidelines on physical activity.[92] After the news broke, CEO Muhtar Kent promised more transparency in the future and the company website outlines corrective measures[93] but such inconsistencies are stark. To think that had it not been caught, Coca-Cola would have continued unabated is not implausible and undermines trust for the organization despite its other accomplishments. On another occasion, Kent himself asserted the need to be authentic, an ironic reminder to his and other organizations today, "No longer is it enough to make a good product. You have to make a product that fulfills more than just one expectation from you as a company. You need to be in line with what they expect your character to be."[94]

Then there is the ongoing investigation of Wells Fargo, one of the oldest banks in the United States that has recently come under fire for reportedly pushing the limits on cross-sell, forcing employees to sell as many as eight financial products to consumers regardless of whether they needed those or not. Pressured to meet company targets, employees reportedly created more than two million bogus accounts without customer consent. Wells Fargo has been fined a combined total of US$185 million and the bank has fired 5,300 employees. Senator Elizabeth Warren took a tough stance on the issue, calling out the CEO John Stumpf for his "gutless leadership," for not having made any of the tough changes—resigning, returning his earnings at the time the scandal was ongoing, scapegoating low-level employees, or making any changes in executive management.[95] Former employees have said that contrary to company statements, management was fully aware of the extent of deceptive practices and would reprimand employees that fell short of company targets.[96]

Soon after the news of the fraud broke, Twitterverse was abuzz with largely negative mentions of Wells Fargo, going quickly from a daily average of 24 percent positive and 31 percent negative to only three percent positive and 74 percent negative.[97] Using hashtag #WellsFargo, different groups voiced their opinion of the bank's toxic culture, support for harsher penalties, called on customers to take their business elsewhere, posted clips from the Senate Committee hearing, and pictures of graffiti around the bank's ATM locations. The company announced that Stumpf will forfeit US$41 million in stock awards and bonuses for 2016, furthering intensifying the demand for his resignation. Soon after, Stumpf resigned.

What should we make of these developments? An article in The Economist titled 'The Openness Revolution' prophesizes that the days of opacity and secrecy are over, and aside from some exceptions ("the world is still full of murky shell companies"), predicts that "…change is coming, like it or not."[98] Companies and their leadership need to adapt to this changing environment of higher expectations and scrutiny, what is called a VUCA (volatile, uncertain, complex, and ambiguous) world. Leading in a VUCA world requires courage and creativity.

Take the case of outdoor clothing company—Patagonia—that has been radical in its approach to engage and lead. With a company mission to "Build the best product, cause no unnecessary harm, use business to inspire and implement solutions to the environmental crisis," activism is not antithetical to the firm. In 2011, Patagonia issued a full-page advertisement in The New York Times on Black Friday (the biggest shopping day in the United States) asking consumers to not buy the company's clothes ("Don't buy this jacket") and to consider the environmental cost of their consumption patterns and decisions.[99] Sounds counterintuitive? Patagonia acknowledged that its action "to do the opposite of every other business today" was driven by a concern for the bigger picture, the sustainability of business and the planet.[100] The message guided consumers to join the Common Threads Initiative to together change consumption patterns and lower the environmental footprint.

The brand is unconventional in other ways. When audits revealed that Patagonia's suppliers in Taiwan were subjecting migrant workers to deplorable working conditions and charging hefty fee in exchange for a factory job,[101] they quickly took action to assess the problem and develop new standards for migrant workers. More important, instead of trying to cover up the problem, Patagonia openly communicated about the issue on its blog[102] and urged customers to "to promote not the action we took, but what caused us to make that action."[103] Patagonia's commitment to its mission and to be transparent is recognized in the apparel industry and among global sustainable brands.[104] Patagonia also a certified B-Corp, a growing movement of for-profit organizations combining purpose and stakeholder orientation.[105]

Specific cases aside, as we look toward social media to potential thwart irresponsible leadership, and reward responsible business practice, we need to develop more sophisticated explanations of transparency in the digital age. Of course, digitally propelled transparency is not a new idea. Studies of CSR reporting in Web 1.0 era were undergirded by the assumption that the Internet (and social, more so) affords an accurate look inside the organization and therefore stymie irresponsible behavior. Is it really that simple? A critical perspective on this issue will tell us that more visibility and/or information does not equal transparency, the sine qua non of CSR. Conflating information and transparency assumes "a simplistic communication model according to which senders [organizations] are compliant information providers, messages are clear and self-evident, and receivers [communication audiences] are consistently interested and involved."[106]

The Internet can create a "psuedo-panopticon"[107] that promotes an illusion of transparency and suspends criticism of corporate claim based on the (misguided) assumption about the power of the Internet to expose wrongdoing. Breaking out of this panopticon requires stakeholders to be active evaluators of CSR information, asking the tough questions, probing organizations for relevant information, and holding them accountable, which requires a high level of (social) media literacy. A combination of stakeholder pressure and interest along with bold leaders who are willing to challenge 'business as usual' is crucial for CSR to remain relevant. Whether social media will provide the much-needed tipping point for this change remains to be seen.

In conclusion, this chapter has discussed the need to refocus attention on CSR or sustainability, mapped key developments in this realm including the ways in which social media are used for CSR, how stakeholders are influencing CSR via social media, and how business confronts heightened scrutiny of its practices, leadership, and ethics in the digital age.

It is clear that CSR or sustainability in the digital age is about emerging from silos and adapting to changing expectations and environments; aligning communication objectives with business strategy; situating brand purpose, leadership, trust, and ethics, center stage; and collaborating with multiple actors to accomplish long-term societal goals.

Chapter Highlights

1. CSR is understood and conceptualized differently across organizations and contexts.
2. A growing spate of business scandals and changing stakeholder expectations have put CSR and/or sustainability firmly on the corporate agenda.
3. Many businesses are aligning with the UN 2030 sustainable development agenda as a way to contribute long-term solutions to societal problems.
4. CSR communication is central to how organizations give meaning to CSR and involve stakeholders in the process. Social media amplify the co-creation and collaboration opportunities for business to 'take people along' in the CSR journey.
5. Organizations are increasingly integrating CSR in their business strategy and/or (re)defining brand purpose in terms of sustainability. In this way, CSR is not detached from business (as its roots suggest) but very much part of how organizations see their role as institutional actors.
6. CSR dialogue is purported to be the defining feature of social media; however, translating dialogue into practice has its challenges, key being the perceived loss of control over CSR conversations.

7. Organizations need to contend with growing stakeholder influence, activism, and demand for transparency. The evolving consumer landscape is, by no means, universal or conclusive, but it can be harnessed as an opportunity if organizations understand and prepare for the risks (e.g., negative exposure).
8. Formally organized or small, marginalized groups, now have the potential to call out powerful corporations on their claims. Social media offer a potential equalizing platform for fringe groups to make themselves noticed and heard.
9. CSR communication via social media can be a reputation enhancer or risk, what has been called the 'wild west' of CSR communication. For the majority, such efforts are in an experimental phase confined to replicating one-way communication. Yet, the illustrative cases show the emergent and innovative ways in which a small handful are leading the way in this space.
10. The role, vision, and support of leadership cannot be underestimated as the crucial driver for embedding CSR in organizational culture. However, the digital age requires leaders to, more than ever, lead by example.
11. Leaders are also responsible for creating an ethical culture. Although social media might not prevent unethical cultures, they can act as a deterrent creating a downward reputation spiral when organizations are caught.
12. Although these terms—visibility and information, and transparency—are often conflated, they are not the same. Assuming that the Internet (and social media) will automatically reduce incidents of whitewash and greenwash creates a false sense of comfort and makes audiences less critical of what companies report.

Activities

1. CSR and/or sustainability have different meanings across organizations and cultural contexts. Examine the different ways in which organizations construct their understanding of CSR across industry/business sector and at the national level. What patterns do you find and what explanations can you offer?
2. In groups, conduct an in-depth case or comparative study of how organizations use social media for CSR communication. Which are the most commonly used social networks; for what purposes are they used; what kinds of conversations can you find; what is missing? In what way do these organizations engage their stakeholders; who are they speaking with?
3. Repeat the same exercise for non-profit and non-government organizations. Compare results.
4. NGOs have also become active users of social media, and they too need to be cognizant of their reputation and legitimacy in the eyes of their supporters and stakeholders, implying that they are also subject to scrutiny and critique. Research how NPOs seek to establish and maintain their legitimacy in social media especially in a crisis.
5. Identify a specific social issue (e.g., refugee crisis in Europe; humanitarian disasters; nutrition) and investigate the rhetorical communication strategies employed. What kinds of stories, narratives, symbols, and visuals are used? How does the nature of the issue influence the possibilities for communication?
6. A large part of the optimism around social media comes from their dialogic potential. However, few organizations are able to realize these benefits. Conduct research to identify and assess the presence, forms, and outcomes of dialogue. Reflect on the process of conducting such research. What challenges did you encounter that might explain the state of CSR dialogue in social media?

7. An outcome of social media is the propensity for digital activism, whether consumer or NGO. Review cases where NGOs have used social media to influence change in business practice. What strategies did they use and what outcomes did they achieve (or not)? Based on the analysis, create a framework of NGO influence in a social-mediated environment.

8. Transnational frameworks such as the UN SDGs offer a guiding framework and a common language around sustainability. As organizations align themselves with such initiatives, they face the paradox of becoming more similar than different. If CSR is a reputation enhancer and a source of differentiator, how are organizations making efforts to be unique while being similar. Examine this paradox by looking at different sources of communication—sustainability reports, website, and social networks.

9. Surveys find that Twitter and Facebook have dominated most organizational communication including sustainability communication. So far, YouTube is underused but growing in prominence as a medium for storytelling. Select examples of companies that have YouTube channels for CSR, and examine how they leverage YouTube for their sustainability communication? As a second step, compare their communication across different media.

10. Taking a cue from Patagonia's candid communication around migrant labor, analyze how other organizations deal with controversial issues? How do they conduct 'difficult conversations' on these issues, be it on their website or social channels?

Discussion Questions

1. Are social media an appropriate avenue for CSR (communication)? What, if anything, do they allow organizations to do that was not possible before? Explain your point of view.

2. What does digital activism imply for organizational efforts to be socially responsible and to derive reputational gains from CSR?

3. With social media and its assumed scrutiny on corporate behavior, it is ever more challenging for organizations to please all stakeholders. What advise can you give to organizations looking to establish trustworthy relationships with their stakeholders?

4. Although all organizations would like to build CSR reputation via social media, the results may differ. Using a specific example, argue your perspective on what makes social media an '(un)equal opportunity' platform? What considerations determine differential outcomes?

5. Critically reflect on the argument for CSR as a driver of employee engagement. Using relevant examples, argue your position on the conditions that are necessary for CSR to become embedded in corporate culture, and the approaches and challenges of employee engagement in CSR.

6. Is the ethical consumer a myth? Millennials are seen as a conscience driver but the results are far from universal or conclusive. Based on a small survey or relevant examples, share your perspective on the role of the consumer in advancing CSR. Do cultural differences matter?

7. The chapter identifies facilitators and constraints for social-mediated CSR dialogue. Some of these constraints challenge organizational 'control' of the CSR agenda. How might organizations overcome these limitations while mitigating risk?

8. Who do you consider model leaders in sustainability? Why? What makes their leadership exemplary and what can others learn from their experiences?

APPENDIX A

DO SOCIAL MEDIA MATTER FOR CSR, AND HOW?

The 2015 Cone Communications/Ebiquity Global CSR Study[108] finds that social media are leading the CSR conversation as consumers seek to speak directly and engage with companies on CSR issues, especially in developing countries.

- 34 percent share positive information about companies and issues.
- 30 percent learn more about companies or issues.
- 25 percent share negative information.

The 6th Annual Social Media Sustainability Index 2015[109] finds that companies using social media for sustainability communication have more than doubled since 2011 (283 in 2015 vs 120 in 2011).

- 4x companies with sustainability reports on social media (15 in 2010 vs 64 in 2015).
- Twitter is the most preferred network.
- The United States and Europe lead this space.
- By category, industrials are the most active followed by consumer goods, food and beverage, and financial services. The auto sector is found lagging.

2014 Lundquist CSR Online Awards Survey[110] in the European context finds similar support for social media with some differing insights:

- LinkedIn most preferred by both corporate and non-corporate stakeholder groups.
- Common uses include sharing news, following experts, staying updated, and commenting on relevant topics.
- Willingness to follow and engage with CSR expert (76%), NGO (61%), company (60%), and CR manager (7%) in that order.
- High interest in CSR case studies (including video cases), updates on CR initiatives, and responses to stakeholder questions. High skepticism for companies that only show themselves in positive light.

APPENDIX B
CASE

VOLKSWAGEN DIESELGATE

News broke on September 18, 2015, that global automaker Volkswagen (VW) had intentionally installed 'defeat devices' (software) in some of its diesel cars in order to cheat on emissions tests.[111] These devices were able to detect when the engines were being tested and changed the performance during tests in order to improve results. An investigation by the United States Environmental Protection Agency (US EPA) reported that affected cars performed flawlessly during tests, but emitted almost 40 times more than the permissible (US) levels of nitrogen oxide on the road.

The defeat devices were first found in 2009–2015, VW and Audi diesel cars that were equipped with 2.0-liter engines, affecting around 499,000 vehicles.[112] On September 22, four days after the EPA's revelation, VW stated that the defeat devices were installed in 11 million cars sold in the United States and Europe.[113] Around 500,000 VW vehicles are affected in the United States and 8.5 million in Europe.[114] On November 2, 2015, the EPA stated that the cheat software had also been found in 3.0-liter engines of diesel cars of brands under VW Group: Audi and Porsche. On November 19, 2015, VW confessed that the defeat devices were installed in all of its US 3.0-liter diesel models since 2009.[115]

As the scandal has unfolded, its organizational, consumer, national, and regulatory ramifications have pointed to systemic issues. The scale of fraud has placed business ethics at the center of attention. Before the crisis, VW stood for a trustworthy brand that ordinary families and business executives could depend on, backed by that the company's promise to deliver 'innovative, responsible mobility to people worldwide' ambition to become the world's economically and ecologically leading carmaker by 2018.[116]

VW suffered its worst-ever annual loss of €1.58 billion in 2015.[117] VW shares dropped by 19 percent on Monday following the revelation and the stock had lost 30 percent within four days.[118] VW has recalled millions of cars worldwide and set aside US$18.32 billion to cover the costs of the scandal's aftermath.[119] As part of the US settlement in court, VW must buy back or repair the affected cars by December 2018.[120] It is yet unknown whether VW will face similar charges in Europe. So far, the company has not offered to buy back cars of European customers affected by defeat devices.[121] Volkswagen sold 9.9 million vehicles in 2015, 2 percent fewer than in 2014.[122] Aside from financial loss for the company, the dieselgate also brought forth questions regarding the company's business culture and ethics.

On September 23, 2015, five days after the scandal was brought to light, Martin Winterkorn, then CEO of VW AG, said to be innocent from any wrongdoing, announced his resignation. Winterkorn was replaced by Matthias Müller, another VW veteran. Since then, the head of VW's American operation Martin Horn stepped down, and several high-ranking executives have been suspended.[123] Like Winterkorn, Horn had testified in October 2015, that he had no knowledge of the defeat devices and shifted the blame to "a couple of software engineers who put this in for whatever reason."[124]

As the enquiry progressed, several reports confirmed that the deception was systemic and not an isolated incident.

A deeper look: The first signs of the fraudulent software were found in 2014 by auto researchers from a non-profit group (International Council on Clean Transportation) that stumbled on strange test results by accident.[125] US regulators raised concerns about the emissions levels of VW in 2014, but these allegations were dismissed by the company as "technical issues" and "unexpected" conditions in the real world versus conditions in laboratories.[126] The decision to install the defeat devices was made a decade earlier when VW employees realized that they could not legally meet US standards for clean air.[127] The defeat devices were created to recognize when the vehicles were driving under controlled laboratory conditions, which typically involve drives on a stationary test rig, after which the device would start a safety mode in which the engine would run below its normal capacity. On normal roads again, the engines reverted back to its normal mode which emitted far more pollutants than was allowed in the United States. In comparison with petrol cars, diesel car fumes are known to contain higher levels of nitrogen oxides and dioxides, which are pollutants linked to harmful health conditions, such as lung diseases, increased heart attacks and strokes.

In the years following the installation of the defeat devices, several high-ranking executives of the company were informed about the software, but the extent of who knew remains a mystery. In May 2014, a memo was sent to the then CEO Martin Winterkorn, highlighting concerns over the discrepancy in test results of diesel cars on the road and in laboratory settings.[128] VW stated that the memo landed in the CEO's "extensive weekend mail" but did not disclose information on who the sender was and whether Winterkorn actually opened the email.[129] VW stated that Winterkorn was later informed again about the problem in November 2014, and was told that fixing the issue in the United States would cost roughly US$21.7 million.[130] The company said that the defeat devices were treated as one of the many product issues that VW was facing and that the diesel problem initially did not garner much attention at all at management level. In August 2015, VW technicians informed a board member that the cars were equipped with illegal defeat devices in order to make the cars seem greener than they actually are and to mislead regulators. Still, the company did not come clean until the revelation made by the EPA in September 2015.

In December 2015, VW Chairman Hans Dieter Pötsch stated that the defeat devices were the result of "a chain of errors" at the company, and that the fault lies within the company as a whole rather than a group of engineers.[131] VW further stated that only a small number of people were actively involved in the design and installment of the deceptive software, but systematic issues within the company enabled the deception to continue. Significant among these was a management style that perpetuated a culture of fear in which confessions of wrongdoing were met with fearsome words or severance.[132] One week after the news of the scandal, Bernd Osterloh, a member of VW's supervisory board, wrote a letter to the staff of VW: "We need in future a climate in which problems aren't hidden but can be openly communicated to superiors. We need a culture in which it's possible and permissible to argue with your superior about the best way to go."[133]

Reactions and response: A flurry of reactions ensued. VW's reputation has taken a beating, dropping from the top 20 in past years to 123 among the top 100 most reputable firms (RepTrak 2016). Ten days after dieselgate, VW's brand value dropped from US$31 billion to US$21 billion, according to Brand Finance.[134]

The news about the diesel scandal caused an uproar in social media. From 53,000 tweets on September 18, the numbers spiraled to 1.3 million tweets in the following week, averaging more than 8,000 new tweets per hour.[135] Before the scandal, there was an average of 10,000 tweets per day that discussed VW. Soon after the revelation and at the peak of the crisis, the number surged to 100,000 tweets per day, using hashtags #vw, #vwscandal, #BuyBackMyTDI, #VWGate, and #VWCares. Many tweeters were disappointed in VW and felt deceived for having brought into the company's false claims of environmental friendliness.

Numerous angry comments appeared on the Facebook page of VW and on other online outlets where customers and dealers took to social media to express their sentiment: "As a someone who has owned, driven and loved Volkswagens for more than 40 years, because of your criminal actions, I will probably NEVER buy another. #BoycottVW Shame on you."[136] A user on the Volkswagen Owner's Club forum, said: "I can't believe Volkswagen pulled this stunt. Very disappointed."[137]

Other companies leaned in to benefit from VW's woes. On Facebook, budget airline Ryan Air promoted winter/holiday fares "with Europe's greenest, cleanest airline." Below the post, the company posted its logo with the tagline *Das Flugzeug* [The Aeroplane], a satirical play on VW's advertising slogan (Das Auto).[138] Greenpeace Deutschland republished a YouTube video that welcomed VW back to the dark side.[139] Germany's biggest news magazines had taken on VW's famous "Das Auto" ad slogan and changed it to "The Suicide" (*Der Spiegel*), "The Drama" (Focus), and "The Lie" (Wirtschaftswoche).[140]

The impact of the crisis is not limited to the organization and its immediate environment. The company employs 50 percent of the 120,000 residents in the city of Wolfsburg, who fear for their livelihood.[141] Although the early pronouncements of the drastic impact on Germany's reputation have now mellowed, the German Chancellor Angela Merkel called for full disclosure while noting that "…the reputation of German industry... is not so shaken that we are no longer considered a good place to do business."[142] Comparisons with previous auto crises—Toyota and General Motors in particular—were rife.[143] Toyota's unintended acceleration problem and GM's faulty ignition posed serious public safety problems (even accidents and deaths in the latter case), and they both suffered financial and reputation loss for not doing enough to address product defects. However, VW's case is worse because of the intentional cheating and attempt to mislead regulators, government, and publics, coupled with the company's past claims of being green. In its 2014 sustainability report, VW pledged that by 2018 it would become "the world's most environmentally compatible automaker," and "The Volkswagen Group has a long tradition of resolute commitment to environmental protection." Citing the breach of trust, Linda Greer, director of the Natural Resources Defense Council's (NRDC) health and environment program, noted that "knowing what we now know, every other sentence [in the sustainability report] is cringe worthy."[144]

VW's first social media response came four days after the deception was made public, on September 22, with a video[145] by former CEO Winterkorn in which he promised swift action to get to the root of the matter (chalking up the issue to the actions of a few) and cooperate with relevant government authorities. Expressing remorse "I am deeply sorry that we have broken this trust," Winterkorn addressed multiple audiences including VW employees, and promised to do "everything necessary to win back your trust, step-by-step." The VW Twitter accounts in the United States remained silent for a week until a statement from Michael Horn, CEO of VW USA, broke the silence while denying personal wrongdoing: "We've totally screwed up. Our company was dishonest with the EPA, and the California Air Resources Board and with all of you.[146] The VW social media accounts were further used to apologize to the public, and employees and long-time owners have stepped in to support VW through the crisis.[147]

Looking ahead: Following the confession of the fraudulent devices, the company had to halt the selling of diesel cars in the United States.[148] The diesel market in the United States has taken a hard hit due to the dieselgate. Before the reveal of dieselgate, diesel sales accounted for almost a quarter of the VW brand sales in the United States. A VW spokesperson stated that the company does "not expect diesel to return to the U.S. with the same significance."[149] In the coming years, the number one priority for VW is to regain the trust of customers and to take correction action.[150] In the European Union, VW has already registered an upswing sales in 2016 although the group's market share has dropped from 26.1 to 25.2 percent.[151] How the company fares in terms of restoring trust and reputation remains to be seen.

Going forward, changes in emission testing methods are expected to include outside road conditions and third-party verification. The exact outcome for VW is yet to be determined as the company still faces further lawsuits from several US states and the Justice Department criminal Investigation. The crisis has also spurred on a bigger debate regarding the effectiveness of the current regulation system now that it is found that test results cannot always be trusted. From 2019, the European Union will include real world driving conditions for emission tests thereby setting stricter standards into place by 2020.[152]

Voices from the Field
by Truus Huisman (TH) and Susanne Stormer (SS)

1. **In the contemporary business landscape, what are the most critical drivers for CSR and/or sustainability?**

TH: For Unilever, the key driver for our Sustainable Living Plan was our insight that the world is reaching its planetary and societal limits:

- Nearly 800 million people are without access to safe drinking water and over 2 billion without access to proper sanitation.
- More than 2 million children die each year from preventable diarrheal disease.
- 1 in 10 adults is obese while almost 1 billion go hungry.
- Climate change is causing extreme weather conditions and changes to the seasons.
- Over a billion people live in water-scarce areas.
- Demand for food is increasing to feed a growing population.
- 767 million live in extreme poverty, subsisting on less than US$1.90 per day.

Governments struggle to agree and implement global solutions on climate change and human development. At Unilever, we believe the world cannot wait, the urgency is now, and that business and brands have to be part of the solution.

Our sustainability strategy is firmly embedded in the business case. To help capture the ways in which sustainability contributes to our business success, we have developed this simple four-point framework:

Through more growth

Sustainability is supporting growth by deepening brand equity, driving sales, and inspiring innovation. Our Sustainable Living brands are a good example—more on those later.

Lower costs

By cutting waste and reducing use of energy, raw materials, and natural resources, we create efficiencies and cut costs. Cost avoidance ultimately helps to improve our margins. We have achieved cumulative cost avoidance of over €600 million through eco-efficiency in our factories since 2008.

Less risk

Sustainable ways of doing business help us mitigate risk across our operations. Operating sustainably helps us to future proof our supply chain against the risks associated with climate change and long-term sourcing of raw materials.

More trust

Placing sustainability at the heart of our business model strengthens our relationships with stakeholders and helps us succeed as a business. It helps us maintain our value and relevance to consumers, whilst inspiring Unilever's current and future employees. Unilever is named number one employer in 34 countries.

SS: Novo Nordisk is an innovations-based pharmaceutical company, and the journey for a successful new product takes 10–13 years from early discovery till it is available for patients. It means that the products we develop must match patients' needs several years out in the future and that grooms us for a long-term perspective.

This goes well hand in hand with our Triple Bottom Line business principle which is anchored in the company bylaws and in the company's values-based management system, the Novo Nordisk Way. It obliges everyone to always make an effort to conduct our activities in a financially, environmentally, and socially responsible way.

I consider it business critical to be able to understand the needs and expectations of stakeholders in a long-term perspective. Not only regarding the products we offer but also when it comes to broader societal expectations, such as how prices are determined and local value creation through local production.

Another business critical factor is the ability to attract the right talent to the company. Although we are facing challenging times at the moment, we still expect to hire many new people over the coming years and in order to attract the right people we need to understand what motivates people. Research has shown that in particular, Millennials want to work for a company that serves a bigger societal purpose, so here I believe that our Triple Bottom Line can be an important company differentiator.

At a global level, I think a critical driver for sustainability will be to link the Global Goals and business priorities. The Global Goals are important for Novo Nordisk, not least because non-communicable diseases, including diabetes, are explicitly mentioned in the goal to provide 'health and well-being for all, of all ages.'

More than ever, I think it is important to demonstrate that 'business' and 'sustainability' are not opposites because it is exactly through our business we can contribute to more sustainable development. And the Global Goals give us a platform from which we can engage local, national, and international stakeholders in discussions on diabetes, and sustainable development as well as on many other topics on our agenda.

2. **Where do new and social media fit in your business strategy as it relates to sustainability? Please share some highlights/specific examples.**

TH: Social media is a powerful way for us to communicate about our Sustainable Living Plan to our internal and external stakeholders. We aim to report transparently on our Sustainable Living Plan progress and social media allows us to provide this in an accessible way. We fundamentally reviewed our website to serve our stakeholders better. We have used a digital platform—the Sustainable Living Lab—to engage our stakeholders on the big challenges we are facing. Toward our internal stakeholders, we developed a bright future in Action Digital Employee Engagement Platform where we used a combination of gaming and active participation to develop solutions.

SS: Novo Nordisk has a long tradition of building and maintaining good relations with our stakeholders and I believe we can use new and social media as a strategic tool to engage more effectively with our stakeholders.

To ensure long-term business success, it is essential that we identify and understand the priorities and perceptions of key stakeholders and take these into account when we shape our business priorities and activities.

Social media have certainly opened up for many new ways to connect with our stakeholders. When you sit in a headquarter staff function, you can sometimes feel a little bit far away from the end user, that is, the patient. One way, we have used social media to engage with patients is through a Twitter chat that we organized last year in collaboration with our Digital Team and Patient Partnering Unit. The purpose was to address myths around diabetes, particularly around the difference between type 1 and 2, and engage in an online conversation with patients about the way we think and talk about diabetes. We invited two online influencers in as panelists—Kelly Close, type 1 and founder, and Chair of the Board of The diaTribe Foundation and Phyllisa Deroze, type 2 blogger at www.diagnosedNOTdefeated.com —and we managed to get a lot of engagement from users and some good insights to take back to the organization. This was the first time we did a Twitter chat like that but hopefully not the last!

3. **What do you perceive to be the biggest (a) opportunities and (b) risks of new media for business–society relations? How do you prepare to leverage the opportunities and mitigate the risks?**

   TH: Social media's strength is that it allows us to engage all stakeholders in an authentic, real-time way and gives us the ability to invite everyone to join us in our movement to make Sustainable Living common place. Social media can also be a tremendous bottom-up power to create a better future. Of course, there are risks too as social media tends to polarize and has the potential to amplify rapidly, also in the case of wrong conclusions or unfounded opinions. The way to mitigate is a combination of being well prepared on potential risks, for example, through simulations, and have an 'always-on' social media monitoring in place. Organizations that are guided by their purpose will in general find it easier to engage stakeholders via social media and manage the risks associated with it.

   SS: When you work in a highly regulated industry like the pharmaceutical industry, you have to be mindful of formal requirements. For example, we are not allowed to talk about our products on social media, which is very different from the way most other companies operate.

   Of course, there are risks associated with new media. Social media is a place where people often exchange very critical views and conflicts can escalate quickly. Here, everyone has the opportunity to create their own reality which may not always be rooted in actual facts—which is very different from the way we operate as a science-based company.

   However, I believe that the benefits outweigh the risks. In Novo Nordisk, we have social media guidelines that we need to follow and a digital team to assist us. I don't believe that a company should be too restrictive about how employees can behave online and, for example, not allow people to access social media at work.

   We are more than 40,000 people working at Novo Nordisk which means that we have 40,000 potential ambassadors. Having them speak up is truly a fantastic way to multiply a company's reach in a very authentic way.

   For example, when our CEO, Lars Rebien Sørensen was named the 'best-performing CEO' by *Harvard Business Review* last year, this was one of the most shared stories by our employees on social media. The fact that colleagues feel proud about this recognition and want to share it in their networks can be worth a lot more than traditional employer branding.

4. **Much CSR scholarship points to the immense dialogic potential of social media especially for stakeholder engagement, involvement, and feedback ... yet many organizations are hesitant to get onboard. What is your perspective and practice (including 'ground rules') regarding dialogue and engagement with stakeholders?**

   TH: Social media is deeply embedded in today's society. Not getting onboard or delaying is not really an option, as social media is becoming so powerful from a communications' perspective. In today's ultra-transparent world, it is no longer possible to hide, if ever this was possible in the past.

Businesses need to be committed to transparency, which coupled with a clearly articulated purpose, strategy and commitment to honesty will enable businesses to build relationships of trust. Yet, it is important to be prepared for potential issues, and also ensure you have the capacity and resources to deal with comments, feedback and suggestions. Once you are part of the social media dialogue, it is not easy or even impossible to leave. So it is a key to understand what it is you are trying to achieve and understand what the resource implications are. Furthermore, with boundaries between personal and professional life fading on social media, it is critical that everyone in the organization understands the implications of social media. Organizations should, therefore, have a set of guidelines in place, which explains the policy but also makes it clear that certain areas belong to business confidential information and that sharing this can have big implications for the organization and the individual involved.

SS: We consider social media to be an effective way to have conversations with stakeholders about what interests them. In that regard, social media are a proxy for face-to-face communication, which is always to be preferred, particularly when you are talking about important matters. And, just like in face-to-face communication there are ground rules. For us, number one is: treat everyone with respect. That means listen actively to what others say, try to understand what they mean and what they expect of you, and then respond, with facts, in your personal voice and always politely.

5. **Using new media, activists and/or marginalized stakeholder groups can now organize to influence change in business practices, and such opposition often transcends geographic boundaries. How do you respond to such possibilities? In what way is this response different from how you may have addressed the issue before?**

TH: Indeed, national issues no longer exist as today's society is hyper-connected and fast moving in real time, giving everyone a voice. The only way to deal with this is to build trust with wide group of stakeholders, communicate how you tackle the big challenges which are material for you, share your counter arguments in an accessible way where this matters, and be transparent on progress or lack of it. Although this is by no way a guarantee that this prevents such opposition, it might mitigate it, provided your communication shows you understand the problem and shows what you have done or what the limits of your actions are.

SS: New media can help us identify emerging trends and better understand what stakeholders expect of us, for example, when it comes to our business model. I think there can be tensions between us as a pharmaceutical company and groups in society who are critical of our business model. I acknowledge that we could be better at explaining why we value our products the way we do and communicating the long-term value to society that we provide.

I believe digital connectivity and social media have also made it more challenging to maneuver due to the vast amount of information exchange. We do our best to respond to the stakeholder inquiries that we get from all over the world via emails, social media, or our website, so that we ensure a two-way dialogue—and you can rest assured that it is always a person answering, not a robot—but it is of course not always that we can accommodate all wishes.

6. **In what way does new media facilitate and constrain corporate efforts to build CSR reputation?**

TH: For Unilever, this is not about CSR reputation, it is about business, as our Sustainable Living Plan and purpose are part of our business model. Social media allows us to engage with a broad audience, including people who are also our consumers. This enables us to create a movement for sustainable growth. It does require a powerful communication approach, as the new media often leaves minimal or no time for nuance or depth. Obviously, the new media will expose businesses that see CSR as a 'nice-to-do' when the times are good. The new media will relentlessly hold business accountable for inconsistencies between what they say and what they do.

SS: New media can definitely facilitate both faster and more interactive ways to build reputation. One example is through Twitter. Back in 2011, we launched a Novo Nordisk Twitter account dedicated to sustainability—@NovoNordiskTBL—which is short for Triple Bottom Line. We use it to share stories and learnings and to stay updated on interesting reads, events, and trends within the field.

I personally joined Twitter in 2012 and I really enjoy using it, but I have to admit that I am active on and off. However, I think it is a fantastic way to connect with people both in and outside the sustainability community and take part in conversations at different events that I attend.

Again, there is of course the risk is that you can be misunderstood—especially when your communication is restricted to 140 characters—but I still believe it primarily strengthens our ability to build trust and reputation.

7. **Organizations communicating their societal commitments have to contend with a 'Catch-22' situation and, often, complete skepticism. How does your organization ensure that stakeholders perceive communication as credible, honest, and transparent?**

TH: In today's ultra-transparent world, any communication from business needs to be consistent, authentic, and clearly linked to its purpose and strategy. Actions will speak louder than words, and will need to demonstrate what business is doing to make a net positive contribution to tackle some of the world biggest challenges. Expectations of business have moved from 'do no harm,' 'shared value' to 'net positive impact.' Research shows that stakeholders and people in general, value the contribution business can make and indeed is making. They also understand the size of the challenges and that business alone cannot solve this.

SS: I believe that organizations in general could become better at explaining how doing business generates value beyond profits. We have an obligation to consider the best interests of shareholders and obviously that includes generating revenue, dividends, and share value. But the way we earn our money matters a lot. In Novo Nordisk, we choose to be responsible because it is the right thing to do and because we are convinced it is right for our long-term business success. I often say that I am not here to save the world but to save Novo Nordisk in the world!

A very simple way to build a stronger and more authentic relationship with our stakeholders is by employees telling small stories about their day, an event, or a colleague's achievement. These stories become vital to showcase who we are, what we do, and why we are committed.

For example, a few years back we created an online sustainability magazine, *TBL Quarterly*. It conveys the actions, challenges, and opportunities of striving to be a sustainable business using a storytelling format. Each issue offers articles, photos, videos, and infographics that can be shared on multiple online platforms.

Another way we are doing it is to increasingly invite external voices into the magazine, so it is not just Novo Nordisk talking about Novo Nordisk. We would also like to address some of the more difficult issues and dilemmas that exist in our industry but could probably do it to a higher degree than we do today.

8. **How do you assess 'success' of your social-mediated efforts?**

TH: Our measurement metrics include outcome KPIs [Key Performance Indicators] that cover both our internal and external audiences. It includes recognition by KOFs for the work we are doing to drive sustainability into the business and understanding with our employees how they contribute to sustainable growth.

SS: Going digital gives us the opportunity to obtain a lot of information about how our content is consumed. Now we can track downloads, likes, shares, etc., and we do that systematically, for example, when it comes to our digital magazine *TBL Quarterly*. However, the challenge is to go from metrics to insights that can inform us about how we can work smarter and I think this is an area where there is room for improvement.

I also think it is important to consider success in both quantitative and qualitative ways. Although one of the measurements of success for our digital magazine is to maintain a high number of downloads, we might still find it more valuable that the 'right' people see and interact with our content rather than just hunt for likes! In a world full of data, we also have to be careful and not over quantify things. As human beings, we still make a lot of decisions based on emotions and gut feeling, and I would like that our communication cater to both the rational and emotional self.

9. **With respect to leadership in the domain of CSR or sustainability, does the contemporary (digital, transparent) business environment necessitate new leadership skills? Under what conditions can organizations succeed in building and strengthening their reputations as trustworthy, responsible, transparent, and authentic enterprises? Please elaborate.**

TH: Yes, the new business environment is deeply and fundamentally changing the skills, and competence requirements leadership will have to respond to. First of all, future leaders need to be familiar with system thinking and understand how 'wicked problems' can or will affect their business, and how they need to respond to this. They also need to be able to engage different stakeholders than customers, suppliers, and shareholders. Furthermore, leaders of the future will be expected to be strong communicators, as their business or organization will be judged on the authenticity and integrity of its leaders. In today's Exponential Organization world, everything will turn around digital, mixed with other technologies—not understanding this and the impact on sustainability, will no longer be an option. Finally, future leaders will be asked to show that their EQ matches their IQ in order to inspire current and future talent.

SS: I think that the use of social media can be a great way to 'humanize' an organization and to have a face and a voice behind the words. This was much more difficult in the days of print media. People are used to engaging with social media platforms privately and it comes natural to be engaged as an employee as well—both at work and outside of work.

The lines between the personal and professional have become more blurred, and although that can pose certain challenges, I also believe it holds great value. Some people would argue that you should not bring your 'non-work life' to work, but I disagree. I think this is where you can tap into people's passion, curiosity, and perseverance that make up some of the most important ingredients of our company culture. If we can bring people's passion to life at their work—whether that passion is studying molecules or finding new ways to save energy in our production facilities—then I believe you will get more motivated employees. At least that is my own personal experience.

On social media, everyone at Novo Nordisk has an opportunity to engage with people about where they work and what they do. I think there is a lot to be proud of and discuss when it comes to your work. It's valuable for Novo Nordisk's reputation and employee engagement.

10. Reflecting on your experience, what have been the positives and negatives of social-mediated presence? Going forward, what would you do differently?

TH: The positives far outweigh the negatives. The expressions of recognition—such as our leadership in the DJSI [Dow Jones Sustainability Index]—and sometimes keen support by stakeholders and the public at large have been tremendously energizing. The negatives have been triggered by our inexperience at first and therefore hesitation to communicate or communicate in an unclear way. Speed in the social media environment is critical, and therefore important that the organization is set up for this. Also, the insight that our own employees are an untapped potential, and of course sometimes risk as well, will require more thought and action. Finally, authenticity is so crucial, and it is therefore critical to review communications on social media through third parties.

SS: We have been fortunate to often be cited as a sustainability leader. That is flattering, and does indeed boost self-confidence, but it can also be delusional. That is why I always make a point of inviting critique and listening to what is really being said. Flattery will lead you nowhere. The way we communicate about sustainability is anchored in what we do, and frankly I and my team spend more time on the doing than on talking.

One thing that I have learned along the way is that in the sustainability world, we have a tendency to get caught up in abstract discussions which might not always be very productive, such as what does the 'S-word' mean. In Novo Nordisk, we have chosen to stick to the Triple Bottom Line as our common language—it's about how we do business in a way that will enable us to be a sustainable business. Some might see this as 'old-fashioned' but I think it is important to stay true to our heritage. I prefer to spend my time making actual change happen rather than discussing definitions.

11. Any other comment or question that you wish to discuss that you believe has not come up and needs to be addressed?

TH: The paradox of social media is that it connects people in a globalizing world—the opportunities to do so are fantastic. Yet, at the same time the potential of polarization and being exposed to the unique views you support through power algorithms are frightening too. This begs the question about what is the role and responsibility of business to ensure that people are exposed to all points of view? Should and can it play a role, and if business chooses to take up this role, how can it best be played?

SS: Despite the rapid technological development, I still believe the digital world cannot replace the important face-to-face engagements that I also enjoy in my work, for example, when attending workshops where I have the chance to discuss implementation of the Global Goals with industry peers or when meeting colleagues in the markets to better understand their business challenges and how I can support them. But connecting online can definitely be a great way to begin a conversation that would not have happened otherwise—and it makes it possible to work across multiple borders and time zones.

Voices from the Field: Activism in the Digital Age
by Martin Lloyd (ML)

How would you describe the role of new and social media for advocacy?

ML: New and social media are essential tools for advocacy organizations. They are not everything, but they have merged with traditional approaches to the point where it does not make a lot of sense to consider them separately.

For instance, Twitter is an essential part of any media outreach operation. So even if your focus is on placing the right stories in the right media, you'll need to be monitoring and using Twitter to ensure your point of view is well represented and picked up.

Likewise any kind of above the line communication. There's an expectation that if an organization wants my attention for something it should be providing opportunities to interact and get more information online. That could be a Facebook page, or a dense website depending on the issues involved but there's an assumption that there will be a next step available online.

In addition to supplementing/reinforcing traditional ways of working new media/social media provide unique channels for campaigning. Mailing lists, Twitter accounts and Facebook pages let organizations effectively bypass the media and share their messages directly with the target audience. For organizations with mailing lists in the millions—potentially more outreach than any given publication could provide—this is very significant and makes it possible to sustain an advocacy effort in the absence of other communications support.

Online campaigning via petitions, hashtags, crowdsourced material, or fundraising efforts are all things that would have been impossible without social media. So it effectively adds new tools to the toolbox—and one of the key qualities is that online campaigning can be extremely efficient, generating significant awareness/returns for relatively little effort.

The targets of campaigns can also be addressed directly via their own social media. This could be individual politicians or entire corporations. And because this happens in public, there's an expectation that a response will be forthcoming.

In what specific ways have you seen NGO advocacy and influence change with new media technologies? Please share some examples.

ML: First, and perhaps most importantly we've seen the emergence of advocacy groups that operate almost entirely online. Avaaz and Sum of Us are examples of this strategy. The climate advocacy group 350.org started out as an online organisation focused on building grassroots participation, and now it boasts a large number of local groups who have driven its hugely successful divestment campaign.

Within more traditional NGOs, new media has dramatically altered the costs of running some types of campaign. For instance, brand attacks, focused on tarnishing an organisation's reputation in front of a large audience have become much cheaper. Greenpeace pioneered this approach with the Green My Apple campaign, a sustained online push to persuade Apple to produce products free from toxic chemicals.[1]

[1] There's an extended case study of this campaign at http://www.greenpeace.org/international/en/news/features/greening-of-apple-310507/

Within Greenpeace, Green My Apple sparked a wave of interest, as the campaign had demonstrated that a major corporation could be moved in relatively little time (12 months), and with that, an online campaign could provide a focus point for traditional media activities and offline non-violent direct action. Subsequent campaigns addressed corporations including Unilever, Nestle, Nike, Adidas, Shell, and Procter and Gamble.

Digital campaigning also creates the possibility of a much more open campaigning approach. Sum of Us and Avaaz both poll their members regularly as part of their strategy setting process. They ask their members which issues they should be working on and how they should divide their resources. At the tactical level, crowd sourcing content has proved effective.

Greenpeace's Arctic Ready campaign asked supporters to produce their own spoofs of Shell's advertising and provided a simple online application to help them. The results were widely reported in the media.[2]

Some are skeptical of the 'power' of new media for fostering weak ties and clicktivism. How do you respond to that critique?

ML: It's true that at the heart of most campaigns you'll find a small group of activists united by strong personal ties, a shared agenda and deep commitment to the issues involved. But that doesn't mean those individuals wouldn't like to be supported by a million weak ties to people who would be prepared to do something on their behalf.

Often that something is awareness raising—turning the actions of a few into an issue of concern for millions. That activists have taken direct action or published a report may not be newsworthy in itself. That this activity has 'gone viral' might be. The media storm *Kony* 2012 attracted wasn't a result of the quality of the video; it was the result of the staggering traffic figures it generated.

There are so many issues for people to be concerned about that meaningful engagement with more than a handful of them is practically impossible. But by maintaining a weak tie with an advocacy group—for instance, liking their Facebook page—you can make yourself available to be activated when something important happens. It also provides a mechanism for you to get information when the issue becomes salient to you.

Successful campaigning and advocacy work will always require good strategy. The emergence of social media hasn't changed that. What it has done is meant that a lot of poorly thought-out campaigns that follow a strategy of "1. Gather petitions 2. ??? 3. Victory" now fail in public, potentially in front of millions, rather than dying in obscurity.

In recent years, there has definitely been an emergence of 'campaign fatigue' in the public who have been asked to care about and fight for so many different causes. This has in turn led to a more discerning public who want to be assured that their participation in a given cause will make a difference. Since that's an essential part of effective advocacy, this is probably a good thing in the long term.

How do you assess the success/effectiveness of digital activism? In what ways is it different from offline activism?

ML: The only meaningful way to measure the success of any form of activism is to ask if it achieved the change in the world it aimed at. If you campaign to protect Indonesian rain forests and they get cut down, you've lost, and no other metric will feel relevant.

[2] See Greenpeace parodies Shell with 'Arctic Ready' adverts - in pictures. (July 19, 2012). *The Guardian*. Retrieved from https://www.theguardian.com/environment/gallery/2012/jul/19/greenpeace-shell-arctic-ready-in-pictures.

But digital activism does lend itself to movement building. As the number of people you have permission to contact grows your potential for winning future campaigns increases. This is also the case for offline activism, but digital campaigning is at its core a database-driven activity. So, online activism has given organisations a chance to build their networks and establish a broader base of support than would otherwise have been possible.

One key difference between digital activism and offline activism is the lack of opportunity for direct action. Meaningful direct action online tends to involve either leaking documents (Wikileaks, Snowdon) or hacking (some anonymous activities). Both of these activities can usually only be carried out by one or two individuals who may expose themselves to significant legal risk by engaging in them. Offline non-violent direct action is frequently protected by the courts and involves relatively small legal penalties—typically for trespass. Equivalent online direct action is frequently covered by laws that could result in heavy fines or incarceration. This also makes it hard for the individuals involved to take responsibility—a key step in legitimizing an act of protest.

How do you see the future of digital advocacy? What lessons can other NGOs learn from your experience?

ML: Digital advocacy will increasingly become a normal part of what we think of as advocacy. We'll see the emergence of coalitions of NGOs who can leverage their supporter bases to put issues on the agenda and decision makers under pressure without recourse to media outlets.

I hope we'll see a profusion of tools that makes it easier for motivated individuals to start and run their own advocacy campaigns. These tools are starting to emerge, but there's a lot of scope for improvement. One of the most interesting developments is governments providing mechanisms for citizens to petition them, for example, the EU Citizen's Initiative or the UK Parliament Petition Site (https://petition.parliament.uk/).

As social networks come and go, advocacy groups will be increasingly concerned with establishing their own databases of persistent contacts. For the last 20 years, this has meant building and maintaining a database of supporter emails. But with some signs, that email is becoming less universal—particularly in Asia, this may change. However, advocacy groups will not want to invest significant effort in building networks that can vanish overnight (e.g., MySpace).

As I alluded to earlier, I think the big thing missing at the moment is an online mechanism for non-violent direct action. It might be that this can't be developed in a digital space, but I'm optimistic that someone somewhere will think of something suitably creative.

From a reputation standpoint, how do you evaluate the effectiveness of new media for digital activism campaigns?

ML: Any well planned campaign is going to be aiming to address a number of different stakeholders. You might be looking to motivate your own supporters to demonstrate that a constituency exists, or you might want to convince investors that a project is more or less risky than they originally thought. You might need to persuade individual politicians or convince their supporter base of the merits of your case.

So assessing the effectiveness of a medium first requires you to have a good understanding of why you're using it in the first place. For instance, online brand attacks often look like they're aimed at reaching large numbers of people in order to damage a brand, but their biggest effect is often on the direct employees or managers of the targeted organisation. It may not matter if a public campaign gets relatively little traction if it succeeds in making a given issue a priority for the targeted institution.

Once you know what you're trying to achieve, you can look for an appropriate metric to measure it. Sometimes that's obvious—numbers of likes, volume of media coverage, changes in opinion polling... Other times it's more complex. If an investor, regulator, or politician changes their mind about something knowing why it is hard, there are often multiple factors at play. One of the nice things about working in a large NGO that operates on a lot of campaigns over a long period is that we're often able to go back years later and talk to key players to find out what really made a difference. That kind of information is often simply not available as the decisions are being made.

What are the challenges you have faced/expect to face with advocacy? What do you need to address or prepare for these challenges?

ML: The audience fatigue I mentioned earlier is definitely a coming challenge. That will challenge NGOs to demonstrate that they are relevant and effective on an ongoing basis. Also important because the online advocacy space is becoming increasingly crowded, so standing out isn't easy.

I'm also concerned that as Facebook orients itself further toward profit making that what has been a very effective low-cost medium will become a less effective medium cost one. That's one of the reasons I think advocacy groups need to build their own 'platform-independent' means of contacting people.

And digital media has increased the expectations of transparency and openness for all parts of society, NGOs included. Supporters and other members of the public expect to be able to have meaningful exchanges with advocacy organizations 'on-demand.' Supporting and facilitating those in a way that is sustainable will be a major challenge for advocacy organizations in the future.

Any other comments?

There's often an unspoken assumption that the tools and techniques developed for online activism will only be used for good. But in recent years, we've seen the downsides of these tools emerge as well. Both in terms of added opportunities for surveillance, as exposed by the Snowden leaks, and in terms of indisputably malign organisations such as ISIS turning publicly available technologies into effective tools for pursuing their own ends.

In the future, I think it is the responsibility of all stakeholders, governments, civil society, and corporations, particularly the ones providing the platforms, to engage in an open and meaningful discussion about how we work with social media. Decisions that support corporate profits are not necessarily going to be ones that provide support for democratic institutions or the good functioning of society.

NOTES

1 Hartogs, J. (2016, April 28). *VW CEO says priority is to "regain trust" after emissions scandal*. Retrieved October 31, 2016, from http://www.cnbc.com/2016/04/28/vw-ceo-says-priority-is-to-regain-trust-after-emissionsscandal.html

2 Kent, M. (2015, August 19). Coca-Cola: We'll do Better. Retrieved May 25, 2017, from http://www.wsj.com/articles/coca-cola-well-do-better-1440024365

3 Journey Staff. (2015). Coca-Cola No. 10 on FORTUNE's 2015 list of world's most admired companies. Retrieved November 26, 2016, from http://www.coca-colacompany.com/coca-cola-unbottled/coca-cola-no-10-on-fortunes-2015-list-of-worlds-most-admired-companies

4 Friedman, M. (1970, September 13). The social responsibility of business is to increase its profits. *New York Times*, pp. 122–126. Retrieved November 26, 2016, from http://www.colorado.edu/studentgroups/libertarians/issues/friedman-soc-resp-business.html

5 van Marrewijk, M. (2003). Concepts and definitions of CSR and corporate sustainability: Between agency and communion. *Journal of Business Ethics, 44*, 95–105.

6 Ignatius, A. & McGinn, D. (Nov 2015). Novo Nordisk CEO Lars Sørensen on What Propelled Him to the Top Retrieved May 25, 2015, from https://hbr.org/2015/11/novo-nordisk-ceo-on-what-propelled-him-to-the-top

7 Carroll, A. B. (1991). The pyramid of corporate social responsibility: Toward the moral management of organizational stakeholders. *Business Horizons*, *34*, 39–48.

8 For a full version of the Companies Act, 2013, see http://www.mca.gov.in/Ministry/pdf/CompaniesAct2013.pdf

9 Definition retrieved May 25, 2017, from https://ec.europa.eu/growth/industry/corporate-social-responsibility_nl

10 Ibid.

11 According to the *Reputation Institute's* RepTrak framework and annual studies. CSR RepTrak scores reflect a firm's performance on three key dimensions: citizenship, governance, and workplace.

12 For a counter perspective, see Crane, A., Palazzo, G., Spence, L. J., & Matten, D. (2014). Contesting the value of "creating shared value." *California Management Review, 56*(2), 130–153.

13 Elkington, J. (2011, May 25). Don't abandon CSR for creating shared value just yet. *The Guardian*. Retrieved from https://www.theguardian.com/sustainable-business/sustainability-with-john-elkington/corporate-socialresposibility-creating-shared-value

14 CSR is dead! What's next? (2016, January 22). Retrieved November 26, 2016, from http://oecdinsights.org/2016/01/22/2016-csr-is-dead-whats-next/

15 Carroll, A. B. (1999). Corporate social responsibility: Evolution of a definitional construct. *Business and Society, 38*, 268–295.

16 Dahlsrud, A. (2008). How corporate social responsibility is defined: An analysis of 37 definitions. *Corporate Social Responsibility and Environmental Management, 15*, 1–13. doi:10.1002/csr.132

17 Company information retrieved November 26, 2016, from http://www.tata.com/sustainability/articlesinside/corporate-social-responsibility

18 Definition retrieved May 25, 2017, from http://www.unece.org/oes/nutshell/2004-2005/focus_sustainable_development.html

19 Definition retrieved November 26, 2016, from http://www.sustainability-indices.com/sustainability-assessment/corporate-sustainability.jsp

20 Definition retrieved November 26, 2016, from http://mvonederland.nl/dossier/definition-background

21 Porter, M. E., & Kramer, M. R. (2011). Creating shared value: How to reinvent capitalism and unleash a wave of innovation and growth. *Harvard Business Review, 89*, 62–77.

22 Reinecke, J., & Ansari, S. (2016). Taming wicked problems: The role of framing in the construction of corporate social responsibility. *Journal of Management Studies, 53*(3), 299–329. doi:10.1111/joms.12137

23 Annual Global CEO Survey. (2016). *Redefining business success in a changing world.* 19th Annual Global CEO Survey/January 2016. Retrieved November 26, 2016, from https://www.pwc.com/gx/en/ceo-survey/2016/landing-page/pwc-19th-annual-global-ceo-survey.pdf

24 IMD, & Burson-Masteller. (2015). *Keeping it real: How authentic is your corporate purpose*. Retrieved May 25, 2017, from http://powerofpurpose.burson-marsteller.com/wp-content/uploads/2015/04/Keeping-it-Real_Brochure.pdf

25 Accenture. (2016). *The UN global compact—Accenture strategy CEO study*. Retrieved November 26, 2016, from https://www.accenture.com/us-en/insight-un-global-compact-ceo-study

26 Annual Global CEO Survey (2016).

27 Retrieved May 25, 2017, from http://www.nielsen.com/ug/en/press-room/2015/consumer-goods-brands-that-demonstrate-commitment-to-sustainability-outperform.html

28 Tench, R., & Jones, B. (2015). Social media: The wild west of CSR communications. *Social Responsibility Journal, 11*(2), 290–305. Quote from p. 301. http://dx.doi.org/10.1108/SRJ-12-2012-0157

29 For example, see Chaudhri, V. (2016). Corporate social responsibility and the communication imperative: Perspectives from CSR managers. *International Journal of Business Communication, 53*(4), 419–442.

30 For example, Schultz, F., & Wehmeier, S. (2010). Institutionalization of corporate social responsibility within corporate communications. Combining institutional, sense making and communication perspectives. *Corporate Communications: An International Journal, 15*, 9–29.

31 KPMG. (2015). *Currents of change: The KPMG Survey of corporate responsibility reporting*. Retrieved May 25, 2017, from http://www.kpmg.com/CN/en/IssuesAndInsights/ArticlesPublications/Documents/kpmg-survey-of-corporateresponsibility-reporting-2015-O-201511.pdf

32 Etter, M., & Fieseler, C. (2010). On relational capital in social media. *Studies in Communication Sciences, 10*(2), 167–189.

33 PwC report retrieved May 25, 2017, from http://www.heromotocorp.com/en-in/about-us.php

34 Jha, S. (2016, July 19). How Vijay Sethi leveraged social media to increase the impact of CSR efforts at Hero Moto Corp. *ETCIO.com*. Retrieved May 25, 2017, from http://cio.economictimes.indiatimes.com/news/case-studies/how-vijay-sethi-leveraged-social-media-to-increase-the-impact-of-csr-efforts-at-hero-moto-corp/53265792

35 Ibid.

36 How Hero MotoCorp is leveraging #RideSafeIndia awareness drive via digital. (2015, October 8). Retrieved May 25, 2017, from http://lighthouseinsights.in/hero-ridesafeindia-tweetchat.html/

37 Jha (2016).

38 Ibid.

39 Xerox. (2016). *Xerox 2016 global citizenship report*. Retrieved May 25, 2017, from https://www.xerox.com/corporate-citizenship/2016/commitment/stakeholders.html

40 Case based on the following sources (Retrieved September 26, 2016):

- http://www.toms.com/corporate-responsibility
- https://www.youtube.com/watch?v=eXiQABwCD6k
- Abbott, K. (2016, February 8). *Tom's #withoutshoes campaign a #socialwin*. Retrieved from http://oustrategicsocialmedia.com/2016/02/08/toms-withoutshoes-campaign-a-socialwin/
- Chandler, I. (2016). Why TOMS shoes is the leader of conscious marketing. *Social Media Explorer*. Retrieved from https://www.socialmediaexplorer.com/content-sections/cases-and-causes/toms-shoes-leader-conscious-marketing/
- McNew, S. (2013). Social media breakdown: TOMS social media marketing. *SocialToaster*. Retrieved from http://www.socialtoaster.com/blog-entry/social-media-breakdown-toms-social-media-marketing
- Rogers, C. (2016). How footwear brand Toms engaged 3.5 million people in one day using tribe power. *Marketing Week*. Retrieved from https://www.marketingweek.com/2016/06/29/how-footwear-brand-tomsengaged-3-5-million-people-in-one-day-using-tribe-power/
- Ali, M. (2015). Toms: Using social media marketing effectively. *Social Media for Business Performance*. Retrieved from https://smbp.uwaterloo.ca/2015/11/toms-using-social-media-marketing-effectively/

41 Lebowitz, S. (2016, July 15). *The creators*. Retrieved from http://www.businessinsider.com/toms-blake-mycoskietalks-growing-a-business-while-balancing-profit-with-purpose-2016-6

42 For example, Chapin, A. (2015). TOMS shoe donations might not be doing any good. *Racked*. Retrieved September 26, 2016, from http://www.racked.com/2015/7/27/9046207/toms-shoes-charity -poverty. Also see Small, D. (2015, February 16). The one-for-one business model: Avoiding unintended consequences. Retrieved May 25, 2017, from http://knowledge.wharton.upenn.edu/article/one-one-business-model-social-impact-avoiding-unintended-consequences/

43 TOMS FAQs: http://www.toms.com/faq

44 PWC report retrieved May 25, 2017, from https://www.pwc.com/us/en/about-us/corporate-responsibility/assets/pwc-employee-engagement.pdf

45 Chaudhri, V., & Kaul, A. (2014). IBM India: 'Localizing' a global model of corporate citizenship. *Harvard Business Publishing* case study (#W14169-PDF-ENG).

46 Greenpeace blog post. Retrieved October 9, 2016, from http://www.greenpeace.org/usa/we-asked-17000-people-what-the-climate-movement-should-do-next-heres-what-you-said/
47 Adapted figure from company document: Unilever. (n.d). Inspiring sustainable living: Expert insights into consumer behavior and Unilever's five levers for change. Retrieved November 2, 2016, from https://www.unilever.com/Images/slp_5-levers-for-change_tcm13-387353_tcm244-409796_en.pdf
48 Korschun, D., & Du, S. (2013). How virtual corporate social responsibility dialogs generate value: A framework and propositions. *Journal of Business Research, 66*, 1494–1504. http://dx.doi.org/10.1016/j.jbusres.2012.09.011
49 Eberle, D., Berens, G., & Li, T. (2013). The impact of interactive corporate social responsibility communication on corporate reputation. *Journal of Business Ethics, 118*, 731–746. doi:10.1007/s10551-013-1957-y
50 Ibid.
51 Kent, M. L., & Taylor, M. (2016). From Homo Economicus to Homo Dialogicus: Rethinking social media use in CSR communication. *Public Relations Review, 42*, 60–67. http://dx.doi.org/10.1016/j.pubrev.2015.11.003
52 Brennan, N. M., Merkl-Davies, D. M., & Beelitz, A. (2013). Dialogism in corporate social responsibility communications: Conceptualising verbal interaction between organisations and their audiences. *Journal of Business Ethics, 115*, 665–679. doi:10.1007/s10551-013-1825-9
53 Lee, K., Oh, W., & Kim, N. (2013). Social media for socially responsible firms: Analysis of Fortune 500's Twitter profiles and their CSR/CSIR ratings. *Journal of Business Ethics, 118*, 791–806. doi:10.1007/s10551-013-1961-2
54 Ihlen, Ø., May, S., & Bartlett, J. (2014). Four Aces: Bringing communication perspectives to corporate social responsibility. In R. Tench, W. Sun, & B. Jones (Eds.), *Communicating corporate social responsibility: Perspectives and practice* (Critical Studies on Corporate Responsibility, Governance and Sustainability, Volume 6; pp. 25–39). http://dx.doi.org/10.1108/S2043-9059(2014)0000006023
55 Illia, L., Romenti, S., Rodrýguez-Canovas, B., Murtarelli, G., & Carroll, C. E. (2015). Exploring corporations' dialogue about CSR in the digital era. *Journal of Business Ethics* (Published Online First). doi:10.1007/s10551-015-2924-6
56 Table compiled using the following sources: Kent and Taylor (2016); Illia et al. (2015); Lane, A. B., & Bartlett, J. (2016). Why dialogic principles don't make it in practice—and what we can do about it. *International Journal of Communication, 10*, 4074–4094; Etter, M., Morsing, M., & Castello, I. (2011). *Barriers to dialogue: Organizational challenges for CSR communication in social media.* Retrieved May 25, 2017, from http://openarchive.cbs.dk/bitstream/handle/10398/8530/Michael_Etter_2_paper.pdf?sequence=1
57 Marico is among India's leading consumer goods company with an international presence in 25 countries across Asia and Africa and boasts an expansive product portfolio spanning personal care, health, and wellness brands including industry leaders such as Parachute, Saffola, and Livon (market shares of ~57%, 60%, and 79% respectively). Case information provided by the company.
58 Varshney, V. (2001). Saffola study, a marketing ploy? Retrieved October 9, 2016, from http://www.downtoearth.org.in/blog/saffola-study-a-marketing-ploy--42334
59 Quote retrieved from https://www.unilever.com/news/speeches/polman-global-citizen-festival-2015.html
60 Note that this is not an unqualified position, and, even as we laud the democratic potential of social media, contextual realities and technological constraints cannot be overlooked. For example, see van Dijck, J., & Poell, T. (2013). Understanding social media logic. *Media and Communication, 1*(1), 2–14.
61 Whelan, G., Moon, J., & Grant, B. (2013). Corporations and citizenship arenas in the age of social media. *Journal of Business Ethics, 118*, 777–790. doi:10.1007/s10551-013-1960-3
62 Ibid.
63 ABP case information retrieved November 9, 2016, from http://gofossilfree.org/about-fossil-free/; http://gofossilfree.org/europe/press-release/more-than-10000-call-on-dutch-pension-fund-to-divest-from-coal-oil-and-gas/; *Dutch News*. (2015, March 19). Thousands of Dutch say ditch fossil fuels from pension fund. Retrieved from http://www.dutchnews.nl/news/archives/2015/03/thousands-of-dutch-say-ditchfossil-fuels-from-pension-fund/; http://gofossilfree.org/nl/has-abp-started-to-divest/
64 http://gofossilfree.org/about-fossil-free/
65 Dutch News (2015).
66 Sea World case information retrieved November 9, 2016, http://www.usatoday.com/story/money/2016/03/17/seaworld-orcas-killer-whales/81900498/; http://news.nationalgeographic.com/2016/03/160317-seaworld-orcas-killer-whales-captivity-breeding-shamu-tilikum/
67 Solomon, M. (2015, November 14). The Year of the Millennial Customer: Is Your Customer Experience Ready? Retrieved May 25, 2017, from http://www.forbes.com/sites/micahsolomon/2015/11/14/2016-is-the-year-of-the-millennial-customer-heres-how-to-be-ready/#4d289a766e72

68 Beucler, P. (2016, Sept 28). Role of Millennials and their Impact on Reputation Management. Retrieved May 25, 2017, from http://blog.mslgroup.com/role-of-millennials-and-their-impact-on-reputation-management/
69 Argenti, P. A. (2016, August 24). *Corporate ethics in the era of millennials*. Retrieved October 9, 2016, from http://www.npr.org/sections/13.7/2016/08/24/490811156/corporate-ethics-in-the-era-of-millennials
70 Charles, D. (2016, June 27). *In quest for happier chickens, Perdue shifts how birds live and die*. Retrieved October 9, 2016, from http://www.npr.org/sections/thesalt/2016/06/27/483724603/in-quest-for-happier-chickensperdue-shifts-how-birds-live-and-die
71 Coombs, W. T., & Holladay, S. J. (2012). Fringe public relations: How activism moves critical PR toward the mainstream. *Public Relations Review, 38*, 880–887. doi:10.1016/j.pubrev.2012.02.008
72 See, for example, International development videos 2016. (2016, June 2). *Social Media for Development*. Retrieved November 20, 2016, from http://social-media-for-development.org/category/unicef/
73 GP Kit-Kat Campaign. Retrieved October 7, 2016, from http://www.greenpeace.org/international/en/campaigns/climate-change/kitkat/
74 Laura, K. (2010, May 25). Social media can save the planet (Blog post). *Greenpeace*. Retrieved May 25, 2017, from http://www.greenpeace.org/international/en/news/Blogs/makingwaves/social-media-can-save-the-planet/blog/11832/
75 Davis, C. B., Glantz, M., & Novak, D. R. (2016). You can't run your SUV on cute. Let's Go!: Internet memes as delegitimizing discourse. *Environmental Communication, 10*, 62–83. doi:10.1080/17524032.2014.991411
76 Ibid., pp. 80–81.
77 Glaser, A. (2015, September 29). *You did it! Shell abandons Arctic drilling*. Retrieved October 7, 2016, from http://www.greenpeace.org/international/en/news/Blogs/makingwaves/save-the-arctic-shell-abandons-arctic-drilling/blog/54263/
78 Greenpeace. (2014). *Greenpeace apologises to the people of Peru for Nazca activity*. Retrieved October 7, 2016, from http://www.greenpeace.org/international/en/press/releases/2014/Greenpeace-apologisesto-the-people-of-Peru-for-Nazca-activity/
79 Chaudhri, V., & Kaul, A. (Accepted). Digital activism: NGOs leveraging social media to influence/challenge corporate social responsibility (CSR). In A. Lindgreen, J. Vanhamme, F. Maon, & R. Watkins (Eds), *Digital Social Responsibility*. Routledge.
80 #UnileverPollutes. Retrieved October 31, 2016, from http://www.visibrain.com/en/blog/unilever-kodaikanal-crisis-twitter-analysis/
81 Jhatkaa petition retrieved October 7, 2016, from https://petitions.whitehouse.gov/petition/uphold-international-law-stop-shielding-dow-chemical-accountability-corporate-crimes-bhopal-india
82 Glinton, S. (2015, September 24). *How a little lab in West Virginia caught Volkswagen's big cheat*. Retrieved September 14, 2016, from http://www.npr.org/2015/09/24/443053672/how-a-little-lab-in-west-virginiacaught-big-cheat
83 Gelles, D. (2015, October 19). *VW scandal puts greenwashing in the spotlight*. Retrieved September 14, 2015, from http://www.livemint.com/Industry/fEpJY11xlB743YIqBZ55uK/VW-scandal-puts-greenwashing-in-thespotlight.html
84 Lyon, T. P., Montgomery, A. W. (2015). The means and end of greenwash. *Organization & Environment, 28*(2), 223–249.
85 Gillespie, E. (2008). Stemming the tide of "greenwash." *Consumer Policy Review, 18*(3), 79–83.
86 European Commission. (2013). *Attitudes of Europeans towards building the single market for green products*. Retrieved May 25, 2017, from http://ec.europa.eu/public_opinion/flash/fl_367_en.pdf
87 Brandalism. (2015). *Brandalism at COP21*. Retrieved September 30, 2016, from http://www.brandalism.org.uk/brandalism-cop21
88 Table based on the following sources:

- Alton, L. (2015, December 2). *How to use social media with your corporate social responsibility efforts*. Retrieved May 25, 2017, from https://socialmediaweek.org/blog/2015/12/corporate-social-responsibility-social-media-efforts/
- Connor, D. (n.d.). *How to use social media for better corporate social responsibility*. Retrieved May 25, 2017, from http://greeneconomypost.com/social-media-corporate-social-responsibility-11551.htm
- Illia, L., Romenti, S., & Zyglidopoulos, S. (2015, September 1). Creating effective dialogue about corporate social responsibility. *MIT Sloan Management Review, 57*(1), 20–22.
- Illia, L., Zyglidopoulos, S., Romenti, S., Rodríguez-Cánovas, B., & González del Valle Brena, A. (2013). Communicating corporate social responsibility to a cynical public. *MIT Sloan Management Review, 54*(3), 16–18.

89 Quote retrieved May 25, 2017, from http://www.brainyquote.com/quotes/quotes/h/howardschu592238.html

90 Chew, J. (2016). Here are some companies accused of dodging taxes in Europe. *Fortune*. Retrieved September 26, 2016, from http://fortune.com/2016/03/11/apple-google-taxes-eu/

91 Coca-Cola case information retrieved October 11, 2016, from http://www.coca-colacompany.com/press-center/press-releases/coca-cola-is-the-first-fortune-500-company-to-replenish-all-the-water-it-uses-globally

92 Coca-Cola case information retrieved October 11, 2016, from http://well.blogs.nytimes.com/2015/08/09/coca-cola-funds-scientists-who-shift-blame-for-obesity-away-from-bad-diets/

93 Coca-Cola case information retrieved October 11, 2016, from http://transparency.coca-colacompany.com/

94 Coca-Cola case information retrieved October 11, 2016, from http://www.coca-colacompany.com/stories/coke-s-muhtar-kent-innovation-starts-and-ends-with-the-consumer

95 Watch video of the Senate Committee hearing here: Retrieved May 25, 2017, from https://www.youtube.com/watch?v=xJhkX74D10M

96 Wells Fargo case information retrieved October 12, 2016, from http://www.npr.org/2016/10/04/496508361/former-wells-fargo-employees-describe-toxic-sales-culture-even-at-hq?utm_source=twitter.com&utm_medium=social&utm_campaign=morningedition&utm_term=nprnews&utm_content=202604

97 Retrieved October 12, 2016, from http://finance.yahoo.com/news/wells-fargo-blasted-social-media-142935760.html

98 *The Economist.* (2014). *The openness revolution.* Retrieved September 22, 2016, from http://www.economist.com/news/business/21636070-multinationals-are-forced-reveal-more-about-themselves-where-should-limits

99 Patagonia. (2011). *Don't buy this jacket.* Retrieved October 12, 2016, from http://patagonia.wpengine.com/wpcontent/uploads/2016/07/nyt_11-25-11.pdf

100 Ibid.

101 Hensel, A. (2015, June 3). *What Patagonia did when it found human slaves in its supply chain.* Retrieved September 23, 2016, from http://www.inc.com/anna-hensel/patagonia-pledges-to-implement-higher-standards-in-factories.html

102 Patagonia. (2015, June 3). The unacceptably high cost of labor—How a deeper dive into our supply chain led to a new migrant worker standard. *Blog Post.* Retrieved May 25, 2017, from http://www.patagonia.com/blog/2015/06/the-unacceptably-high-cost-of-labor-a-new-migrant-worker-standard-from-patagonia/

103 Lorenz, J. (2015, November 10). *Hacking Patagonia's PR strategy: How to improve your brand's voice and influence.* Retrieved September 23, 2016, from http://sherpablog.marketingsherpa.com/marketing/improve-your-brandvoice-and-influence/

104 Watson, B. (2015, May 28). Unilever, Patagonia cement their positions as the world's most sustainable brands, says new report. *The Guardian.* Retrieved September 23, 2016, from https://www.theguardian.com/sustainable-business/2015/may/28/sustainability-leaders-report-unilever-patagonia-ikea-nestle

105 What are B-Corps? Retrieved June 2, 2017, from https://www.bcorporation.net/

106 Christensen, L. T., & Cheney, G. (2015). Peering into transparency: Challenging ideals, proxies, and organizational practices. *Communication Theory, 25*, 70–90.

107 Coombs, W. T., & Holladay, S. J. (2013). The pseudo-panopticon: The illusion created by CSR-related transparency and the internet *Corporate Communications: An International Journal, 18*, 212–227. http://dx.doi.org/10.1108/13563281311319490

108 Survey report retrieved September 14, 2016, from http://www.conecomm.com/news-blog/2015-cone-ebiquity-csr-study-press-release

109 Survey report retrieved September 14, 2016, from https://sustainly.com/sites/default/files/The%206th%20Annual%20Social%20Media%20Sustainability%20Index.pdf

110 Survey report retrieved September 14, 2016, from http://www.lundquist.it/wp-content/uploads/2014/05/CSROA_SurveySummary_220514.pdf

111 Gates, G., Ewing, J., Russell, K., & Watkins, D. (2016, November 4). *How Volkswagen is grappling with its diesel scandal.* Retrieved November 6, 2016, from http://www.nytimes.com/interactive/2015/business/international/vw-diesel-emissions-scandal-explained.html?_r=0

112 EPA. (n.d.). Volkswagen light duty diesel vehicle violations for model years 2009–2016. Retrieved October 31, 2016, from https://www.epa.gov/vw

113 Ewing, J. (2015, September 22). *Volkswagen says 11 million cars worldwide are affected in diesel deception.* Retrieved May 25, 2017, from http://www.nytimes.com/2015/09/23/business/international/volkswagen-diesel-car-scandal.html

114 Gates et al. (2016).
115 EPA (n.d.).
116 Economia (2015). *VW scandal: Ethics versus profit*. Retrieved October 31, 2016, from http://economia.icaew.com/business/december-2015/ethics-versus-profit
117 Boston, W. (2016, April 28). *Bad news? What bad news? Volkswagen bullish despite emissions costs*. Retrieved October 31, 2016, from http://www.wsj.com/articles/volkswagen-says-diesel-car-buy-backs-to-cost-almost-9-billion-1461831943
118 Clothier, M. (2015, September 22). *VW's U.S. chief apologizes for diesel dupe: "We screwed up."* Retrieved October 31, 2016, from http://www.bloomberg.com/news/articles/2015-09-22/vw-s-u-s-chief-apologizesfor-diesel-cheating-we-screwed-up-
119 Boston (2016).
120 Gates et al. (2016).
121 Boston (2016).
122 Hartogs, J. (2016, April 28). *VW CEO says priority is to "regain trust" after emissions scandal*. Retrieved October 31, 2016, from http://www.cnbc.com/2016/04/28/vw-ceo-says-priority-is-to-regain-trust-after-emissionsscandal.html
123 Gates et al. (2016).
124 Wattles, J. (2016, March 9). *Volkswagen America's CEO resigns*. Retrieved October 31, 2016, from http://money.cnn.com/2016/03/09/news/companies/volkswagen-america-ceo-resignation/
125 Vlassic, B., & Kessler, A. M. (2015, September 21). *It took E.P.A. pressure to get VW to admit fault*. Retrieved October 31, 2016, from http://www.nytimes.com/2015/09/22/business/it-took-epa-pressure-to-get-vw-toadmit-fault.html
126 Hotten, R. (2015, December 10). *Volkswagen: The scandal explained*. Retrieved October 31, 2016, from http://www.bbc.com/news/business-34324772
127 Gates et al. (2016).
128 Steitz, C., Cremer, A., & Shepardson, D. (2016, March 2). *Update 1-VW says 2014 diesel warnings did not get CEO's attention*. Retrieved October 31, 2016, from http://www.reuters.com/article/volkswagen-emissionsidUSL2N16A252
129 Ibid.
130 Neate, R. (2016, March 3). *VW's chief executive was told about the illegal emissions crisis a year before it admitted cheating tests*. Retrieved October 31, 2016, from http://www.businessinsider.com/vw-emissionscrisis-martin-winterkorn-company-cheating-tests-2016-3?international=true&r=US&IR=T#comment-56dac7bc8fe4de2a527b23c7
131 Domonoske, C. (2015, December 10). *Volkswagen chairman says emissions cheating sprang from "chain of errors."* Retrieved October 31, 2016, from http://www.npr.org/sections/thetwo-way/2015/12/10/459195558/volkswagen-chairman-says-emissions-cheating-sprang-from-chain-of-errors
132 Cremer, A., & Bergin, T. (2015, October 10). *Fear and respect: VW's culture under Winterkorn*. Retrieved October 31, 2016, from http://www.reuters.com/article/us-volkswagen-emissions-culture-idUSKCN0S40MT20151010
133 Ibid.
134 Comen, E., & Sauter, M. B. (2016, May 12). *Companies with the best (and worst) reputations*. Retrieved October 31, 2016, from http://247wallst.com/special-report/2016/05/12/companies-with-the-best-and-worst-reputations-4/
135 David, J. D. (2015, November 17). *The implosion of a brand: A social media analysis of the Volkswagen emissions scandal*. Retrieved October 31, 2016, from http://www.marketingtechnews.net/news/2015/nov/17/implosion-brand-social-media-analysis-volkswagen-emissions-scandal/
136 Preston, B. (2015, September 25). *Volkswagen scandal tarnishes hard-won US reputation as green company*. Retrieved October 31, 2016, from https://www.theguardian.com/business/2015/sep/25/volkswagen-scandal-usreputation-emissions
137 Ibid.
138 Laue, J. (2015, November 4). *Dieselgate—Reactions from the web and how other brands jumped on the Volkswagen*. Retrieved October 31, 2016, from https://www.searchlaboratory.com/2015/11/dieselgate-reactions from-the-web-and-how-other-brands-jumped-on-the-volkswagen/
139 Ibid.

140 Ibid.
141 DW. (2016, April 28). *VW scandal: A city's future at stake*. Retrieved October 31, 2016, from http://www.dw.com/en/vw-scandal-a-citys-future-at-stake/a-19223430
142 BBC. (2015, October 4). *Merkel: VW scandal won't damage Germany's reputation*. Retrieved October 31, 2016, from http://www.bbc.com/news/business-34438031
143 Murphy, S. (2015, September 29). *VW scandal: How it compares to Toyota's recall crisis*. Retrieved October 31, 2016, from https://yougov.co.uk/news/2015/09/29/volkswagen-crisis-lessons-history/; Liker, J. (2015, September 24). Assessing the sins of Volkswagen, Toyota, and General Motors. *Harvard Business Review* (digital article). Retrieved from https://hbr.org/2015/09/assessing-the-sins-of-volkswagentoyota-and-general-motors
144 Preston (2015).
145 Ewing (2015).
146 Clothier (2015).
147 Brandbastion. (n.d.). Volkswagen scandal on social media. Retrieved October 31, 2016, from https://www.brandbastion.com/volkswagen-scandal-on-social-media
148 Shepardson, D. (2016, September 14). *Volkswagen says it might not resume U.S. sales of diesel vehicles*. Retrieved October 31, 2016, from http://www.reuters.com/article/us-volkswagen-emissions-diesel-idUSKCN11K2LN
149 Ibid.
150 Domonoske (2015).
151 Kollewe, J. (2016, May 13). *VW sales rise for first time since emissions scandal*. Retrieved October 31, 2016, from https://www.theguardian.com/business/2016/may/13/vw-sales-rise-diesel-emissions-scandal
152 *Reuters*. (2016). *EU proposes stricter tests on car emissions from 2017 in wake of VW scandal*. Retrieved October 31, 2016, from http://www.reuters.com/article/us-eu-autos-tests-idUSKCN0Z11E5

CHAPTER 6

MEASURING THE $ SPEND ON SOCIAL MEDIA

CHAPTER OBJECTIVES

- Understand what constitutes ROI of social media.
- Examine tools for measurement of social media ROI.
- Build understanding of campaign objectives.
- Evaluate the relationship between organizational goals, social media campaigns, and performance outcomes.

Keywords

Acquisition	Evangelism	Run
Activity	Goals	Sentiment
Campaigns	Intangible investments	Socio-media-logy
Conversation	Interactivity	Tangible investments
Conversion	Measurement	Thrive
Crawl	Performance metrics	Walk
Data analysis	Reputational currency	Web metrics
Engagement	ROI	WOM

INTRODUCTION

You can now measure everything, but you won't survive without the metrics that matter to your business.

Katie Delahaye Paine[1]

In 2006, Tom Dickinson, founder of Blendtec, launched a viral marketing campaign "Will it Blend?"[2] in the form of YouTube videos. The first in the series was a low-cost YouTube video that asked, "I love my iPhone, but will it blend?"[3] that gained immediate traction. Subsequently, Dickinson demonstrated the power of his *Total Blender* by blending various items that were selected on the basis of the requests sent by his followers on the official Facebook page.[4] After the products were churned, the contents of the blender were emptied onto the table with the subtitle "Yes, it Blends!"[5]

A definitive visual statement by the company! The success of the experiment was evidenced in the form of numbers that favored Blendtec. The first "Will It Blend?" video became the thirty-third most-viewed series ever on YouTube. Almost 50 percent of these viewers logged on to the company website, and 15 percent made a purchase. In 2006, sales of the US$399 high-end consumer blender went up by 500 percent. Since the introduction of the videos the company website traffic increased 650 percent and there was a five-fold increase in the online sales.[6] Blendtec used the videos to present infomercials with product range of blenders and what they were able to blend.

This is just one of the many documented examples that show tangible and intangible investments in social media for gainful returns. Yet, there is considerable debate on return on investments (ROI), measurement techniques and objectives of employing social media. What should measurement/assessment focus on? Business objectives or communication output (coverage and visibility of the message)? Differing views have been posited and the scales are in favor of organizational objectives. However, we submit that before a discussion on ROI can be initiated, reflection on the following questions is imperative.

What is the ROI of social media? (See Appendix A for researcher views on what constitutes social media ROI.) Why is there a buzz around measuring social media ROI? Does it help in assessing company reputation? Can it help a company acquire reputational currency? Is it a measurement tool in the hands of the marketers or a PR exercise to assess market condition and understand consumer mind space?

The questions gain credence as we argue in favor of changed consumer preferences, behaviors, and attitudes governed by online opinions. With a proliferation of social tools to measure online conversations on products, services, and companies, it has become mandatory for companies, ranging from the most technically savvy to the most ordinary, to indulge in assessment and measurement. Thus, positioned to essentially communicate in the digital era, organizations have been forced to develop performance metrics that measure the success of products and processes in terms of consumer and customer behavior.

Yet another measurement challenge faced by organizations as they grapple with developing performance metrics, is of cognizing, developing and enhancing relationships in different business models as business to business, business to customers, and customer to customer. What are the processes to be followed? Does a 'counting' of number of stakeholders suffice or should a measurement technique be introduced that considers processes, results, and provides a clue on the prudent choice of social media investments, or can there be a third category through which relationships, precursor to building a good reputation, are measured?[7]

'CAN'T-LIVE-WITH-IT–CAN'T-LIVE-WITHOUT-IT': THEN WHY MEASURE?

> The goal is to turn data into information, and information into insight.
>
> *Carly Fiorina*[8]

LEARNING OBJECTIVES

- Understand the difference between traditional and social media.
- Develop a goal-based approach to social media.
- Comprehend the 'why' of measuring returns.

In today's complex media environment, traditional media measurement techniques have become almost archaic. There is a constant struggle with social media measurement as marketers are still driven by assessment of reach and frequency instead of focusing on the interactive nature of this new medium. The struggle is more evident as there are differing perceptions about the value of social media in quantitative terms. In the search for gainful returns, organizations have increased the social media spend. While all are in agreement over the need to spend more, the question rests on the 'why' to measure the returns.

Organizations have different goals for ROI assessment which may be as varied as collecting competitive intelligence, generating sales, strengthening brand, monitoring business, acquiring contacts, and creating advocates. It could be market driven or initiative focused. The advantage of a goal-based approach to ROI is that it helps in understanding the 'why' instead of the 'how' of marketing initiatives. To further elaborate, why do I [organization] want to go ahead with a particular campaign instead of which social media channel should I [organization] use. If we are in agreement on this point then we can, with alacrity, state that in an ideal condition, goal of social media dialogue synergizes with the objectives of the company. Unfortunately, this 'ideal condition' is a distant reality as organizations are still caught up in promoting and advertising their products through monologues.

Effective social media measurement requires a new approach that is distinct from traditional media. The difference in the two media has majorly been accredited to objectives, spend, and delivery. The objectives of traditional media can be defined as knowledge, recall, and purchase decisions. Stratified objectives of social media can be listed as conversation, interactivity, engagement, evangelism, etcetera. The expense for traditional media is a direct cost for increasing sales and hence, the delivery is direct from the marketer. The same for social media is more intangible as building social currency, trustworthiness, authenticity, transparency with the delivery directly stem from the source. Being conversational, continuous, and consumer-led brings in a large amount of difficulty in measurement of social media ROI.

For instance, marketers are now faced with the dual responsibility of understanding customer behavior and motivations as they engage with the organization. The relationship oriented nature of social media has motivated users to create their social currency which is invested through a process they find useful.

With an increase in the social media spend, ROI measurement has become an imperative. Measurement provides organizations a handle to identify what works and what does not. Historically, the investments required in social media campaigns were much lower than those for traditional media as TV and print. With passage of time, organizations realized the potential of high returns. They stepped up their social media game plan by increasing investments in external evangelists and content generation. Organizations though have not been very successful in devising a concrete measurement plan. The reason can be attributed to the dialogic nature of the medium that requires co-creation, collaboration and synergistic content generation bordering on the motivational and engagement levels of consumers.

There is an opportunity for organizations to tap into areas as building awareness, enhancing engagement, and spreading messages through WOM. Developing a set of metrics that link to a set of proxy benchmark can align company objectives with the desired returns. An interesting case in point is of Kellogg. In 2007, Kellogg created a "Special K Challenge" for its Special K Cereal. The challenge was supported by a website that provided customers an opportunity to customize their diet with the cereal and to participate in online forums getting advice from guides and experts. The product could be purchased at Amazon.com. Kellogg was able to translate the market response over a period of 18 months by analysis of web interactions and clicks. The company found that the online response for the product was twice as high as that from television.[9]

From the above example it is evident that there appears to be a need to move beyond the traditional objectives such as sales, cost reductions, or increase in market share. Objectives may be as varied as interactivity or building customer loyalty by establishing rapport and engagement. A simple approach as this can positively impact the bottom line of the organization and improve its efficiency of market research when online prediction markets are set up to crowdsource ideas or mine online forums that provide the consumer an opportunity to comment on the existing product line of the company or suggest improvements. These are all obvious objectives.

What more can organizations track with social media?

WHAT ARE YOU OUT TO TRACK: WHY AND HOW?

> Figure out what you want to track, where you can track it, think about both current customers and new customers, and go do it.
>
> *Kevan Lee*[10]

LEARNING OBJECTIVES

- Examine different measurement techniques.
- Understand the importance of web analytics.
- Develop in consumers a willingness to participate.

In today's fast-paced world, creation and exchange of user-generated content has been facilitated by social media.[11] Business-related research on social media has focused on the use of public social media initiatives for increasing revenue and sales. It has helped companies in engaging with communities leading to increase in not only sales but also brand loyalty, co-creation activities, and firm trust.[12] Implicit user-generated content such as users' search queries on Google are being used as a measure for investor intention.[13] Researchers have also found predictive power of stock microblog sentiment among the investment communities.[14]

Social media ROI which was earlier measured in terms of fans, followers, and engagement is now being assessed in terms of tweets, followers, comments, posts, shares, likes, mentions, channels used, and engagement.

"Social media ROI = [(tweets – followers) ÷ (comments × average monthly posts)] ÷ (Facebook shares × Facebook likes) ÷ (mentions × channels used) × engagement"[15]

In contrast with traditional media, social media provides an opportunity to measure every footprint of the journey of the audience. The audience leaves imprints where it goes. Different channels create different paths and output at each stage of the journey. There are measurement opportunities at every stage. The measurement can be based on (a) activity, (b) reach, (c) engagement, (d) acquisition, (e) conversion, and (f) retention and advocacy.[16] (For details, see Appendix B.)

There is now greater emphasis on engagement. However, there are challenges in operationalizing engagement. Deliberations on what is the right metrics or what can help an organization be successful are now being assessed through activities that increase leads, sales, and loyalty. The old model of "Willingness to Pay" has given way to the new model of success, the "Willingness to Participate."[17] Benefits associated with customer motivation and engagement reflect a willingness to associate with the brand or the organization through activities as content creation.

Arguably, at this juncture, we need to underscore the relevance of engaging customers which can be linked to the Internet 'pull' strategy in which customers are attracted through relevant content. The objectives may be varied as repositioning, branding, content creation, or seeking engagement. A case in point is Unilever's Dove campaign on YouTube titled, *Evolution*, presenting the transformation of a plain model into a beautiful woman through light effects. This campaign, which added US$1.2 billion value to the brand, was viewed over 12 million times.[18]

In today's fast paced world which is data driven and data centric, collation of real-time data provides organizations a platform for creation of opportunities translated in greater efficiency and improved campaign outcomes. Evaluations and assessments at three levels—pre-market, in-market, and post-campaign—can help in re-sketching and re-strategizing social media strategy. Let us consider the example of Kellogg (Box 6.1).

Box 6.1: Kellogg's and Digital Marketing

Kellogg's allocates a major share of its advertising money in digital marketing and is of the view that the right 'pull' strategy, measurement, and optimization are critical components in measuring the success of digital advertising. The company has defined three stages in the strategy—premarket, inmarket, and post-campaign. The pre-market strategy first, defines a common set of goals and formulates the Key Performance Index (KPI) that helps track the goals. A digital framework is developed and communicated to help track digital data and capture KPI results. The pre-market strategy includes design, mode of delivery, and cost per effective audience impression.[19]

The in-market strategy relies on programmatic buying. Continuous monitoring of each campaign using comScore validated Campaign Essentials (vCE) proves very helpful as the data received is almost real-time. These data are used to create brand awareness, build purchase interest, enable message association, and facilitate direct response. The campaign is constantly tweaked in response to the feedback received to improve overall delivery of the media plan.[20]

Post-campaign evaluates the actual branding impact of its campaigns with the help of Brand Survey Lift (comScore's branding effectiveness solution) or Offline Sales Lift. With these tools, Kellogg's is able to measure changes in key branding and equity metrics in addition to the in-store sales lift generated by its campaigns. The evaluation brings to light the critical analyses of the campaign run as well as helps future campaign planning and execution.

Summing up the whole Digital marketing goal of Kellogg, Aaron Fetters, Director KNA insights and Analytics Solutions Center says, "At Kellogg we are continually seeking to improve the overall effectiveness of every media dollar spent. Key to enabling our decisions is understanding who each impression reaches, how visible our ads are, and where the greatest efficiencies exist. Being able to validate our media delivery through a single source with vCE creates opportunities for both near real-time optimizations as well as enhanced future planning."

Source: McConnell (2015).[21]

Kellogg's brings forth a very important point in digital marketing where programmatic buying can increase pricing efficiency through improvement in targeting efficiency and higher ROI. Identifying users, enhancing visibility, and targeting the right audience can be achieved through a simple seven-stage process. Implementation of this process can facilitate a smooth transition from no or little presence to active dialogue and reputational currency (Table 6.1).

TABLE 6.1 *Seven-step Model to Implementing Effective Social Media Campaigns*

Steps	Advantage
1. Monitoring conversations	By listening to the conversations and monitoring them companies and brands can engage with customers and influencers in the cyberspace.
2. Identifying influential individuals with potential to spread messages	Identify influencers who can impact and transmit the message.
3. Identifying commonalities between influential individuals	Companies should identify the commonalities among influencers that will help the message spread and influence.
4. Locating high potential influencers with impact on the campaign	It is not sufficient to identify individuals who have clout in the social media space but also who would like to talk on a topic or brand.
5. Recruiting influencers with who can share opinion on the campaign and talk about the company's product or service	Enlist these influencers to spread positive WOM.
6. Incentivizing influencers to develop positive sentiment and conversations on the product or service	By incentivizing (through tangible benefits) these influencers to talk about a product or a brand, a buzz can be created.
7. Reaping the rewards from effective social media campaigns	Social media ROI can be measured by linking the buzz to performance success of the campaigns. Further, tracking can be done to measure performance.

Source: Kumar and Mirchandani (2012).[22]

A case in point is Lenovo India which partnered with YUWA to bring tribal girls from a non descript village in Jharkhand to the World platform in the field of Football. Lenovo used a digital platform to garner support for the YUWA girls. These girls represented India at the Donosti Cup in Spain. A video series was aired on these *Girls with Goals*, which touched the hearts of the viewers through vivid presentations of their trials and failures in Spain.[23] Lenovo released a series of videos depicting their journey of sheer determination. With a lot of buzz on social media with the unscripted live recording of the girls' journey to Spain, the viewers kept following the matches with interest. Lenovo also leveraged Facebook Live, Twitter, and Snapchat to keep people glued to the matches.

Additionally, Lenovo India initiated an online campaign #Kickforbrick, with the objective of adding bricks to an envisioned new school for the girls. Viewers were asked to record themselves kicking a ball and share the video on social media and nominate a friend. Soon the girls received huge social and economic support from the local agents. The results were positive and new classrooms were built in the school to provide education to the girls.[24]

Clearly, the intangible rewards of the Lenovo campaign are evident for the consumers at large. However, at this point we need to reflect on the measures, if any, to assess data points and objectively analyze the process of social media campaign.

Data Analysis

With social media the availability of publicly available, user-generated text, on the World Wide Web has increased manifold. It is possible to measure the success metrics, a study of relevant data on the net related to the process of a campaign. There are four stages in this process: sourcing and scraping of data, text cleaning and storing, text transformation, and analysis. The most important and most difficult step in ROI measurement is the analysis of data.

The process for analysis requires sourcing and scraping/searching the data first from the web. Various tools such as Google trends and Social Mention can come to the rescue of inexperienced hands. The next logical steps are to refine, clean, sort, and then analyze the data. There are numerous tools available for all of these steps, some of the most important being Data Wrangler and Google Fusion tables. Further, there are tools that aggregate mention of company, product, or individual on the net and try to assess if the mentions are positive, negative, or neutral. "Sentiment analysis is a set of methods, typically (but not always) implemented in computer software, that detect, measure, report, and exploit attitudes, opinions, and emotions in online, social, and enterprise information sources."[25] It is a study of automated techniques for extracting sentiments from written languages and can potentially be used to provide real-time insights into the sentiments of people.[26] This technique is used effectively by organizations keen to market products, identify new opportunities, and build their reputation.

Web metrics and analytics

There are myriad of metrics available suitable only to a particular type of media. Some more commonly used metrics are as follows:

1. **Blogs and micro-blogs:** Number of references in other media, number of reblogs, number of likes.
2. **Networks:** Appearance on timelines, number of posts, reposts, shares, responses to invites.
3. **Videos and photos:** Number of embeds, incoming links, references, likes.
4. **Product reviews:** Number and valence of reviews, number of references, visits.

Javascript is used to collate web metrics that enable organizations track visitor behavior as number of unique visitors, visits, page views, goals reached (downloads, registrations, orders) time on site, bounce rate (percentage of visitors who leave after visiting one page), and conversion rate (number of goals reached divided by number of unique visitors).

The relevance of web analytics cannot be debated or disputed. The analysis would benefit PR in carving out a niche social media strategy for the company. Analytics for PR are concerned with traffic information as direct traffic, natural or organic and paid search (e.g., Google Ad Words), earned media, email campaigns etcetera referring search keywords, email campaigns, digital advertisements (e.g., banner Engagement metrics include the number of "unique visitors coming to the organization's site from a story, the amount of time visitors referred from a story spend on the site, how many pages or which pages they read, and if visitors from the story are helping the organizations reach a goal, such as purchasing a product, registering for email alerts, or downloading white papers."[27]

Web analytics can facilitate comparison of marketing activities and can inform a PR strategy based on evidence. It is finally, an affordable alternative to marketing mix modeling. Though not a substitute, web analytics is a cost-effective method for measuring the relative contribution of PR to business goals.[28]

There are two methods for using web analytics for communications: Basic and Advanced.

Basic

Basic method deals with measuring and understanding the traffic the web portal generates and attempts to provide an answer to the following points:

- Traditional media (i.e., sites with a print or broadcast companion) and social media sites that possess the potential of driving traffic to an organization's website.

- Sites (e.g., traditional media, blogs, forums, etcetera) that can drive visitors and promote engagement at the organization website.
- Conversion rates for earned media.

This analysis can be done with the help of integrated solutions like Radian6 and WebTrends, or Omniture's SiteCatalyst and can be conducted by PR practitioners.

- **Downloading relevant data:** Web analytics software systems provide facilities to download data into a .csv file or similar format. Depending on the software you might be able to organize paid and unpaid sources.
- **Data cleaning and quality control:** Raw data from web analytics software can be huge, and may require special skills to organize this data on excel.
- **Analysis of media types:** Media type analysis can be performed by categorizing the media sources from the cleaned data.

Two basic categories for this analysis can be:

- Site Type (Mainstream Media, Online media, Blogs, Forums, Video, Microblogs, Bookmarking sites, and Social Networking).
- Site Content (National News, Regional News, Business Press, Investor Sites, Lifestyle, Personal/biographical, and Consumer review).

Once we have categorized the data, the metrics need to be compared across site categories.

Advanced

This method involves integrating different types of data, and conducting advanced statistical analysis. As these methods are highly technical, it may help a PR practitioner to secure support from external experts.

These analyses address issues as:

- Audiences to be targeted (e.g., individuals of a specific age, gender, or income level). Questions such as these emphasize marketing concepts of segmentation and targeting, and are based on demographics (age, sex, and occupation) and psychographics (audience profiling).
- Messages to be created which are effective in driving traffic and securing engagement.
- Framing of messages to specific audience requirements.

The advanced analytics requires expertise in data management and statistical skills. A single model is used to integrate wide range of data types which can help PR practitioners in selecting their online strategies.

Some goals for using advanced statistical applications to integrate PR and Web Metrics are as follows:

- Effectiveness of site and post attributes.
- Cause—effect relationships between site and post attributes to objectives of the PR exercise.
- Future strategy.

CONVERTING THE $ SPEND ON BUILDING REPUTATIONAL CURRENCY

> It's about reaching the right eyeballs, not all the eyeballs.
>
> *Katie Delahaye Paine*[29]

FIGURE 6.1 *Objectives Identification*

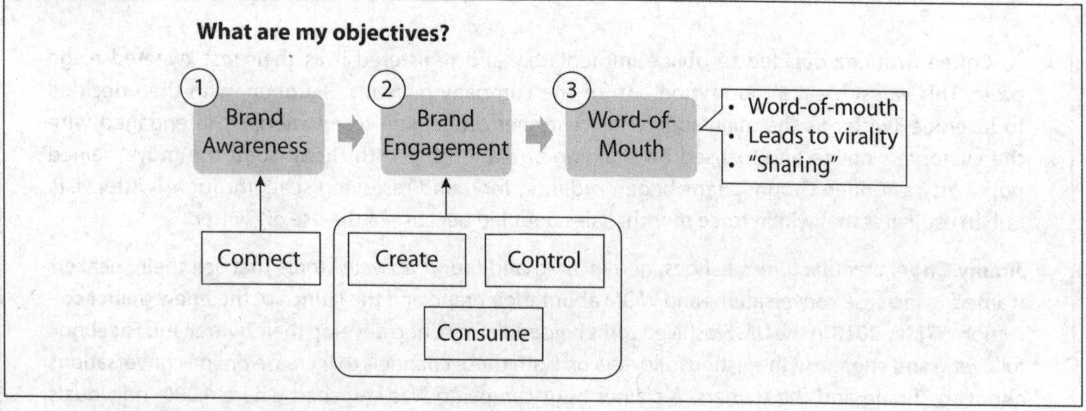

Source: Adapted by authors from multiple sources.

LEARNING OBJECTIVES

- Understand the imperative of social media presence.
- Learn the process of a campaign journey.
- Identify the social media objectives for maximum returns.

With the advent of social media, companies no longer face the challenge to be or not to be. Their presence on social media is no longer a choice but an imperative. The question now underscores the importance of 'how' of the process of securing the 'right eyeballs.'

We argue that for success of any social media campaign, there should be clarity on objectives of the campaign. Is the objective to connect (brand awareness), create, control, or consume (brand engagement) or spread message by word-of-mouth (WOM) that leads to virality and sharing of information (Figure 6.1)? Is the outcome or the expected return always tangible or intangible and how does it link with the overall organizational objectives? Some interesting examples (Box 6.2) are cited below which show tangible and intangible benefits for organizations.

Box 6.2: Linking Company Objectives to Social Media ROI

On October 31, 2008, the Twitter landscape was changed by one message from a **Coffee Groundz** customer:

> **@coffeegroundz** I want to pre order a bkfast wrap so i can zip thru to get back for gas man. c'est possible?
> *07:27 AM October 31, 2008 from mobile web*

(Box 6.2 Continued)

(Box 6.2 Continued)

Coffee Groundz decided to oblige immediately and registered it as their first tweeted to-go order. This was a breakthrough moment for the company owner, J. R. Cohen, who then decided to leverage Twitter as the main source for customer orders and reservations.[30] He engaged with the customers online and focused on building a relationship with them. Soon the move gained popularity as Coffee Groundz fans began ordering food and reserving seats through Twitter. J. R. Cohen estimates that within three months sales doubled because of the use of Twitter.[31]

Jimmy Choo, manufacturer of shoes, geo-located and found upscale stores that sell their sneakers wanted to increase conversations and WOM about their brand and the launch of their new trainer collection on May 2010 in the UK. FreshNetworks helped Jimmy Choo develop their Twitter and Facebook following and engage with existing followers on both these channels to increase online conversations about the brand and the trainers. A trainer hunt campaign was launched where 4,000 individuals participated on Foursquare, Twitter, and Facebook in just under three weeks. The competition details were viewed on Facebook 285,000 times and mentioned over 4,000 times on Twitter. The online buzz translated into sales as their sneakers purchase increased by 33 percent with a 40 percent increase in positive tweets and messages (measurements taken between 19 April and 6 May).[32]

In 2007, **Toblerone** used the company website of its maker Kraft Foods and other social networks used in the Philippines to establish October 20 as the country's "National Thank You Day." The campaign generated nearly 500,000 hits and the sales for Toblerone increased by 132 percent. This led to Philippines becoming the number one market in Asia for the brand.

The main objective driving this campaign was to develop a link between Toblerone and the feeling of gratitude.[33] To create the initial buzz around the campaign thousands of Toblerones were given away and the stamp of success was achieved when the campaign got government support and they declared October 20 as National Thank You Day. The company got 40 percent of the total sales with Toblerone products.[34]

Foiled Cupcakes was started by Mari Luangrath in spring 2009. She created a Facebook page and Twitter account in April for Foiled Cupcakes and by June, when the business was officially opened, she had amassed hundreds of followers on Facebook and thousands on Twitter. Today, the company also has a blog that Ms Luangrath uses to solicit feedback from her audience related to the flavors or naming of the cupcakes.[35]

The various other channels used to further connect with the potential and existing clients were Pinterest, LinkedIn, and Yelp. They received an order for 40,000 cupcakes and today 97 percent of their customers are from social media. The same exceeded forecasts by 600 percent in the first year.[36]

Cadbury Wispa was petitioned by the customers to bring back the Wispa bar. In response to the overwhelming demand, Cadbury decided to relaunch the Wispa on a trial basis in October 2007. The results were astounding as Cadbury sold an impressive 20 million bars in the first seven weeks of the trial. This prompted the brand to permanently relaunch the bars in 2008. Soon the public started campaigning to bring back Wispa Gold. Cadbury decided to capitalize on this demand and turned to social media to build an enthusiastic following in preparation for the Wispa Gold relaunch. The campaign was a huge success as 40 million bars were sent to the market and in 18 weeks after responding to the petition all the bars were sold which added 30 percent to their annual profit.[37]

FIGURE 6.2 *Campaign Journey*

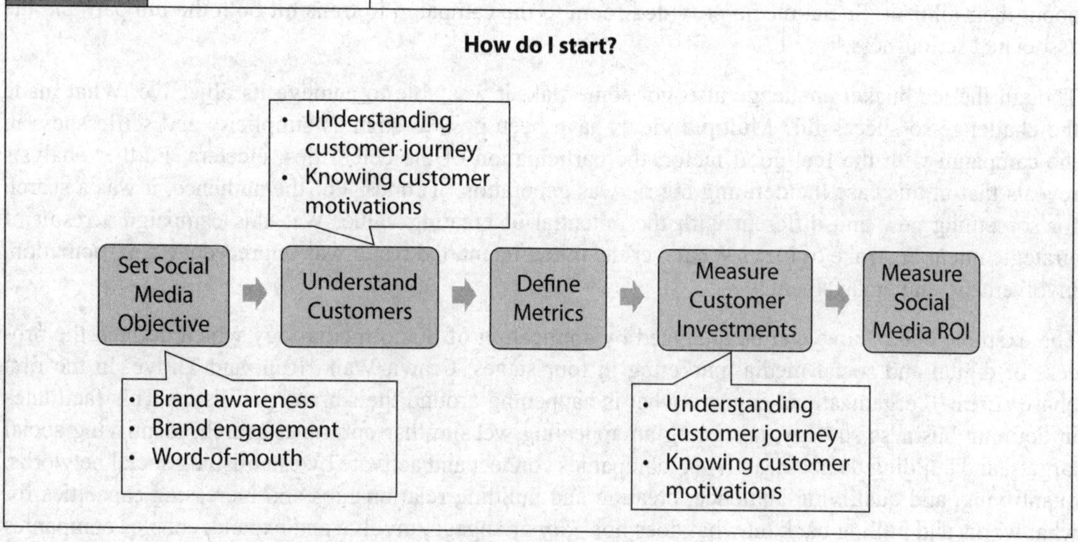

Source: Adapted by the authors from multiple sources.

In all the examples presented above, the users adopted a process that helped companies invest in crediting social currency through conversation, sharing, supportiveness, and helpfulness. Apart from these there can be other promotion techniques as (a) finding opinion leaders or high influencers to spread the message, and (b) employing promotions, contests, etcetera.[38] As seen in the above examples, it is advisable that to achieve a better ROI, tangible or intangible, organizations should follow a process which first sets objectives, defines the strategy, and then measures the ROI on a frequent basis.[39]

The diagram (Figure 6.2) enunciates the organizational journey from setting objectives to measuring ROI. Interestingly, in social media the key player is no longer the company but the customer/consumer whose purchase journey or investments are studied vis-à-vis motivation to make a decision.

A diagram that traces the journey of a campaign can be a good starting point for understanding the 'how' of the process.

Take the example of amyotrophic lateral sclerosis (ALS) (Refer Appendix C) where the objective of the campaign was to build awareness and generate funds for ALS. Pouring a bucket of cold water on the head did not capture the fancy of many Americans who preferred to make a donation. In less than two months the campaign went viral with many stars and celebrities actively taking the challenge. The campaign was a huge success. Some numbers which validate the findings are as follows: there were 3.17 million videos created with more people participating in it than Super Bowl and Oscars combined. As the campaign became viral, participation expanded to 159 countries with 50 political figures, 200 notable actors, 200 musicians, and 200 athletes participating in the campaign. There were 70 billion counted views. Over 440 million people viewed it without any extra cost. There was no money spent on the campaign but accrued benefits of US$220 million.[40]

What made the campaign so successful? Participation of celebrities gave the campaign a required boost. The two critical objectives, raising awareness and funds, were met. Through this campaign ALS association was able to raise money which was over 40 times the amount raised in 2013 over the same period. Researchers state that in 2014, the awareness spike for "ALS" was much higher than cancer. Additionally, the component of challenge and making it "challenging" for other participants added the required spice to the campaign. Finally, it gave people, who had the disease, an opportunity to talk about their ailment. Social media provided room to the campaign to transmit both the fun part and the associated seriousness.[41]

Though the ice bucket challenge also got some flak, it was able to achieve its objective. What made the challenge so successful? Multiple views have been posited such as simplicity and selflessness in the campaign with the feel good factor, the participation of the celebrities, etcetera. Further analysis reveals that in this case the defining metric was generation of funds. For the audience, it was a search for something new and different with the potential of creating value. Was this campaign a result of strategic intent or stroke of luck? Whatever the initial intent, the result was unprecedented participation, involvement, and engagement.

The example cited above can be analyzed by application of Socio-media-logy which defined the process of digital and social media marketing in four stages: Crawl, Walk, Run, and Thrive. In the first phase *(Crawl),* organizations cognize what is happening around their brand and listen. This facilitates in defining business strategy, designing an appealing website that optimizes search, identifying social targets, and building database. In *Walk,* companies connect and activate by establishing social networks, quantifying, and qualifying audience, creating and building relationships and increasing capacities for what works and pulling back on what does not. *Run* or engage, involve and expand, enables companies to make the content more appealing by indulging with content on videos, podcasts, webinars, apps, etcetera. In the final stage of *Thrive,* fans or followers act as advocates.[42]

Did the the Ice Bucket Challenge crawl, walk, run and thrive? Yes! Much of its success can be attributed to the listening, connecting with people and activating support with social targets, creating engaging content and securing support from fans, followers and advocates.

However, managing conversations in the social media is not simple. Challenges and hurdles abound which though tough are not impossible to overcome.

MAKING A CASE FOR MEASURING SOCIAL MEDIA RETURNS

> We cannot measure, what it is we do not know to value.
>
> *Brian Solis*[43]

LEARNING OBJECTIVES

- Understand the different perspectives and challenges in using social media.
- Appreciate a process-approach to implementing and measuring returns.
- Learn about select models of influence/learn about select models for measurement of social media ROI.

Today, organizations have begun to feel that social media are an essential part of the commerce fabric and all must be actively involved in the process. However, the constant demand for 'proof' of return on investment emphasizes the uncertainty in the effort and the budget for social media spent.[44] Still unable to break free from the chains of control and objective as purchase, marketers are finding it difficult to focus on social objectives where expectations and returns are different. Additionally, French innovators[45] emphatically assert that social media technologies cannot be a substitute for traditional forms of connecting. In an interesting study[46] French CEOs met with customers and consumers and found that the best possible method of fueling relationships was through offline techniques. Social media technologies could only complement traditional media but not add value.

Missing in this analysis of the French innovators is the uncertainty of outcome, speed with which messages become viral, the reach, and the share of voice. Undoubtedly, this is a medium which excites love and hate at first sight. Absence on social media implies that all conversations happen without you, competition gains precedence and rank in search engines begins to fall. In short, the 24×7 world becomes oblivious to your existence. Presence does not necessarily entail success. The outcome is often unpredictable, negative or intangible.

Considerable resources, such as money, effort and time, are required for purpose of assessments. Large-sized organizations have forayed in the interactive domain of social media and can afford the luxury of measurement. Mid-sized and small companies are taking small steps in this direction. As on date, single silver bullet matrix is being employed. However, with social media new metrics and dashboards are being innovated for content creation and co-creation of ties and relationships. This paradigmatic shift to participatory forms of communication where control gives way to influence is obviously difficult and time consuming.

Lack of information on processes to be followed has led many organizations to use matrix created by social operators which may not be specific to their requirements or help them make informed marketing decisions. Definition of company goals and measurement of degrees of deviation, if any, and implementation of measures for improvement are part of the matrix.[47] New forms of content can be developed that can lead to engagement and dyadic ties with customers and consumers.

Effectiveness of social media is generally accepted but corporations differ on the results it yields for them. It is also a journey that every company undertakes with unsure steps, even though social media is now an essential part of the communication mix. Approaches to social media are a combination of the objectivity of the measurement and the manager's subjective assessment about the performance of their social media efforts.

Most organizations start at the stage of Naïve Optimism. They begin their social media campaign and feel that it is not working for them. At this stage, it would be prudent to state that organizations have either limited ability or are uncertain about the measurement of social media efforts. They believe that social media are good for their business, but are unsure about measurement. This is a position of bliss and lasts as long as the investments are not large and the results not specific. Within no time realization dawns that though there is a lot of noise and buzz, there has really not been much progress. They may decide to measure and adjust their strategies. As measurement is fuzzy and there are no specific measures to ascertain the effectiveness of the effort, the managers initiate arbitrary changes which in no way help in measuring impact. Some organizations which feel that their social media efforts are not working reach a dead end and stop their campaigns. In most cases, the performance is related to small amount of money being spent. It is only when they believe that social media is effective, more budgets are allocated and the organization begins developing measurement metrics which can help it move from a subjective to objective domain. It is at this stage that the organization has moved to "iterate for success" from "naïve optimism."[48] The attempt is to move in the known domain and get a handle on what will work and what will not and chalk out a path.

Considering the inability of organizations to devise suitable measurement models, scholars and PR agencies have proposed the following (see Box 6.3).

Box 6.3: Models for Measuring ROI of Social Media

1. **Amplification Model:** This model measures the dollar value of social media activity as if it were purchased through traditional paid advertising means.
2. **Value of Social Traffic versus Display:** This model allows brand marketers to compare the cost of website traffic from social media to the cost of website traffic from display advertising.
3. **Quality of Visitors from Social Media:** While Model 2 compares the cost per visitor, this model evaluates the quality of visitors that come from social media versus those who come from other means.
4. **Revenue from Facebook Fans Model:** Using published data on the propensity for fans to change purchase behavior after becoming a fan, this model provides a framework for estimating the business value from new Facebook fans.
5. **Revenue from Social Media Marketing:** This model allows brands to calculate the estimated sales impact of their various social media marketing efforts in part by evaluating the impact on traffic to business-driving "goal" pages.
6. **Social Promotions Sales ROI:** Using data from Model 5, this final model provides a framework for measuring the return on investment from a given social promotion.

Source: Tobin (2014).[49]

Based on these models we can deduce the following: First, ROI is mostly measured in terms of tangible returns. Second, measurement of ROI from social media helps assess the traffic and compares it to display advertising. Third, securing eyeballs through select group of visitors is critical. Fourth, increasing existing customer base and enhancing business value is critical for assessing tangible returns. The last and final model then provides a framework for measuring the tangible ROI from a social promotion.

All these models are interlinked and point toward tangible returns from campaigns. Interestingly, these models point to a conversion of qualitative data to quantitative. For many users beginning with a click of the mouse on the 'like' and 'dislike' to indicate (un)favorable disposition toward a product or service often translates to a measure of making a purchase decision. Some are guided by the high intensity of the traffic which connotes an immediate interest. But what is of concern to the organization is the visibility that a particular campaign accords. By visibility we mean reaching the right target audience. Can this translate to purchase decisions and tangible outcomes? A yes and a no! If the outcome is negative and the objective of translating a neutral perspective to positive does not materialize, the company is burdened with addressing issues of negative ROI which can damage reputation and negatively impact the balance sheet. The impact of negative ROI in social media is as swift as positive but more damaging to organizational reputation than any other medium. Measuring both positive and negative ROI are critical but the why, what, and how need to be addressed.

To measure the ROI of a campaign and use the learning to predict, strategize, or implement future action is as on date a very difficult proposition. Altimer Group's analysis succinctly and quantitatively posits its findings on difficulties in measuring social media ROI—inability of 56 percent marketers to link social media to business outcomes. Some of the other issues highlighted in the study are "lack of analytics expertise and/or resources, poor tools, inconsistent analytical approaches and unreliable data."[50]

Practically, when we begin study of social media and its effect on an organization we realize that analysis of short-term effects can be misleading. One of the reasons for the same is lack of historical data which often makes the analysis skewed or inconclusive. At the superficial level, this seems a lost opportunity and wasted effort. We argue that no matter how uncertain may be the current terrain of social media ROI measurement, there is light at the end of the tunnel as scholars and researchers partner with practitioners to provide empirical evidence to the issue and problem of measurement.

Chapter Highlights

1. There has been in recent times a surge in measuring ROI of social media. However, as on date, there is uncertainty on what comprises ROI of social media.
2. Challenges faced by organizations are in terms of cognizing, developing and enhancing relationships in different business models. Associated challenges can be in terms of understanding the appropriate measurement techniques.
3. The measurement techniques need to focus on objectives of social media which can be stratified as conversation, interactivity, engagement, evangelism, etcetera.
4. As social media is conversational, continuous, and consumer-led there are difficulties in measurement.
5. A goal based approach to ROI helps in understanding the 'why' of the marketing initiative instead of just the 'how.'
6. With social media there is an opportunity for organizations to develop a set of matrices that link to a set of proxy benchmark which can align company objectives with the desired returns.
7. Social media ROI which was earlier measured in terms of fans, followers, and engagement is now being assessed as tweets, followers, comments, posts, shares, likes, mentions, channels used, and engagement.
8. There are tools to evaluate mentions on the net and assess if they are positive, negative, or neutral.
9. Most measures strive to ascertain levels of engagement. Organizations though have realized the challenges associated with operationalizing engagement. There has been a shift in perception of organizations in changing the consumer perspective from "Willingness to Pay" to "Willingness to Participate."
10. Organizations are indulging in data analysis which can be through myriads of available metrics.
11. Organizations are initiating multiple campaigns with clear-cut objectives as brand engagement, brand awareness, and WOM.
12. The processes adopted by companies can be in terms of developing conversational threads, sharing, being supportive and helpful; finding opinion leaders or high influencers for spreading the message; and employing techniques as promotion, contests, and the like to stimulate messages by others.
13. The outcome or the result is measured both in terms of tangibles and intangibles.
14. Occasionally, incorrect perceptions are created in the minds of consumers which lead to a loss of face, faith, and reputational currency.
15. There are multiple models for measuring social media ROI. Most of them are interlinked and point toward tangible returns. Most point toward conversion of qualitative data to quantitative.
16. The qualitative aspects, though, are critical and cannot be ignored.

Activities

1. Companies have often used influential bloggers to run campaigns and in most cases have been successful. Study any one company and share techniques used in requisitioning bloggers and other influencers for promoting the product.
2. Select any five companies and study their social media campaigns. Share similarities and differences in terms of objectives and outcome.
3. Recently, many organizations have been in the news for generating positive and negative sentiment. Present a summary overview of what these organizations did right or not to solicit these views. You may decide to compare and contrast companies in the same business sector.
4. Create groups of four. Select any one company for study of Socio media-logy. Divide the four steps amongst the group members. One will study strategies related to Crawl, one for Walk, one for Run, and one for Thrive. Knit together the presentation and share your findings.
5. Study three to five campaigns which went viral. What were the objectives of the company/companies? What made these campaigns go viral? To what extent were they able to match the company objectives?
6. In your groups, compare any two campaigns—try to pick campaigns that make distinct use of a specific social network (e.g., blogs, Facebook, Pinterest, Twitter, Instagram). What were the campaign objectives, how did the specific platform align with those objectives, and what engagement strategies were used? Assess how platform affordances contributed to the outcomes of these campaigns.
7. Study five campaigns which failed to gather momentum. Present reasons for the same.
8. Study the seven-step model to implementing social media campaigns. Apply the model to any situation/ campaign and discuss merits of implementation. Based on your analysis present what is missing/what more would you add to the model?
9. Imagine that you are a start-up focusing on a specific societal issue (e.g., environmental preservation or education) or a business problem. With limited funds, you turn to social media. Using knowledge from the chapter and your own research, prepare a detailed campaign plan starting with social media objectives, activities, channel, communication processes, and assessment of performance. Groups may reflect on how and whether campaign plans differ or follow the same logic for all kinds of organizations, profit or non-profit.
10. In small groups, select different fictional scenarios and conduct an experiment to assess stakeholder response to social-mediated campaign communication. Under what conditions are stakeholders (e.g., consumers) likely to read, like, share, and pass on the message? Compare findings and prepare a model to help companies (re)design strategies for optimum results.

Discussion Questions

1. Should the ROI always be measured in terms of tangibles or intangibles? Discuss citing examples.
2. The measurement of ROI has been divided into the following categories: (a) Activity, (b) Reach, (c) Engagement, (d) Acquisition, (e) Conversion, (f) Retention and advocacy. Which according to you is the most important? Elaborate citing examples.
3. Discuss how sentiment analysis can be employed by businesses for marketing products, identifying opportunities and managing reputation.

4. Why is it important to measure both positive and negative sentiments? Discuss how organizations can leverage this information to their benefit.
5. Present a campaign journey bearing in mind the company objectives. Illustrate with the help of an example.
6. Conversation, sharing, supportiveness, and helpfulness are important social currencies for an organization. Do you agree with the statement? Present your arguments in favor or against citing examples from the corporate world.
7. Corporate messages are more effective when spread by opinion leaders or high influencers than through promotions, contests, etcetera. Take a stand and argue in favor of your position.
8. Why is it difficult to measure the ROI of a campaign and use the learning to predict, strategize, or implement future action?

APPENDIX A

WHAT CONSTITUTES SOCIAL MEDIA ROI?

Author	View	Comment
Filisko (2011)[51]	It is difficult to measure social media ROI	ROI cannot be measured in quantitative terms as social media are about developing relationships, and making connections.
Manguic (2009)[52]	If social media ROI is well defined, there are methods of measuring the same	Based on the traditional methods of measurement, detailed costs, 'hard' and 'soft' benefits can be worked out.
Blanchard (2009)[53]	ROI can be measured in financial terms	As ROI is a financial transaction it can be measured when the less tangible measures are converted into meaningful data.
Murdough (2009)[54]	ROI can be measured if it is part of a larger system or framework	There are five steps to the framework: concept, definition, design, deployment, and optimization that are contingent on how a brand wishes to engage with its customers.
Campbell (2011)[55]	ROI can readily be measured	There are tools available for measurement that must be suitably deployed.

APPENDIX B

ILLUSTRATIVE LIST OF MEASUREMENT METRICS

Type	Metrics	Nature of Responses
1. Activity	Average response time, Content rate	The average time taken by a company to respond to comments and inquiries from its social media audience; The number of pieces of content produced per period o Blog posts per period o Presentations per period

(Appendix B Continued)

(Appendix B Continued)

Type	Metrics	Nature of Responses
	Post rate, etcetera	Number of social media posts per period o Tweets per period o Facebook posts o LinkedIn updates per period
2. Reach: The current and potential audience touched	Audience growth rate	The rate at which a company adds (or loses) audience members per channel
	Average position	The average position where a company's ad or posts appeared on a search engine results page
3. Engagement: Interactions and interest in the brand	Amplification rate	The number of shares on average for each post o Twitter retweets o Facebook shares
	Applause rate	The number of approval actions, or virtual "applause," from audience per period, such as +1s, likes, thumbs-up and favorites
4. Acquisition: Creating a relationship	Blog subscribers	Number of subscribers to the company's blog
	Bounce rate	The percentage of visitors who only went to a single page of the company site, bouncing back to the place they came from rather than clicking further into the site
5. Conversion: Actions, sales, and results	Average purchase value/ average order value	The average value of each purchase made by the customers of a company
	Average revenue per customer	How much the average customer spends, found by dividing yearly revenue by yearly customer count
6. Retention and advocacy: Happy customers and evangelists	Brand evangelists	Number of users considered evangelists based on their social media advocacy
	Customer annual or lifetime value	A prediction of the net profit attributed to the entire future relationship with a customer

Source: Adapted from Seiter (2015).[56]

APPENDIX C
CASE

ALS ICE BUCKET CHALLENGE

ALS Ice Bucket Challenge and its positive and negative impact on the stakeholders have often been cited as an example of ROI assessment based on stakeholder sentiment.

It is difficult to state the origins of the campaign or the idea of dumping cold water on one's head to raise money for charity. Multiple sources have been attributed for the same. The most commonly accepted origin credits Pete Frates, a Boston College student who was diagnosed with ALS in March 2012 and Pat Quinn, a friend of Frates, who was diagnosed with ALS in 2013. Another friend of Frates, Corey Griffin, has been recognized as a "co-founder" of the challenge.

The original idea of the ice bucket challenge has been differently attributed to Pete Frates who was diagnosed with ALS (a.k.a. Lou Gehrig's disease) in March 2012 and Pat Quinn who was diagnosed with ALS in 2013. The challenge was initiated in June 2014 with the objective of building awareness about ALS. The rules of the challenge were simple. A bucket of ice was to be poured on the head and two or three people were nominated to follow a similar rule. In case of inability to accept the challenge, a donation of US$100 had to be made to an ALS association. It was like a game of "Would-You-Rather involving the entire internet where, appallingly, most Americans would rather dump ice water on their head than donate to charity."[57] Once the challenge was accepted, the process was video filmed and posted on social media.

By July 2014, the challenge began to gain steam and soon changed hue and shifted from "The #icebucketchallengeto #ALSicebucketchallenge."[58]

By early August 2014, the ALS Ice Bucket Challenge went viral. Famous personalities across USA, such as Mark Zuckerberg, Oprah, Bill Gates, the Kennedy family, Tim Cook, Jimmy Fallon, Kate Upton, and George Bush took up the challenge. Obama declined but donated to the charity. By mid-August, the statistics published by The *New York Times* revealed that a sum of over US$13.3 million dollars had been raised by the participants. ALS had registered 260,000 new donors and there were over 2.2 million mentions of the campaign on Twitter. Slate.com reported that as of August 24, the ALS Association had received over US$70 million in pledges.[59] Referring to the success of the campaign, ALS Association President Barbara Newhouse said, "It's huge. It's a game changer for the ALS Association."[60]

In less than two months social media went live with criticism based on grounds of water wastage. Other negative comments underscored money being taken away from other charities. Arielle Pardes, a writer for *Vice* called it "narcissism masked as altruism." The believers of this dictum stated that indulging in Facebook activity only led to "'hashtag activism' and was of no real consequence."[61] By mid- to late August 2014, some people started tweaking the challenge and some copying it. Following negative sentiments on social media, by late August–September, the challenge saw a natural death.

A year later critics and sceptics openly mocked the challenge. However, the mockery was a tad premature and the very next year in 2016, a gene was discovered to fight ALS and social media was abuzz with the following message: "August is for raising awareness and funds to fight ALS!"[62]

Voices from the Field
by Rohan Mirchandani (RM) and Karlijn Vogel-Meijer (KVM)

1. **How are investments and returns defined in the social media space? How is the ROI of social media measured? Please elucidate using examples from your own company.**

   RM: Social Media Investments can be described differently for every company but mainly we could define it as return on innovation as well as return on engagement. ROI of social media can be measured depending on the efficiency of the campaign that is live and also what exactly is the goal of your campaign. At Drumsfood, at times many campaigns are launched only to gain awareness within our target audience and hence it is difficult to measure the ROI on an actual basis in such cases. To effectively measure ROI, you have to correctly determine and define all of the various inputs and outputs, as well as how that return actually ties into the bigger picture of your organizational strategy.

   KVM: Investments and returns can be defined in several ways, because campaigns can have different goals. You can invest money in order to sell tickets or bring new people to our website.

   For example, in our organization we re-target people who haven't completed their booking yet. The goal of the retargeting is that those people will make eventually a conversion. In this case we invest money to get money in return. We also have several campaigns where we invest money to collect website traffic, so we can reach those people later on with a different campaign.

   There are a lot of different measurements for ROI. We have an internal system that measures last click sale based on 28-day-cookie time. However, we see that systems like that have trouble measuring the role of social and cross device in particular. We also use Facebook pixels and Twitter pixels to measure ROI; however, these are not de-duplicated.

2. **What strategies are deployed to improve the ROI of social media?**

   RM: ROI can be correctly defined only if all the variables are in place and quantifiable including the investments and return. In many cases, there might not be financial outcomes and hence there are other ways to define and improve the ROI including tracking what kind of things did the target audience interact with after the campaign. Different actions done by the audience can be tracked and checked if they are aligned with our goals as well as if they did not then devise ways to improve the next campaign. The main strategy is to make sure what are the metrics that you are actually measuring and mapping for that duration. Social media is never static and to meet your social media ROI goals, you'll need to update and adapt your strategy constantly, taking into account the analytics data you're tracking.

   KVM: First of all, on social visual and copy are extremely important. You are in the timeline of other people, between their friends and family so your post—especially when it's commercial—needs to blend in perfectly and be relevant and worth sharing.

   Furthermore, we are always trying to find the sweet spot where the lowest investment can get the highest return. The ROI can tell us if and where our social media budget is spent effectively.

   For example, we compare the CPA, website clicks, conversions, revenue, and spend in order to optimize budget and revenue. It gives us insight to change or to quit campaigns based on predefined KPIs, so we can use the budget in a different way.

We also receive updates from our advertising agency multiple times a week with the results of the running campaigns so far. We use this to divide the budget on the most relevant audience, quit campaigns, or expand them. All in order to improve results.

3. **What are some of the challenges in measuring the ROI of social media?**

   RM: As described above ROI can only be measured in an efficient manner if there is a financial outcome. The campaigns a lot of times revolve around generating leads, creating awareness and engagement among target audience and so on. In such cases the value of likes, shares, and retweets is more important but it doesn't translate into traditional ROI.

   KVM: There are multiple challenges in measuring the ROI in social media. Cross device and cross channel are still badly integrated in some media channels and reporting. A customer can be triggered to buy a ticket via Facebook on his mobile phone and eventually buys a ticket on his Laptop. This sale won't be visible as a social sale. Customers are using several devices and channels and that makes it difficult to measure the value of social media within to the purchase journey. Second, social media channels such as Facebook and Twitter give good insights on ROI but these results are not de-duplicated.

4. **Why do companies (such as yours) want to use social media? List four to five key objectives.**

   RM:

   - Direct engagement with target audience
   - Problem solving and complaint handling on an immediate basis with customers
   - Increase customer acquisition on the website
   - Increase brand awareness
   - Content generated by the audience and low cost to promote

   KVM: Social media are very important for us, and we actually use the following objectives that are the basis of our social strategy.

   - Be where your customers are: we know that everybody is on mobile and we know that people use 5–6 apps on a daily basis. These are for the most part social platforms such as Facebook, Twitter, and for instance, WhatsApp. If you want to reach your customers, then you have to be where they are.
   - As your customers are on social, you want to give them the opportunity to interact with you and answer all their questions. This way you know what they are dealing with, etc.
   - Via social we can reach all those people that have never heard of KLM before, and expand our footprint. Via Facebook and Twitter we can practically reach the Western world. Via WeChat we can reach the Chinese market, etc. By posting engaging content that is relevant and worth sharing, we keep them informed and make them interact with us.
   - And if you do servicing and engagement right, if those people know you, then you have a basis for commerce. We sell tickets via social.

5. **How is success defined in the digital realm?**

   RM: It can be described on the basis of number of qualified and targeted conversations and relationships we are able to create and build, which will have a direct impact on our ability to generate leads, be exposed to great business opportunities, and at the end of the day add real value to our organization.

   KVM: Success is reaching your goals and learning from your failures. It's that simple.

6. **As it is a new domain, what are the common mistakes made by practitioners in defining the metrics and measurement?**

   RM: There are so many different measures of using social media and promoting different products online but marketers always give importance to metrics that don't matter as much. For example, on Facebook, everybody was focusing on how many fans and how many followers they had. But that was a mistake, because today we know that in general, from one million fans, just one percent are interacting with the brand. Many people try using offline measurement tools to see the effectiveness of social media which is another huge problem as simply measuring sales leads is not at all appropriate in today's online marketing world.

   KVM: Starting on social media without having a clear goal. Be sure to know what the purpose of your campaign is and look at the relevant metrics. If website clicks is your goal, then you don't have to take likes and shares into account.

7. **Is ROI always measured in dollar terms or can there be other criterion for measurement?**

   RM: Social media ROI can be defined as the return on your social media goals. ROI can be anything that you want it to be depending on what your goal is and value you want to derive from the campaign. It is important for people to understand that what somebody considers an industry standard or what somebody says is a best practice can be completely wrong, because one might be measuring the wrong things. Customer yield, customer advocacy, customer engagement, brand reputation can be used as different metrics to measure returns on the digital campaigns.

   KVM: There are a lot of different measurements for ROI. It depends on the goal of your campaign. ROI can be measured in revenue, reach, site traffic, conversions, sign-ups, website views, etc. It is not always about getting money in return, brand awareness and building a good reputation and can have the same value.

8. **What are some of the lessons learned? Reflecting on your experience, what would be your top advice to a new entrant?**

   RM: One of the major lessons learnt is not to go after mindless likes and increasing followers but concentrate on gaining quality fans and followers who are the actual target audience. This can be achieved mainly by creating content that will resonate with the target group as well as urge them to share and interact with the brand. It is necessary to develop a personality on social media which is extremely approachable so that the communication is clear and consumers enjoy interacting with you.

   KVM: Don't be afraid to fail. If you are afraid of making mistakes, then don't go on social. The developments on social go extremely fast. Go with the flow and try out new stuff, but be sure to fail some time.

9. **What more do practitioners want/need to know as social media become further embedded?**

   RM: PR in a way is totally moving towards social media and it is acting as new distribution channel for all kinds of information. The digital format has given rise to an evolution of multiple networks that can be used for focus or specific campaigns and will be of a greater value for us in the future. The main thing that marketers need to know is that social media platforms will continue to evolve and it is critical to stay innovative, on top of the latest and greatest, and make recommendations based on the customer's needs.

KVM: You have to be where your customers are and that's on social. Social is turning into a third entry point for customers next to .com and app. By opening up your APIs and connecting them to the APIs of social platforms, your customers will be able to perform all activities without leaving the platform of their choice.

10. **What are some of the questions related to social media that keep you up at night/give you sleepless nights?**

    RM: The main debate topic that still has not been solved for me is "Does social media have a direct impact on sales?"

    "Can social media be a boon or a bane to a company's reputation?"

    "How many are actual qualified leads, and how many of them actually become customers?"

    The best way to find out what type of content and strategy on the digital field is most effective for you is to test, tweak, and test again until you find the right fit.

    KVM: Sleepless nights? None. It is a big adventure and so far it has been a great pleasure. It is very interesting to see where the digital and social world is heading to. The developments (e.g., the movement to chat apps for 'real' conversations) are going extremely fast and to keep track you have to keep your eyes wide open and absorb everything.

NOTES

1 Paine, K. D. (2011). You can now measure everything, but you won't survive without the metrics that matter to your business. In K. D. Paine (Ed.), *Measure what matters: Online tools for understanding customers, social media, engagement and key relationships* (pp. 3–17). Wiley Publishing.
2 Minkovsky, N. (2015, June 28). Will It blend? Company embarks on new influencer marketing program. Retrieved on June 20, 2016, from http://contentmarketinginstitute.com/2015/06/blendtec-influencer-marketing/
3 Albarran, A. B. (2013). *The social media industries*. Routledge. Retrieved June 20, 2016, from https://books.google.co.in/books?id=0TxXb9Of4fEC&pg=PA99&lpg=PA99&dq=five+fold+increase+in+Blendtec+sales&source=bl&ots=jJvGRcop4D&sig=Fh9-xi0DPZve-Tl_67BVVc8GXQs&hl=en&sa=X&ved=0ahUKEwjYov7zODMAhXn3KYKHaooBm4Q6AEIKTAC#v=onepage&q=five%20fold%20increase%20in%20Blendtec%20sales&f=false
4 Campaign Goes Viral. (2011). Blendtec's will it blend? Campaign goes viral. Retrieved June 20, 2016, from http://www.grandsocialcentral.com/hustler-marketers/brand-managers/blendtec/will-it-blend-that-is-the-question
5 Viral Marketing. (2011). Viral Marketing, A Success Story: "Will it blend" That is the Question. (2011, February 20). Retrieved June 20, 2016, from https://soni1220.wordpress.com/2011/02/20/viral-marketing-a-success-story-will-it-blend-that-is-the-question/
6 Albarran (2013).
7 Paine (2011).
8 Fiorina, C. (2012, October 25). 31 Essential quotes on analytics and data. Retrieved June 25, 2016, from http://www.analyticshero.com/2012/10/25/31-essential-quotes-on-analytics-and-data/
9 Hoffman, D. L., & Fodor, M. (2010). Can you measure the ROI of your social media marketing? *MIT Sloan Management Review, 52*(1), 41–49.
10 Lee, K. (2015, March 26). The delightfully short guide to social media ROI. Retrieved June 25, 2016, from https://blog.bufferapp.com/guide-calculate-social-media-roi
11 Kaplan, A. M., & Haenlein, M. (2010). Users of the world, unite! The challenges and opportunities of social media. *Business Horizons*, *53*(1), 59–68. doi:10.1016/j.bushor.2009.09.00
12 Adjei, M. T., Noble, S. M., & Noble, C. H. (2010). The influence of C2C communications in online brand communities on customer purchase behavior. *Journal of the Academy of Marketing Science, 38*(5), 634–653. doi:10.1007/s11747-009-0178-5
13 Da, Z., Engelberg, J., & Gao, P. (2011). In search of attention. *The Journal of Finance*, *66*(5), 1461–1499.
14 Oh, C., & Sheng, O. (2011, December 6). Investigating predictive power of stock micro blog sentiment in forecasting future stock price directional movement.
15 Ibid.
16 Seiter, C. (2015, March 12). 61 Key social media metrics, defined. Retrieved June 30, 2016, from https://blog.bufferapp.com/social-media-metrics
17 Parent, M., Plangger, K., & Bal, A. (2011). The new WTP: Willingness to participate. *Business Horizons*, *54*(3), 219–229. doi:10.1016/j.bushor.2011.01.003
18 Ibid.
19 Fetters, A., & Smith, J. (2012, February 9). How Kellogg's brands work their digital strategies. Retrieved June 30, 2016, from http://www.slideshare.net/imediaconnection/how-kelloggs-brands-work-their-digital-strategies
20 Ibid.
21 McConnell, T. (2015). The Programmatic Primer: A Marketer's Guide to The Online Advertising Ecosystem. Retrieved June 30, 2016, from http://www.warc.com/PDFFilesTmp/cab43353-dcb2-4972-9601-63b34d8b-8ffc.PDF
22 Kumar, V., & Mirchandani, R. (2012). Increasing the ROI of social media marketing. *MIT Sloan Management Review*, *54*(1), 55–61.
23 Girls with Goals. (n.d.). Lenovo and Yuwa. Retrieved August 31, 2016, from http://www.girlswithgoals.in/
24 Donosti Cup. (n.d.). The Indian YUWA team will be the second team invited by in its 25th anniversary. Retrieved June 30, 2016, from http://www.donosticup.com/donosticup/de/the-indian-yuwa-team-will-be-the-secondteam-invited-by-donosti-cup-in-its-25th-anniversary.asp?nombre=7957&sesion=1347&cod=7957
25 Helweh, A. (2011, November 2). *The Future of Sentiment Analysis.* Retrieved June 30, 2016, from https://www.socialmediaexplorer.com/content-sections/news-and-noise/sentiment-analysis/

26 Jayasanka, R. A. S. C., Madhushani, M. D. T., Marcus, E. R., Aberathne, I. A. A. U., & Premaratne, S. C. (2013). Sentiment analysis for social media. *ITRU Research Symposium*, 25–30.

27 Duncan, S. (2010). Using web analytics to measure the impact of earned online media on business outcomes: A methodological approach. *Institute for Public Relations*, 1–22.

28 Ibid.

29 Paine (2011).

30 Britz, P. C. (2009, July 20). Profile: Coffee Groundz. Retrieved June 30, 2016, from https://twitter09.wordpress.com/2009/07/20/profile-coffee-groundz/

31 Underkofler, A. (2009, October 27). Twitter for business case study: The coffee groundz. Retrieved June 30, 2016, from http://www.squaremartinimedia.com/twitter-business-case-study-coffee-groundz/

32 Social Media Case Study. (n.d.). Social Media Case Study: The Jimmy Choo Trainer Hunt. Retrieved June 30, 2016, from http://www.evancarmichael.com/library/jo-stratmann/social-media-case-study-the-jimmy-chootrainer-hunt.html

33 Digital Strategy Consulting. (n.d.). Toblerone boosts sales 132% with national 'Thank You' day. (2014, February 24). Retrieved June 30, 2016, from http://www.digitalstrategyconsulting.com/intelligence/2014/02/toblerone_boosts_sales_132_with_national_thank_you_day.php

34 Thank you, Toblerone. (2013, June 10). Retrieved June 30, 2016, from https://alaabogari86.wordpress.com/2013/10/06/thank-you-toblerone/

35 Hendershot, S. (2011, January 1). Doing social marketing right: Foiled Cupcakes has that personal touch. Retrieved June 15, 2016, from http://www.chicagobusiness.com/article/20110101/ISSUE02/301019998/doing-social-marketing-right-foiled-cupcakes-has-that-personal-touch

36 Dawkins, J. (2014, November 5). Cupcakes anyone? How one entrepreneur used Twitter to build successful online start-up. Retrieved June 15, 2016, from https://smbp.uwaterloo.ca/2014/11/cupcakes-anyone-howone-entrepreneur-used-twitter-to-build-successful-online-start-up/

37 Cadbury's Wispa Relaunch: A Twitter Campaign That Exploded. (n.d.). Retrieved June 10, 2016, from http://mavsocial.com/case-study-twitter-cadbury-relaunch-wispia/

38 Weinberg, B. D., & Pehlivan, E. (2011). Social spending: Managing the social media mix. *Business Horizons, 54*(3), 275–282. doi:10.1016/j.bushor.2011.01.008

39 Petersen, R. (2014, April 27). 166 Case studies prove social media ROI. *Barn Raisers*. Retrieved June 15, 2016, from http://barnraisersllc.com/2014/04/166-case-studies-prove-social-media-roi/

40 Sawant, R. Ice Bucket Challenge–campaign analysis. Retrieved August 29, 2016, from http://www.slideshare.net/RachanaSawant1/als-ice-bucket-challenge-campaign-analysis

41 Billing, A. (2014, September). Is the ALS Ice Bucket Challenge Working? Numbers Say Yes! Retrieved August 29, 2016, from http://smallbiztrends.com/2014/09/als-ice-bucket-challenge-marketingcampaign.html

42 Peterson, R. (2014). Socio media-logy-how digital and social media marketing work. Retrieved June 15, 2016, from http://www.slideshare.net/91654/socio-medialogy-34821235

43 Solis, B. (n.d.). Retrieved August 15, 2016, from http://www.inspiringquotes.us/quotes/uU3G_86jplkwA

44 Weinberg and Pehlivan (2011).

45 Kramer, L. (2010). How French innovators are putting the "social" back in social networking. *Harvard Business Review, 88*, 121–124.

46 Ibid.

47 Farris, P. W., Bendle, N. T., Pfeifer P. E., & Reibstein, D. J. (2006). Marketing metrics: 50+ metrics every executive should master. Upper Saddle River, NJ: Prentice Hall.

48 Hoffman and Fodor (2010).

49 Tobin, J. (2014). Whitepaper: 6 Models for measuring the ROI of social media marketing. Retrieved from http://www.ignitesocialmedia.com/social-media-measurement/whitepaper-6-models-for-measuring-theroi-of-social-media-marketing/

50 Etlinger, S. (2016). The social media ROI cookbook: Six ingredients top brands use to measure the revenue impact of social media. Retrieved August 31, 2016, from http://www.altimetergroup.com/2012/07/the-social-media-roi-cookbook-how-brands-measure-the-revenue-impact-of-social-media/

51 Filisko, G. M. (2011). Social media or snake oil. *ABA Journal, 97*(1), 26–27.

52 Manguic, D. M. (2009). Measuring web 2.0 efficiency. *Annales Universitatis Apulensis: Series Oeconomica, 11*(1), 74–87.

53 Blanchard, O. (2011). *Social media ROI: Managing and measuring social media efforts in your organization*. Boston: Pearson Education, Inc.
54 Murdough, C. (2009). Social media measurement: It's not impossible. *Journal of Interactive Advertising, 10*(1), 94–99.
55 Campbell, C. (2011). Social analytics tools for measuring the impact of your social media marketing campaign. Retrieved June 14, 2012, from http://www.lakeshorebranding.com/company/blog/social-analyticstools-for-measuring-the-impact-of-your-social-media-marketing-campaign/
56 Seiter (2015).
57 Pardes, A. (2014). Dumping a bucket of ice on your head does not make you a philanthropist. Retrieved August 16, 2016, from http://www.vice.com/read/dumping-a-bucket-of-ice-on-your-head-does-not-make-you-a-philanthropist-813
58 Just Allie. (2016). The Ice Bucket Challenge Timeline. Retrieved August 20, 2016, from http://justallie.com/2014/08/the-ice-bucket-challenge-timeline/
59 Ibid.
60 Worland, J. (2014, August 18). The viral ice bucket challenge has raised $15.6 Million for ALS. Retrieved August 15, 2016, from http://time.com/3136458/viral-als-ice-bucket-challenge-funds-raised-15-million/
61 Just Allie. (2016).
62 Ice Bucket Challenge-The ALS Association. Retrieved August 27, 2016, from http://www.alsa.org/fight-als/icebucket-challenge.html

EPILOGUE

THE BEGINNING OF A NEW COMMUNICATION ERA

In the *Ballad of the East and West*, Rudyard Kipling wrote, "East is East and West is West and never the twain shall meet."[1] With passage of time, this line became an aphorism and was frequently invoked to emphasize insurmountable global differences. And, then came social media! Transcending geographical boundaries, relationships developed and networking increased. Much before realization could dawn, organizations began communicating under a global umbrella which followed a similar search for patterns and models for reaching out to consumers and initiating a dialogic process.

The amalgamation of the metaphorical East and West has been attributed to the changed interactions between marketers and consumers and their changing expectations. Further, the communication landscape has metamorphosed and riveted by almost 360 degrees and the Internet boom has brought about greater consumer awareness of products and services. As a consequence, there has been a role reversal and consumers have turned into initiators and controllers of social dialogue. Cognizant of this change, organizations too have changed gears and attempted a nouveau approach of increased presence over social media that accentuates their position in the market space and reduces (wishfully) negativity spill-overs. A paradigmatic shift? Probably, still too early to ascertain! But what is confirmed is the current requirement of the digital space and the rise of the walled gardens, which have forced organizations to rethink from the consumer perspective, be relevant and deliver a great experience which may or may not be accepted or appreciated.

Based on the aforementioned argument, let us probe the following question: Have the interactions between organizations and consumers changed or are in the process of changing? The winds of change cannot be denied although 'fully' grasping the nature and extent of change remains a challenge. What is certain is that almost all organizations have joined the bandwagon though most are yet in the exploratory stage gingerly testing the social media waters before making additions and amends to their existing policies. Notwithstanding a recognition of the fact that in this new terrain populated by recent entrants—marketers and digital natives—organizations are evolving patterns of connection and communication to establish a digital footprint.

All organizations, large or small, MNCs, B2B, B2C, are gripped in a frenzy of excitement, adventure, and speed, each laboring under anxiety and uncertainty to capture the social media space that is no longer restricted to marketing. Algorithms are being modified by organizations on an hourly, daily, weekly, and monthly basis for creation of space to include new ideas and newer technologies. The communication expanse has stretched to include recruitment, product development, service design, and organizational culture.

What are the key drivers of this shift in media strategies? Changes in technology and consumer behavior, "velocity, intertwinedness"[2] and the "use of digital technologies to create an integrated, targeted and measurable communication which helps to acquire and retain customers while building deeper relationships with them."[3] An analysis of the statements reflects the importance of measurement and integration for they emphasize the strategic underpinning to any social media approach as well as focus on relationships and communication. We argue that these theoretically sound propositions are practically under consideration for organizations and marketers are pondering the metrics for measuring the success quotient.

Let us unpack and probe some questions related to the 'success' factors which yet need a nested response as: What will tick and what will not? How can all consumers be reached? What will help increase sales? What will help build relationships and manage reputation? Is there a 'wish' segment which can amend or add to the existing approach to social media? The "biggest wish" question in a social media and social media marketing survey in 2016 revealed some interesting findings.[4]

- "A meeting of the minds...business executive acumen meets Millennial social savvy. If we can close the gap on the business objectives for communicating through social media with the social talent of the younger generation, then brands would be unstoppable, not only creating attention but also sales, loyalty and advocacy."[5]
- "My three wishes if I rubbed on a genie lamp would be: 1. I wish for the ability to measure the social media tactics individually and in aggregate over my entire business 2. I wish for more marketers who are savvy customer success managers and technologists 3. I wish for more executives to 'get it'."[6]
- "We move from a world where people no longer look for a social strategy, but for social deeply embedded within their strategy."[7]
- "To break down the silos and stop putting mobile second. Almost all the most interesting things that can be done with social media overlap with other parts and functions of the business but still they operate as distinct units. For example, the website, not just for working out how to make Social part of the broader customer journey but utilising CRM and web analytics to determine if social is driving valuable data capture and then using that information to create more effective social campaigns."[8]

These and similar wishes reflect what has been achieved and what remains to be achieved. Some of these concern the strategic and others operational and tactical decisions with the potential to revolutionize the social media space. Many of the governing perspectives are in the knowledge space, for instance, how do you embed the social in business strategy and deploy measurement techniques that are truly representative of the input and output equation. Wishes as use of social media for business promotion, and a meeting of the minds, clearly point to the need for a greater understanding of the consumer en masse.

To be relevant and understanding requires a change in mind-set, ideation, implementation, and execution. Consider the plaintive cries by younger professionals on the inability of digital immigrants (Baby boomers)[9] to keep pace with the changing technologies. Not surprising is this ruse in the challenging and volatile business environment which has created hurdles in the adaptation and adoption of strategic imperatives. Net result? Failed or half-baked attempts at juggling to balance a multitude of social media mix with the internal requirements of stakeholders and external pressures of the environment. Not all is lost though! What is known and is a certainty is that the use of social media will increase in the coming years and impact reputation. Starting with this premise then, it is not difficult to decipher the new mantra for success—an integration of social media designs in strategic organizational plans, for enhancing consumer interactions and building relationships.

The question is 'how' to proceed?

Prior to delving deep into questions probed in this section, let us take a peek into the changing/changed communication landscape.

CHANGING/CHANGED LANDSCAPE

"The digitization of media represents a phase change in the history of communications"[10] be it from the perspective of the audience, the versatility of the content, the immediacy effect, the accuracy of the content, or the dialogic nature of the medium. Waging war, on an unfamiliar turf, between traditional and social media has made it imperative for organizations to amend their strategic objectives, bring about a shift in resource allocation and spending decisions, techniques of engagement with consumers, and consumer evangelism (e.g., generating positive word-of-mouth, engaging conversations about a brand), half-life and depth of information. The change is reflected in the monitoring of social-space activity and engagement with and analysis of organizations in real-time by creation of social media 'mission control' centers.[11]

The story of social media—their growth and success—is continually being penned. "Compared to non-interactive media, a distinctive feature of social media is the opportunity to integrate a 'human voice' into social media platforms, which plays an important role in social media communications."[12] In consonance with existing literature, we posit in the book that in the age of social media 'dialogue' and not 'monologue' is the mantra with which either party can initiate communication and take it to a (il)logical conclusion. Let us not for a moment consider that adoption of social media technologies obliterate chances of miscommunication or crises. On the contrary, the speed, reach, and volume have increased the reputational risk, leading to higher evidence of communication collapse and consumer negativity.

Given the power of social media, organizations are grappling with definitive agreement on time and money to be allocated for this channel. Other points of contention are development of concrete objectives as co-creation, building a team of evangelists, crowdsourcing, etcetera, that are still in the experimental phase. Furthermore, attempts are afoot to find correlations between interactive social media activities and conversational human voice that will impact organizational reputation.

While there are challenges to communication through social media, opportunities too abound. More so, with excellent strategy, creative intent, and great communication organizations can underscore the importance of managing reputation while selling products and retaining customers through social media. Easier said than done!

Can social media actually impact reputational capital?

MANAGING REPUTATION THROUGH SOCIAL MEDIA

Corporate reputation lies at the core of an organization's business strategy. Development of a powerful image enhances organizational reputation and develops links with consumers, builds loyalty, promotes the brand, and wards off competition. Image and impression management shape stakeholder perceptions who then pronounce the company as worthy of a good reputation which has its attendant benefits as increase in sales, better financial performance, employee support etcetera.

Interestingly, social media hold sway over social expectations and perceptions. Direct experience of and with an organization, shared in the digital environment as 'electronic word of mouth' (eWOM) with groups and communities generating opinions and views. Consequently, perceptual biases can be created as this medium is perceived to be more reliable and the onus lies on the consumer to talk positively or otherwise about a brand, product, or service.[13] Not all is lost for eWOM also emphasizes purchase intentions of customers. Not much is known about the effects of eWOM on the reputation of an organization. What is known though, is that engagement can be viewed as "cognitive aspects (e.g., being interested in a company's activities), behavioral activities (participation in the company's activities), and/or emotional aspects (feeling positive about a company's activities)."[14]

A question frequently probed in the corporate circles attempts to understand the organizational social media strategy that impacts reputational capital. The question gains credence when we comprehend the application and adoption of social media communication strategies that address different hierarchies of reputation (high, medium, and low). Let us consider the high reputation organizations: These may decide to opt for informal communication channels with customers without being perceived as unprofessional. The same strategy would be avoided by organizations with a medium or low reputation. Clearly, the above observation validates the diversity in the nature of social media which is both "an inhibiting and a driving factor regarding evolution of corporate reputation."[15]

If the organizations have to manage reputation through social media, they have to synergize efforts to harness skills of reputation management, while maintaining perspective on reality, expectations, and perceptions of consumers. Can consumer engagement be the solution to this question? A yes and a no! The benefits of consumer engagement have been extolled in reputation literature. Developing online communities and creating cross-referenced communities that are strategically designed and perceived to be purposeful for the consumers can fortify relationships. To convert the aforementioned to a meaningful relation, organizations should cognize and address issues at the ground level.

GRAPPLING WITH REALITY

Organizations have shed concerns on the importance of presence on social media for it has become an imperative and cannot be easily dismissed. With a shift in emphasis from the need to be on social media to an understanding of their functionality, the net savvy consumers—their use of social media platforms and developing relationships—there is yet much to be experienced and learned in this space. A good beginning point may be a comprehension of gaps in existing communication patterns and development of key competencies and skill sets.

In a McKinsey study, 68 percent of respondents claimed that digital marketing and social tools were top priority of an organizational strategic agenda.[16] Most of the corporate honchos agreed that digital had changed the way in which business was conducted. Preparedness, though, to address challenges as increasing visibility, sales and profitability, and retaining customers was reported to be low. Seventy percent of the organizations lacked clear objectives or guidelines to strategize and implement their social media intent.[17] While many were still grappling with the truth of the social media tsunami, few were aware of concrete measures to establish checks and controls. Extant literature on social media, still in stages of infancy, does postulate measures of managing processes. However, their validation in practice is still a far cry.

Let us explore some of the persistent questions that torment researchers and practitioners alike.

Strategizing Social Media Communication

Currently social media are being deployed as a tool for integration of conventional marketing strategies and strategic organizational goals. The ease in approach is evident as consumers are simultaneously present on social media and on conventional media like TV and Radio. Now organizational communication outreach is made possible by what is called 'Purpose driven platform strategies' facilitating a greater level of organization-consumer dialogue, building relationships, gathering news, creativity, and entertainment.[18]

Reliance on social media for interaction with online customers and building relationships is on the increase. Disseminating news and information about the organization is made easier and quicker through social media channels. Attempts are afoot to develop 'Cross-platform integration strategies' by creating a brand personality. The fact cannot be denied that the cornerstones of this creation would be consistency, customization, commitment, and caution. "Social channels serve a distinct benefit, as compared to existing traditional media channels, in that utilizing social media at specific touchpoints can help brand managers direct customers and prospects to an online location matching the consumer's interests and needs."[19]

Creation of a genuine brand personality in which the true character of the brand is recognizable is a slow but sure process in which the greatest aid is consistency and uniformity in approach. Further, to attract and hold attention, social media messages have to be modified and tuned to address customer interests and needs, relation between a brand and its audience. Simultaneously, comprehension of the platform strength for communication can be a huge driver in creating a space for online brand presence in which conversations become meaningful and purposeful.

Content generated on the brand's online platform must be relevant, adequate, and should evolve with the brand.

> Brand managers are encouraged to utilize a number of social channels in building relationships while keeping in mind that it is less important for a brand to be represented on every platform than it is for a brand to be well represented on a few popular platforms that are closely aligned with consumers' needs and the firm's strategic goals.[20]

Unfortunately, many social media users tend to use the public medium to air individual grievances, some of which can be extreme at times, leading to negativity. On the positive side, social media grants brand managers the liberty to respond in a personal manner which again must be used cautiously. Managers must ensure that the same personal communication is not misused in advertisements and promoted content to pitch for sales for it would amount to infringement of trust and may provoke a backlash from consumers.

Different platforms can be used to convey different kinds of information about the same organization, defined by the need to have more user engagement, or to promote the brand through offers and sales. A game of perception management! Controlled and channelized content has often been credited to manage perceptions. New or improved perceptions for reputation enhancement can be created through identification of consumer preferences and tailoring of brand communication through 'social listening.'

Social media integration is thus required from a strategic and creative perspective keeping alive the scope for measurement. Organizations that have under-invested in social are probably still trying to discern the value and design of appropriate strategies. Those that have moved quickly in the space are grappling with attempts to balance integration through creation of 'always on' models. The associated challenges though are of integrating and updating Key Performance Indicators (KPIs) and coordinating paid efforts with the emergence of new techniques as sponsored editorials and native advertising.

How Can Engagement Be Strategized?

A big challenge before organizations is to initiate strategic real-time engagement with consumers demonstrating an understanding of all the consumers. Engaging with them is the first in the series of knowledge securing tactics of current trends, mind-sets, and behaviors. The series can range from securing ideas for new products, co-creation to modifying existing products. The more the engagement, the greater the belief in the company and higher the probability of consumers engaging in positive word-of-mouth.

What are the returns on investments made by companies in terms of seeking consumer engagement? Unfortunately, there is little clarity in research and practice on how measurement should be attempted.

Measurement of return on investment (ROI) is like a Damocles sword for marketers who make furtive attempts to capture, analyze, and present data to C-level executives who though cognizant of the significance of social media are still not conversant with the right approach. Lack of standards and defined metrics coupled with the obsession of measuring ROI seems to be trending. Irrespective of the uncertainty, organizations and practitioners are venturing forth with their measurement techniques. Can granularity be achieved in the measurement techniques? Currently, public relation actioners are unsure on this parameter and torn between strategizing engagement and measuring ROI, they are trying to fathom if synergy can be achieved between expectations and results to create a positive experience for all stakeholders.

Can a Positive Experience Be Created for the Stakeholders?

Advancement in communication technologies has made social media a viable platform for sharing messages and information not just with individuals but also with organizations in advanced stages of dialogue with online communities. Message dissemination through online platforms is subject to decoding by opinion leaders with the ability to act "as the connective communication tissue that alert their peers to what matters among political events, social issues and consumer choices."[21]

Economic, legal, and ethical considerations crowd the consumer mind together with the personality, presence, and performance (the three P's) of an organization. An image is created in the mind of the consumer that is based on the attention the consumer accords to these dimensions and the online experience. Organizations attempt to address the challenge of managing the corporate image and yet staying relevant by offering core promises as—convenience, achievement, fun and adventure, self-expression and recognition, and belonging—for a truly distinctive value proposition that has appeal to the target consumers.

The need to stay relevant in the Internet era has posed a challenge for the corporate culture and has led to restructuring of the organization to adopt a more dynamic leadership identity. Leadership practices within an organization, it has been found, often drive communication, and the internal and external communication system of an organization can be shaped by higher-order authorities like the CEO. Literature validates the influence of the CEO, the image and leadership charisma to have an impact on corporate reputation.[22]

Electronic platforms (i.e., email, intranet, teleconference, streamline video/audio) and social media tools (i.e., blogs and social networking sites) are becoming increasingly popular among CEOs. Use of Facebook, Twitter, LinkedIn, YouTube, and blogs is perceived to be essential for management of online presence and build brand personality. Notwithstanding is the fact that traditional face-to-face channels (i.e., employee meetings) and print media are still being commonly deployed by CEOs. As on date, the organizational communication by the CEO and the social media presence is moderate and needs to be ramped up. There is research evidence supporting a positive correlation between stakeholder perception of organizational communication and stakeholder relational outcomes. Specifically, CEOs who maintain a stronger social media presence are more likely to be "perceived as responsive communicators who are sincere, friendly, agreeable, compassionate, understanding, and willing to listen."[23]

Yet, the questions prevail: How can a positive enriching experience be created that will attract and retain consumers? What can be appealing, interesting, and exciting enough to generate conversation? The answers to these questions are not easily knowable as implicit and explicit consumer requirements have made it difficult for marketers to zero in on their likes and dislikes. Less than two decades ago marketers knew how, where, and when to interact with consumers. With a role change, consumers are now defining the scope and mode of interaction. Combatting the challenge, organizations have begun on a travail seeking answers to the 'how' and 'what' of content generation.

How Should Content Be Created?

The central theme in social media communication and the key driver for leading publics to join or follow a social media site has been credited to content creation and its relevancy for organizational communication is now dominated by voice messages, images, and video providing a real time experience to the stakeholders. Facebook Live, Snapchat, and Periscope have made it imperative for organizations to realign their strategic processes to meet the demands of the plan-and-launch, the always-on models and to capture attention through compelling, transparent and "in the moment story."[24]

The three major trends in social media for enabling content creation are: to disseminate tailored messages, provide entertainment and online experiences, and gather opinion on products and services.[25] Digital technologies, apps, and well created and conceptualized content allow organizations to gain visibility on the net. The ensuing impact can well boost sharing on the net, create a ripple effect, improve conversations, and appeal for the product.

To go back in time, when print media was the one and only source of communication, informational and promotional appeals were key elements in the success matrix of an organization. Come social media and all success measure undergo a radical change. Emotional appeal emerged as the winner in gaining organizational credence. Funny and engaging videos were created to generate discussion on specific topics.[26] There was an increase in bragging or braggadocian online behavior[27] with its attendant advantages and disadvantages. A careful analysis created awareness in organizations on happenings in the public space, and its receptivity by the consumers.

Can content be created and disseminated simultaneously? Yes, and with speed. Delay of an hour or a few minutes due to unforeseen circumstances can backtrack on organizational intent of 'first' in reaching consumers. As on the road so also in the social media space, speed thrills but (also) kills! In the rush to churn out content, correctness, and appropriateness to different segments of society should not be sacrificed at the altar of speed.

Keeping the potential of two-way communication between organizations and customers alive, co-creation and sharing of content is the beginning in the short journey of reaching consumers. Starting advice for securing customer support in the digital information space includes:

- Be creative
- Narrate a story
- Improvise on visual content
- Create organic traffic
- Churn quality content
- Develop native content
- Indulge in co-branding

The pointers are indicative. In addition to the skills, an acquaintance with the rules, code of conduct, and ethical behavior on social media will positively add value. All these three parameters are shrouded in web of uncertainty. Queries have been raised in various forums on what is ethical and what is not in the social media space, for supposedly it has been perceived that ethical rights are being flaunted by individuals and organizations. Ambiguity on this dimension has made it tough to address ethical detours and instances of lack of social ethic or "anomie"[28] are on the increase. The term "anomie" (originally coined by Durkheim, 1951) has been defined by Bowen (2013) as a "state of disconnectedness, social isolation, or the lack of a social ethic"[29] which paradoxically connects people at a distance but isolates those in the near vicinity. Linking this concept to ethics, it has been postulated that ethics is socially constructed. As an understanding of ethics may vary across cultures, a critical attempt at managing what is universally good and truthful, adds value to the self and the organization, should ideally be used in social media.

The silver lining is the knowledge that interactions and conversations between and by individuals can create networks for initiation of dialogic processes. Building on the notion of connectedness, social media can combat anomie and develop greater cohesiveness within and outside communities. One of the techniques of doing it is creation of enabling and facilitating environment that can bring organizations in direct contact with influencers who are also part of the organizational success story. Also referred to as opinion leaders and brand advocates, these influencers can provide free publicity to products, act as champions for a company, spread positivity through word-of-mouth and also prevent attacks and intrusions from unknown quarters.

Given the nature of the challenges and constraints facing organizations, many are still undecided on their stand on social media use and its value-add. The resonant narrative of values and beliefs that organizations stand for still has to be completed; creation of an enriching, yet consistent experience for the consumers is in stages of infancy. Can then organizations declare 'checkmate'?

THE WAY FORWARD

Trudging on an unknown yet desired path, organizations are in the revelation mood. With some claiming victory over one facet and others over another, it is difficult for us as researchers and readers to gauge the overall impact of techniques and strategies. Hence, the need for dialogue to continue through the epilogue. Reminiscing over the known traditional media, let us reflect on the emergence of the social media and chalk the path ahead.

Not so long ago, a coming together of the words, 'social' and 'media,' gave birth to a new science of communication—social media. As the name implies, social refers to a coming together of individuals or minds with similar disposition. Media or medium is the vehicle for bringing together these similar minded people for creation and exchange of ideas and content, socialization, networking, and building relationships. By their very nature, social media grant greater exposure to organizations and their businesses, potentially increasing partnerships, reducing expenses, and improving market intelligence. With little knowledge or information on how social media can be used to achieve targets and manage reputational assets, markets and marketers are struggling to achieve the unknown and the untold.

This new science has excited organizations to embrace social media for ubiquitous use and deploy them for direct interaction with existing and new consumers and communication of products and services. As they progress on this trajectory, they develop a loyal fan following and gain market intelligence. What now? With the end of the era of catchy slogans and wordy ads to impress and draw consumers and with more power vested in the hands of the consumer, danger to the brand and the organization looms larger than otherwise. The word-of-mouth has made content and contextual meaning more relevant and 'always' available. Though people are constantly updated on different streams of information, organizations are tinkering with data to find a solution to what makes a social media message tick—the content, the level of engagement, the skills, and the consistency with which messages are transmitted?

With competition heating up, winning in the social media age is no longer marketer's play. Communication strategies have metamorphosed with continuous, ongoing dialogue that shares information, builds trust, and showcases values and integrity. Notwithstanding the fact is the knowledge that viral diffusion of information can reach a much higher audience than the "short tail" media as TV, print, or radio.[30] No longer is media communication as discrete as it was in yesteryears. The changing nature of expectations and objectives has modified all platforms and made them tools for connecting and sharing almost everything that is and can be done in the privacy of the homes. Most of the platforms on social media have accelerated to everything platforms. For instance, no longer is Twitter a platform for tweeting 140 character updates. Recall the case of Maggi? Facebook has moved up from being a tool for sharing between friends to a platform for video sharing, marketing of products, and sharing of grievances. United Breaks Guitar? Part of the problem lies with the nature of the medium and part with the skills gap. Consequences of social media skills gap do widen the chasm between the organizations and consumers leading to gaffes, "misused hashtags to scheduled posts gone awry, not to mention trillions of dollars (yes, trillions) in lost productivity and business value."[31] Is the panacea to all social media challenges a studied and combined approach from experiential learning of all organizations?

Compounding is the challenge posed by the "Dark Social." Coined by Madrigal in the year 2012, the "dark social" is a description of all the unaccounted social network sites or direct traffic from Google search. Where does this direct traffic come from? Ever attempted analysis with the help of web analytics? If yes, then in all probability you have not got your answer for much of the traffic in social media is "dark social" meaning it has no referrer. A referrer is a URL which the user frequents before clicking onto the desired page to be viewed. A major chunk of the referral traffic, though valuable, is difficult to track accurately. In the analytics, one could always take into account the direct traffic links which may give us an idea about the source of the traffic. Unfortunately, this would not provide information on where and how the content was shared.

Some major network sites do not attach referral information. For instance, Facebook makes no pretense of carrying information on the social media referrer or provide links when there is user engagement on the app. Madrigal adds, "A story's shareability is now largely determined by its shareability on Facebook, with all its attendant quirks and feedback loops."[32] This phenomenon has gained ground with the increasing use of private messaging apps.

With native mobile apps, emails, chat, secure browsing, and organic search, visitors can go to sites in many indirect ways. Assessment of amplification of efforts is proving to be a challenge as almost 70 percent[33] of social efforts are dark. The paradigm shift is from Facebook, where sharing is one to many, to sharing which is one-is-to-one, as in the case of a private forum. Measurement of the dark social can be a challenge but is not an impossible feat. Inclusion of unified threat management (UTM) parameters to the share buttons on the site may be helpful to a certain extent. However, this will take you up only to a certain point and not beyond that! Much of the sharing is really URL copy/paste implying that in such cases, the UTM parameters would not be present.

Is there a solution for this? Not really. Sixty-nine percent of the referrals are from dark, 20 percent from Facebook and six percent from Twitter.[34] What does this imply? Can we really optimize this finding? Operationally, the revelations would be only part of the truth for optimization of the social media spread would lie in an assessment of the social, uncut content which may be difficult to measure. Furthermore, the act of sharing and publishing on the Internet has come a long way, making it more visible, searchable with much metadata added to the link.

Where does this take us? On the road to discourse and dialogue which we have attempted in this book by probing issues. The epilogue is a 'dialogue in progress' to understand challenges and seek solutions/drivers designed to propel social media communication to greater heights. The most critical part of this process is establishing a digital footprint by generating a loyal following, and subsequently setting up measures through which control can (not) be ceded to stakeholders.

The move is to look beyond the creation and mastering of social media tools. To establish a digital footprint, we need greater clarity on defining and determining parameters.

1. Visibility: Increasing the visibility by moving in the user domain. The first step is to explore and shift to a space where we have competitors. What are their strategies? How are they drawing the crowd? Have they been able to capture the masses? How close are we to their strategies? Can we learn and emulate or redefine and realign?
2. Listening: Are we listening to what is being said and what is not? There are dialogues in the social media space which may be favorable or unfavorable. It is critical to listen harder to the unfavorable, assess the winds of change and proceed accordingly. What is the nature of the message? Which platform would be the best to share? Where would the recipient read it—mobile, laptop, or desktop? Answers to these questions may just be a beginning point for implementing change in current strategies.
3. Measuring: Constantly measuring, creating benchmarks, and then devising strategies has helped organizations 'up' their products and services. While we do discuss corporate reputation from the intangible perspective, there is also a quantitative dimension that spells out the need to measure, strategize, and then implement.

There are risks and challenges in embracing social media unconditionally. The question is not if social media are good or bad—it is their use and purpose that can make social entertaining, informative, and socially relevant.

NOTES

1 Kipling, R. (2016, November 1). Retrieved November 1, 2016, from http://www.bartleby.com/246/1129.html

2 Kung, L. (2008). *Strategic management in the media: Theory to practice.* London: SAGE.

3 Smith, K. (2007, October 5). What is digital marketing? Retrieved January 3, 2016, from New Marketing: http://digitalmarketing101.blogspot.com/2007/10/what-is-digital-marketing.html

4 Ward, W.J. et al. (2016). Social media marketing trends 2016. Retrieved December 31, 2016, from https://www2.canneslions.com/resources/downloads/Cannes_Lions_School_Social_Media_Diploma.pdf

5 Breakenridge, D. (2016). Social media marketing trends 2016. Retrieved December 31, 2016, from https://www2.canneslions.com/resources/downloads/Cannes_Lions_School_Social_Media_Diploma.pdf

6 Carter, S. (2016). Social media marketing trends 2016. Retrieved December 31, 2016, from https://www2.canneslions.com/resources/downloads/Cannes_Lions_School_Social_Media_Diploma.pdf

7 Crampton, T. (2016). Social media marketing trends 2016. Retrieved December 31, 2016, from https://www2.canneslions.com/resources/downloads/Cannes_Lions_School_Social_Media_Diploma.pdf

8 Gaffney, K. (2016). Social media marketing trends 2016. Retrieved December 31, 2016, from https://www2.canneslions.com/resources/downloads/Cannes_Lions_School_Social_Media_Diploma.pdf

9 Dumeresque, D. (2013). The corporate digital footprint: Exactly who owns and controls it? The emergence of the digital director. *Strategic Direction, 29*(7), 34–36. doi:http://dx.doi.org/10.1108/SD-04-2013-0011

10 Mulhern, F. (2009). Integrated marketing communications: From media channels to digital connectivity. *Journal of Marketing Communications, 15*(2–3), 85–101. doi:10.1080/13527260902757506

11 Weinberg, B. D., & Pehlivan, E. (2011). Social spending: Managing the social media mix. *Business Horizons, 54*(3), 275–282. doi:http://dx.doi.org/10.1016/j.bushor.2011.01.008

12 Kelleher, T. (2009). Conversational voice, communicated commitment, and public relations outcomes in interactive online communication. *Journal of Communication, 59*(1), 172–188. doi:http://doi.org/10.1111/j.1460-2466.2008.01410

13 Silverman, G. (1997). How to harness the awesome power of word of mouth. *Direct Marketing, 60*(7), 32–37.

14 Dijkmans, C., Kerkhof, P., & Beukeboom, C. J. (2015). A stage to engage: Social media use and corporate reputation. *Tourism Management, 47*, 58–67. doi:http://doi.org/10.1016/j.tourman.2014.09.005

15 Floreddu, P. B., Cabiddu, F., & Evaristo, R. (2014). Inside your social media ring: How to optimize online corporate reputation. *Business Horizons, 57*(6), 737–745. doi:http://dx.doi.org/10.1016/j.bushor.2014.07.007

16 Brown, B., & Sikes, J. (2012, May). Minding your digital business: McKinsey Global Survey results. Retrieved June 16, 2016, from http://www.mckinsey.com/business-functions/digital-mckinsey/our-insights/minding-your-digital-business-mckinsey-global-survey-resultsb

17 Ployhart, R. (2012). Social media in the workplace: Issues and strategic questions. Retrieved July 26, 2016, from www.shrm.org/about/foundation/products/Documents/Social%20Media%20Briefing%20FINAL.pdf
18 Killian, G., & McManus, K. (2015). A marketing communications approach for the digital era: Managerial guidelines for social media integration. *Business Horizons, 58*(5), 539–549. doi:http://dx.doi.org/10.1016/j.bushor.2015.05.006
19 Ibid.
20 Ibid.
21 Uzunoğlu, E. and Misci Kip, S. (2014). Brand communication through digital influencers: Leveraging blogger engagement. *International Journal of Information Management, 34* (5), 592–602. doi:http://org/10.1016/j.ijinfomgt.2014.04.007
22 Cravens, K., Oliver, E. G., & Ramamoorti, S. (2003). The reputation index: Measuring and managing corporate reputation. *European Management Journal, 21*(2), 201–212. doi:http://dx.doi.org/10.1016/S0263-2373(03)00015-X
23 Men, L. R. (2015). The internal communication role of the chief executive officer: Communication channels, style and effectiveness. *Public Relations Review, 41*(4), 461–471. doi:http://doi:10.1016/j.pubrev.2015.06.021
24 Breakenridge (2016).
25 Carim, L., & Warwick, C. (2013). Use of social media for corporate communications by research-funding organisations in the UK. *Public Relations Review, 39*(5), 521–525. doi:http://dx.doi.org/10.1016/j.pubrev.2013.08.006
26 Men, R. L., & Tsai, W. H. S. (2013). Beyond liking or following: Understanding public engagement on social networking sites in China. *Public Relations Review, 39*(1), 13–22. doi:http://dx.doi.org/10.1016/j.pubrev.2012.09.013
27 Valentini, C. (2015). Is using social media 'good' for the public relations profession? A critical reflection. *Public Relations Review, 41*(2), 170–177. doi:http://doi.org/10.1016/j.pubrev.2014.11.009
28 Durkheim, E. (1951). *Suicide, a study in sociology*. Glencoe, IL: The Free Press.
29 Bowen, S. A. (2013). Using classic social media cases to distill ethical guidelines for digital engagement. *Journal of Mass Media Ethics, 28*(2), 119–133. doi:http://dx.doi.org/10.1080/08900523.2013.793523.
30 Kelleher, T. (2009). Conversational voice, communicated commitment, and public relations outcomes in interactive online communication. *Journal of Communication, 59*(1), 172–188. doi:http://doi.org/10.1111/j.1460-2466.2008.01410
31 Holmes, R. (2016, February 11). 5 trends that will change how we use social media in 2016. Retrieved June 15, 2016, from https://www.weforum.org/agenda/2016/02/5-trends-thatwill-change-how-we-use-social-media-in-2016/
32 Madrigal, A. C. (2016). Dark social: We have the whole history of the web wrong. Retrieved January 4, 2016, from http://www.theatlantic.com/technology/archive/2012/10/dark-social-we-have-the-whole-historyof-theweb-wrong/263523/
33 Stanislaw, B. (2016). What is 'Dark social' and is it something you should care about? Retrieved January 4, 2016, from http://simplymeasured.com/blog/what-is-dark-social-and-is-it-something-you-should-care-about/#sm.00011jbbwpiscf8zvfj1mx6zpnhuu
34 Madrigal, A. C. (2016).